Paul Cooper's work brings together East and West in co-nourishing ways. Instead of opposition and antagonism, Cooper emphasizes interweaving. His particular focus is Zen Buddhism and psychoanalysis, how they add to and support each other, a profound journey of appreciation, deepening, opening. We are in a time of cross-fertilization and this work takes up the challenge in stimulating, growth producing ways. You will experience yourself anew you as feel the living waters this work points to.
– **Michael Eigen**, PhD, author of *Faith*, *The Psychoanalytic Mystic*, and *Image, Sense, Infinities, and Everyday Life*.

Zen Insight, Psychoanalytic Action

Drawing from original source material, contemporary scholarship, and Wilfred Bion's psychoanalytic writings, *Zen Insight, Psychoanalytic Action: Two Arrows Meeting* introduces the Zen notion of "*gūjin*," or total exertion, and elaborates a realizational perspective that integrates Zen Buddhism and psychoanalysis.

Developed by the thirteenth century Zen teacher and founder of the Japanese Soto Zen school, Eihei Dogen, *gūjin* finds expression and is referenced in various contemporary scholarly and religious commentaries. This book explains this pivotal Zen concept and addresses themes by drawing from translated source material, academic scholarship, traditional Zen *kōans* and teaching stories, extensive commentarial literature, interpretive writings by contemporary Soto Zen teachers, psychoanalytic theory, clinical material, and poetry, as well as the author's thirty years of personal experience as a psychoanalyst, supervisor, psychoanalytic educator, ordained Soto Zen priest, and transmitted Soto Zen teacher.

From a realizational perspective that integrates Zen and psychoanalytic concepts, the book addresses anxiety-driven interferences to deepened Zen practice, extends the scope and increases the effectiveness of clinical work for the psychotherapist, and facilitates deepened experiences for both the Buddhist and the secular meditation practitioner. *Two Arrows Meeting* will be of great interest to researchers in the fields of Zen Buddhism and psychoanalysis. It will also appeal to meditation practitioners and psychoanalysts in practice and training.

Seiso Paul Cooper is an ordained Soto Zen Buddhist priest and transmitted teacher and Director of the Two Rivers Zen Community in Narrowsburg, NY, and the Realizational Practice Studies Group in New York City, which serves as a unique venue for psychotherapists to engage in Zen practice and to study psychotherapy from a Zen perspective. Cooper continues to be an innovative contributor to the integration of Buddhism and psychoanalysis. He is Former Dean of Training at the National Psychological Association for Psychoanalysis (NPAP), New York, and maintains a private practice in Manhattan and Narrowsburg, NY, USA.

Zen Insight, Psychoanalytic Action

Two Arrows Meeting

Seiso Paul Cooper

LONDON AND NEW YORK

First published 2019
by Routledge
2 Park Square, Milton Park, Abingdon, Oxon OX14 4RN

and by Routledge
711 Third Avenue, New York, NY 10017

Routledge is an imprint of the Taylor & Francis Group, an informa business

© 2019 Seiso Paul Cooper

The right of Seiso Paul Cooper to be identified as author of this work has been asserted by him in accordance with sections 77 and 78 of the Copyright, Designs and Patents Act 1988.

All rights reserved. No part of this book may be reprinted or reproduced or utilised in any form or by any electronic, mechanical, or other means, now known or hereafter invented, including photocopying and recording, or in any information storage or retrieval system, without permission in writing from the publishers.

Trademark notice: Product or corporate names may be trademarks or registered trademarks, and are used only for identification and explanation without intent to infringe.

British Library Cataloguing in Publication Data
A catalogue record for this book is available from the British Library

Library of Congress Cataloging in Publication Data
Names: Cooper, Seiso Paul, author.
Title: Zen insight, psychoanalytic action : two arrows meeting / Seiso Paul Cooper.
Description: Abingdon, Oxon ; New York, NY : Routledge, 2018. | Includes bibliographical references.
Identifiers: LCCN 2018013224 (print) | LCCN 2018013683 (ebook) | ISBN 9780429458606 (Master e-book) | ISBN 9781138614949 (hardback) | ISBN 9781782205784 (pbk.)
Subjects: LCSH: Zen Buddhism–Psychology. | Psychoanalysis and religion.
Classification: LCC BQ9265.8 (ebook) | LCC BQ9265.8 .C66 2018 (print) | DDC 294.3/3615–dc23
LC record available at https://lccn.loc.gov/2018013224

ISBN: 978-1-138-61494-9 (hbk)
ISBN: 978-1-78220-578-4 (pbk)
ISBN: 978-0-429-45860-6 (ebk)

Typeset in Times New Roman
by Out of House Publishing

*The absolute works together with the relative
like two arrows meeting in mid-air.
Reading words you should grasp the great reality.
Do not judge by any standards.
If you do not see the Way, you do not see it even as you walk on it.
When you walk the Way, it is not near, it is not far.
If you are deluded, you are mountains and rivers away from it.
I respectfully say to those who wish to be enlightened:
Do not waste your time by night or day.*

– Sekito Kisen

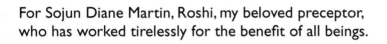

For Sojun Diane Martin, Roshi, my beloved preceptor, who has worked tirelessly for the benefit of all beings.

Contents

Acknowledgments xii
About the author xiv

Introduction 1

1 Total exertion: definition and use 9

2 Simply sitting: origins 23

3 Dogen Zen: radical reformulation 37

4 Total exertion as intuition 49

5 Realization and delusion 65

6 Thinking, not thinking, beyond thought 80

7 Zen musings on Bion's "O" and "K" 96

8 Two arrows meeting: Zen insight, psychoanalytic action 114

9 Taste the strawberries 129

10 The abyss becoming well 143

References 159
Index 168

Acknowledgments

This present edition has emerged with the kind and generous inspiration, encouragement, creative suggestions, and support of many individuals, including my students, who never fail to inspire and motivate me. My Zen and psychoanalytic teachers have provided generously with their teachings and ongoing encouragement, support, and feedback. I am deeply grateful for the opportunity to engage in deep practice and study into the writings and teachings of Eihei Dogen on numerous retreats with Shohaku Okumura, Roshi, who provided an integration and balance between scholarship and authentic practice. I am especially appreciative of my psychoanalytic mentors, Alan Roland, Arthur Robbins, and Michael Eigen, who encouraged and guided me through my initial forays into both areas of self-investigation and expression in these two highly subjective disciplines. My gratitude extends to my colleague and friend, Mel Miller, for engaging in countless and fruitful hours of constructive conversation and for our collaborations on a number of panels and conferences. My appreciation extends to James Grotstein for his enthusiastic, valuable, and encouraging response to my writing. I am indebted to Eric Rhode for his original intellectual peregrinations, his creative insights, and his encouragement, which served as a wellspring of inspiration for many of the ideas presented in the original version of Chapter 10, "The abyss becoming well." Stimulating conversations and collaborations with Mark Finn continue to serve as a rich source of inspiration and clarity of vision. Rod Tweedy and Elliot Morsia at Karnac have both offered consistent encouragement, quick responses to my queries, and positive support for this project. John Marr has applied a close, fine-tuned, and intuitive eye to the details of the original draft, both structurally and conceptually. Last but not least, I am deeply grateful to Karen Morris, my loving wife, for her ongoing, consistent encouragement, thoughtful responses, and close reading of the early drafts of this offering and through this entire process. I gratefully acknowledge permission to reprint the following material:

The translated poem beginning with the line "Mystical cries of monkeys"
    from *The Zen Poetry of Dogen: Verses from the Mountain of Eternal*

Peace translated by Steven Heine, Rutland, VT: Tuttle Publishing Co. (1997, p. 97). All rights reserved. Used by permission of Steven Heine.

The poem beginning with the line "black coffee" from *Still Standing: Three Stones Haiku* by Seiso Paul Cooper, Honesdale, PA: Three Stones Press (2014, p. 2). All rights reserved. Used by permission of the author.

The poem beginning with the line "drifting in and out of dreams" from *Still Standing: Three Stones Haiku* by Seiso Paul Cooper, Honesdale, PA: Three Stones Press (2014, p. 5). All rights reserved. Used by permission of the author.

Chapter 1, "Total exertion: definition and use," is a revised and expanded version of the article originally published as "Total exertion: Zen, psychoanalysis, life," by Paul C. Cooper in the *Journal of Religion and Health* (2011) 50 (3): 592–601 by permission of Springer.

Chapter 7, "Zen musings on Bion's 'O' and 'K'," is a revised and expanded version originally presented at the Two Rivers Zen Community retreat: "Actualizing a Realizational Practice: Zen Meditation and Psychoanalysis", September 27–29, 2015, Himalayan Institute, Honesdale, PA and published as "Zen musings on Bion's O and K," by Paul C. Cooper in the *Psychoanalytic Review* (2016) 103 (4): 515–538 by permission of Guilford Press.

Chapter 8, "Two arrows meeting: Zen insight, psychoanalytic action," is an expanded and revised version of "Zen meditation, reverie and psychoanalytic listening," by Paul C. Cooper originally published in the *Psychoanalytic Review* (2014) 101 (6): 795–813 by permission of Guilford Press.

Chapter 9, "Taste the strawberries," is a revised version of "Dreaming Terror, Delight & the Liminal In-Between," presented at the International Forum for Psychoanalytic Education's Nineteenth Annual Interdisciplinary Conference: "Encounters & Escapes: Danger & Desire in the Psychoanalytic Connection," November 21, 2008, Boston, MA. originally published as "Taste the strawberries," by Paul C. Cooper in the *American Journal of Psychoanalysis* (2014) 74 (2): 147–161 reprinted by permission of Palgrave.

Chapter 10, "The abyss becoming well," is a revised and expanded version originally published as "The abyss becoming well: psychoanalysis and reversals in perspective," by Paul C. Cooper in the *Psychoanalytic Review* (2004) 91 (2): 158–177 by permission of Guilford Press.

About the author

Seiso Paul Cooper is an ordained priest and transmitted teacher in the Soto Zen Buddhist Lineage of Dainin Katagiri, Roshi. He is the co-founder of the Two Rivers Zen Community in Narrowsburg, NY, and the Realizational Practice Group in New York City. He serves as the guiding teacher of the Lincoln Zen Center in Lincoln, NE. He serves as a training analyst, supervisor, and faculty member at various psychoanalytic institutes and previously served as Dean of Training at the National Psychological Association for Psychoanalysis, where he received his psychoanalytic training. Seiso has had many articles published on the relation between Buddhism and psychoanalysis and is an award-winning poet. His books include: *The Zen Impulse and the Psychoanalytic Encounter* and *Into the Mountain Stream: Psychotherapy and Buddhist Experience*. His poetry collections include: *Still Standing: Three Stones Haiku* and *Solitary Moon: New Waka*.

He maintains psychotherapy practices in New York City and in Narrowsburg, NY.

Introduction

Two arrows meeting: Zen insight/psychoanalytic action

Previously, I described the Zen impulse as an inner directed force that propels and energizes the individual toward actualizing and expressing the salvational aims of religious practice and influences the psychoanalytic encounter both consciously and unconsciously. I noted that this impulse is not limited exclusively to Zen alone, but manifests in many forms. I wrote:

> The Zen impulse is a universal that is not limited to one culture, time or place, a particular language or religious system. It is more a frame of mind and a mode of perceiving, experiencing, being in the world and relating to others with sensitivity, understanding and compassion. In short, it is a way of living our lives.
>
> (2010, p. 6)

D.T. Suzuki has observed that the Zen impulse is the force that "… makes all these religions and philosophies vital and inspiring keeping up their influence and efficiency" (1949, p. 268). The Zen impulse has been expressed, for instance, as "Original Face," "True source of all Buddhas," and "Infinite Becoming." These various expressions point to the energetic expression of this impulse internally as rising and falling internal subjective states and externally as objectified experiences. The complete perfection that Zen teaches is our original endowment and finds full expression in the notion of *gūjin*, or total exertion (total penetration, or total immersion), which, in relation to the psychoanalytic encounter, is the subject of this offering.

Despite the universality of the Zen impulse, I don't want to convey the impression that I am subscribing to perennialism or, for instance, the *Sanatana Dharma* of Hinduism as advocated by the Indian sage and mystic Ramakrishna and his followers or that was popularized by Aldous Huxley (1945). Different religious systems articulate different goals. Zen is no exception.

Additionally, from the Zen perspective, it is important to understand that this force or impulse does not operate or exist separately or as a distinct entity from our concrete lived being. That is, total exertion – the central thread in this present offering – of the Zen impulse should not be confused for animism or thought of as a force, spirit, soul, or impulse separate from physical existence and that somehow moves on and exists after the death and decay of the physical body.

The Japanese monk, Eihei Dogen (1200–1253), was the founder of the Japanese Soto Zen school that he imported from China, where he journeyed in search of authentic Buddhism due to his disillusionment with Kamakura-era Buddhism in Japan. Dogen's disillusionment left him with fundamental questions central to Buddhist beliefs and practice unanswered. Dogen's Zen promotes a radical non-dualism. It is from this orientation that the views described above assert a reification and a dualistic separation between the physical and the spiritual aspects of being and between notions of delusion and realization. From the paradoxical Zen perspective, the total exertion of the Zen impulse is neither immanence nor transcendence, yet it is both. Freedom emerges and is experienced through deep immersion in experience. I will tackle these concerns from different vantage points in the ensuing chapters. Simply stated, the Zen impulse is a way of describing realization in terms of activity and relationships in the moment-to-moment experience of our everyday lives.

I also exemplified, through an exploration of Zen kōans, clinical vignettes, and extended case studies, how the Zen impulse influences the psychoanalytic encounter. In this text I add texture, deepen, and expand my previous work in greater detail by focusing on *gūjin*, a notion that serves as a focal point, background theme, and loose organizing structure for this edition.

Briefly stated, *gūjin* refers to the ability of an individual to totally penetrate the nature of an experience, which, from the Zen perspective, is the hallmark of authentic selfhood. I propose that the potential for freedom resides in our capacity for exercising *gūjin* and for realizing the ongoing total exertion and presencing of all phenomena. In this respect, total exertion becomes an affirmation and an expression of the moment-to-moment situation itself and, ultimately, of life.

I will explicate this pivotal Zen notion by drawing from Dogen's extensive writings. His use of *gūjin* finds expression in his monumental *Shōbōgenzō* (True Dharma Eye) and in various contemporary, scholarly, and religious commentaries (Bielefeldt, 1988; Cook, 1977, 1985, 1989; Heine, 2012; Kim, 1985, 2004, 2007; Okumura, 2010; Stambaugh, 1999). *Gūjin* is the activity that facilitates the full functioning of this inner directed force and that, when actualized through practice, influences every aspect of life, including personal religious development, relationships, creative endeavors, and the psychoanalytic encounter. I will further define and elaborate *gūjin* in Chapter 1, "Total exertion: definition and use."

Motivation

The primary motivating factor that encouraged this edition developed out of a series of formal presentations, workshops, and classes that I facilitated in different venues over the past twenty or so years. This experience includes a class on psychoanalytic technique that I have taught at The National Psychological Association for Psychoanalysis (NPAP) in New York City annually since 1996 and where I served as Dean of Training from 2008 to 2010. Additionally, I was invited to develop and facilitate a course on Buddhism and psychoanalysis for the Institute for Expressive Analysis, for NPAP and for the Metropolitan Institute for Training in Psychoanalysis and Psychotherapy in New York City.

During several presentations sponsored by the Cafh Foundation, the Association for Spirituality and Psychotherapy in New York City, the International Forum for Psychoanalytic Education, and, more recently, Zen meditation retreats tailored specifically for the needs of psychoanalysts, psychotherapists, and mental health professionals, I became acutely aware of a need to explicate material that requires more extensive elaboration than was realistically possible within the limitations of such venues. In dialogue with colleagues (most notably Robert Gunn, Mel Miller, Alan Roland, and Mark Finn), with my preceptor – the psychoanalyst and Zen master Sojin Diane Martin – and upon subsequent self-reflection, I realize that my language and presentation style in some of my previous offerings can tend to be intensely condensed, partly due to the limitations of conference parameters, and as a result, can unintentionally become enigmatically terse, bordering on the elliptical. This style can make clear comprehension difficult for the participant or reader, especially for individuals who are not well-versed or familiar with these two highly subjective and rarified areas of inquiry and practice.

For instance, with regard to the long-term effects of Zen practice, I noted in my previous writing that the transformation and amelioration of negative emotional states occurs through a process that eventuates in a radical alteration of perception, mixed with a simultaneous and gradual process of transformation extending over an individual's lifetime. In this offering, I intend to elaborate on this experience beyond pointing to the subject/object split that occurs through the unconscious and active operation of *avidya* ("not-knowing") processes that defend the individual from experiencing fundamental anxiety. For instance, to stay with the same example, in this work I detail this process more closely in Chapter 5, "Realization and delusion," and I return to this theme in subsequent chapters, which provide detailed and extensive clinical material that explicates the conceptual and abstract aspects of the discussion.

The territory ahead

The material that follows is loosely divided into separate chapters. Each chapter addresses total exertion in relation to a different area of inquiry including religious beliefs and practices, psychoanalytic theory, clinical practice, the interplay of subjectivity and objectivity in psychoanalytic listening, creativity, and daily life. The topics are intimately and inextricably intertwined, so that the chapter separations outlined here are somewhat arbitrary. The reader will find areas of overlap, with various threads repeated within the context of the specific topic presented in each chapter. For example, Chapter 4, "Total exertion as intuition," includes clinical material in order to clarify and exemplify the abstract concepts under discussion. Additionally, clinical vignettes that serve to clarify the material presented in each chapter are sprinkled throughout the text.

The material under discussion in this edition draws from the extensive academic and sectarian Zen literature, poetry, psychoanalytic theory, personal encounters with Zen teachers, clinical material, and life experience to exemplify the practical significance of total exertion. These various and diverse sources provide rich material for what I describe as "spontaneously arising alternative intuitive models" (Cooper, 2014a) from which the clinician can draw useful parallels to the psychotherapeutic encounter. For example, Chapter 9, "Taste the strawberries," defines and exemplifies the clinical use of a Zen story as an alternative intuitive model within the context of a dream reported by a patient. Chapter 10, "The abyss becoming well," serves to demonstrate the notion of intuitive models in terms of a patient's spontaneously arising water-well image – an image that was highly condensed with both religious and psychotherapeutic meanings and implications for this patient and that furthered his psychic and spiritual development. Both academic and practical/popular writings serve to support my discussion of meditation practice in Chapter 1, "Total exertion: definition and use," Chapter 2, "Simply sitting: origins," Chapter 3, "Dogen Zen: radical reformulation," Chapter 5, "Realization and delusion," Chapter 6, "Thinking, not thinking, beyond thought," and Chapter 8, "Two arrows meeting: Zen insight, psychoanalytic action."

Additionally, I trace the influence of foundational Zen principles in our everyday lives. Various Zen strands of thought conceptualize the practice-generated alteration in perception that I referred to above differently, which in turn influences how the individual approaches *zazen* (sitting meditation), as well as how the experience of *zazen* and associated states of mind will shift as the practitioner's experience and insight deepen over time. In turn, such differences will influence the therapist who practices Zen in terms of how clinical practice and responses to patients are formulated and then articulated. For example, my fairly consistent use of the question to patients, "What is that like for you?" rather than, "How does that make you feel?", "What do you think about that?" or otherwise prematurely telling the patient what I think, upon scrutiny, is deeply rooted in my Zen practice and, upon further reflection, demonstrates clear and deep connections to foundational principles and associated religious practices. I will pursue this further in my discussion of clinical implications in Chapter 4, "Total exertion as intuition," Chapter 7, "Zen musings on Bion's 'O' and 'K'," and Chapter 8, "Two arrows meeting: Zen insight, psychoanalytic action."

Similarly, related to this alteration in perception, in Chapter 6, "Thinking, not thinking, beyond thought," I elaborate on the relationship between these notions and discuss the role of *prajna* as "quick knowing" in relation to the British psychoanalyst Wilfred Bion's (1970) "intuition of 'O'." I argue that it is important not to lose the importance, for instance, of cognitive capacities that are essential for the accurate discrimination and thought required for clear and effective clinical interpretations. Bion studies and Zen studies often tend to over-emphasize intuition in a manner that can devalue, dismiss, or, in general, pay short shrift to cognitive functions. This is in part due to the influence of D.T. Suzuki's pioneering effort to make Zen accessible to the Western reader based on his Rinzai Zen background, which promulgates a radical refutation of language, cognitive capacities, and an associated critique of reasoning processes. This misconception was further fueled by Eric Fromm's critique of language in his discussion of Zen and psychoanalysis (1960). Ideally, both capacities should be well integrated and internalized by the practitioner so that they operate spontaneously, thoughtfully, and as authentic expressions of being in the world. In Chapter 7, "Zen musings on Bion's 'O' and 'K'," I review the integrative literature on Bion and Buddhism and explicate basic identities, similarities, and differences.

Finally, but no less importantly, I emphasize the highly experiential and practice-oriented agenda of Zen practice. In this context, for instance, the Buddhist scholar Carl Bielefeldt writes that "The Zen school is the meditation school, and the character of Zen can be traced in the tradition of its meditation teaching" (1988, p. 1). With this orientation in mind, I will discuss *zazen* in detail in Chapter 2, "Simply sitting: origins," and Chapter 3, "Dogen Zen: radical reformulation."

A word on language

I will now return briefly to the issue of language that I mentioned above. The Japanese Zen scholar, Masao Abe, writes: "Zen is a double-edged sword, killing words and thoughts, yet at the same time, giving them life" (1985, p. 23). Abe's paradoxical reflection on language tersely summarizes the problem with a largely apophetic communication style in Zen and perhaps all religious traditions and that is clearly evidenced in many psychoanalytic writings. The contemporary American Buddhist scholar, Steven Heine, traces this issue throughout Zen's rich history and he unpacks it in salvational terms. The challenge for both the psychoanalyst and for the Zen practitioner becomes one of developing a cogent, clear, and convincing style of language, whether written or spoken, which effectively addresses the causes of suffering. This language strives to be at once informative and performative. For Heine, the problem becomes one of developing a style of communication:

> ... to convey the truth of subjectivity by creating a style of expression that can suggest just enough to get the appropriate message across, but not too much in a way that might obfuscate or distort through objectification the fundamental subjectivity of spiritual attainment.
> (1994, p. 53)

In other words, to address this point from a psychoanalytic perspective, the issue becomes, as Antonino Ferro (2006) points out, one of offering "unsaturated" interpretations to the analysand and avoiding "saturated interpretations." Following Bion's work (1970), I have described this notion previously as an "oversaturation of psychic space" (2010).

This style becomes problematic in terms of integrating religious and psychoanalytic perspectives because we are dealing with two radically different language styles. At the extreme, the former presents as performative and the latter appears as informative, although typically both disciplines are infused with varying interpenetrations of both styles depending on the orientation of the writer (speaker). The linear, logical, and systematic style of exposition demanded by the psychoanalyst aligned with the scientific model concerns itself with detailed precision. Kavanaugh (2003, 2004, 2005, 2009, 2010), for instance, offers a persistent, detailed, cogent, and convincing critique of this style and approach to psychoanalysis.

However, this style, which privileges an assumed objectivity and rational thought processes, can saturate the reader's psychic space, leaving no room for subjective intuitive realization. In contrast, at the other end of the spectrum, there is a tendency in religious dialogue to be purposely terse, elliptical, and obscure. This style is intended to keep the psychic space open in a way that will mobilize the reader's (listener's) active involvement in the text, engage the reader's intuitive capacities and intentionally engender what Heine characterizes as "a 'leap' into the realm of subjectivity" (1994, p. 54). This style has been the hallmark and defining feature of Zen oral discourse as reflected in the distinctive, unique, and enigmatic Zen kōan.

I will briefly mention another example that centers on the role and function of language in Zen practice drawn from the *Madhyamika* or "middle way" school, founded by the influential Indian sage, Nagarjuna (150–250 CE), and which refutes the absolutist and nihilist extremism espoused by other religious philosophies of the time.

Nagarjuna viewed language as limited to everyday, ordinary, or relative reality, but was considered to be an obstacle to clear experiencing of ultimate or absolute reality. Therefore, from this perspective, language must be cut through. This point of view finds graphic expression in the Zen literature through, for instance, Ta-hui (1089–1163) beating his students with a stick whether they answered his questions with either a yes or a no.

On this point, the Korean Zen scholar, Soeng, notes, "The fallacy of using language to describe human experience in broad general categories like 'suffering' or 'happiness' is likely to turn into metaphysical or ideological statements that many traditions take for granted" (2004, p. 28). Soeng's statement is not simply a condemnation of language; rather, it is a warning of the dangers inherent in misuse, as Kim notes when he writes: "To be sure, Dogen vehemently attacked those who were entrapped and victimized by the words and doctrines they themselves created; he abhorred a deadly literalism" (2004, p. 84). The freedom to use words and letters derives from non-attachment, not through exclusion, as Abe notes:

> Not relying on words and letters, however, does not, as is often misunderstood even by Zen practitioners, indicate a mere exclusion of words or letters, but rather signifies the necessity of not clinging to them. Insofar as one is not attached to words and letters, one can use them freely even in the realm of Zen.
> (1985, p. 23)

In this regard, we could view Te-shan, who, as legend has it, carried the *Diamond Sutra* and his extensive notes with him in a backpack, as representative of attachment. Whether or not this story is true does not matter as much as the symbolic value it conveys in regard to the potential for attachment to scriptures, and which from the Zen perspective obscures experiential truth. (For elaboration and analysis, see Heine, 1994, pp. 32–33). Alternatively, Dogen promulgated a contrasting view. He finds truth in all experience, including language. Further, taking a radically non-anthropomorphic stance, he does not limit language to human experience, but frequently speaks of the language of grasses, mountains, rivers, etc. This all-inclusive, non-anthropocentric view finds expression in his poem:

> The mystical cry of monkeys
> Resounding from the mountain peaks,
> Echoing in the valleys below:
> The sound of the
> The sutra being preached.
> (Heine, 1997, p. 97)

The shifting relationship between realization and delusion, which I discuss in Chapter 5, "Realization and delusion," serves as a central example of such controversies and holds significant implications for both religious practice and for the psychotherapeutic situation. Misunderstandings to some extent derive through a misreading of the translated teachings, which, as I noted above, requires an understanding of the historical, socio-political context in which the original commentaries were developed and how they might have been used or misused to meet the specific agendas of the followers of the original teacher. Bielefeldt (1988), Faure (1991, 1993), Gunn (2000), Heine (1994), and Kim (2004), among others, provide detailed, thorough, and thought-provoking discussions regarding personal experiences, sectarian concerns, political pressures, and the socio-cultural matrix through thorough analyses of the material in question. For instance, Gunn (2000) provides a poignant and moving account of how the tragic losses in Dogen's life influenced his thinking about emptiness. Similarly, Kim (2004), for example, describes the turmoil of Kamakura-era Japan (1185–1333) and its influence on Dogen's views on transience. The etymological origin of the term "Zen" serves as a case in point and will be examined thoroughly in Chapter 2, "Simply sitting: origins."

In conclusion, I hope that with the careful unpacking on my part that this material demands, the writing in this edition will be clear and will benefit the reader, as well as all beings with whom the reader comes in contact, as much as the self-scrutiny involved in the writing process has benefited me.

Chapter 1

Total exertion: definition and use

Introduction

Zen is primarily a practice-oriented discipline. Zen defines practice and practice defines Zen. The term "Zen" derives from the Chinese Ch'an, which in turn derives from the Indian *dhyāna*, the fifth of the six perfections, and is translated as "concentration" or "meditation." The complexities and inaccuracy of this etymological translation will be explicated in Chapter 2, "Simply sitting: origins." For the purposes of the present chapter, suffice it to say that "Zen" as a name for a religious system points to this practice orientation and defines Zen as a highly subjective and experiential discipline.

Gūjin (total exertion, manifestation, penetration, immersion, diligence, or thorough investigation), a central notion in Soto Zen, points to this practice orientation. *Gūjin* is short for *ippo gūjin* or "total exertion of a single thing." With regard to each dharma, or each individual moment of existence, the Japanese philosopher, Masao Abe, notes:

> In the self-awakening of Zen, each individual existence – whether person, animal, plant or thing – manifests itself in its particularity as expressed in the formulation, "willows are green, flowers are red," and yet each is interpenetrating harmoniously as expressed in the formulation, "when Lee drinks wine, Chang gets drunk." This is not an end but a *ground* on which our being and activity must be properly based.
>
> (1985, p. 21, emphasis in original)

The Dogen scholar, Hee-Jin Kim, defines *gūjin* as an ongoing expression of a "... radically non-dualistic mode of living and thinking" (1985, p. 55). He describes *gūjin* as "... Dogen's appropriation of the traditional Mahayana principle of non-duality/absolute emptiness; it is the core of the realization kōan and, for that matter, of single-minded sitting" (1985, p. 59). *Shikantaza* (just sitting, only sitting), which will be discussed in Chapter 3, "Dogen Zen: radical reformulation," functions as an experiential and operationalized expression of this truth of non-duality.

In clinical terms, we might ask: "Who is the patient now, at this very moment?" or, as Bion put it, "The psychoanalyst should aim at achieving a state of mind so that at every session he feels he has not seen the patient before. If he feels he has, he is treating the wrong patient" (1967, pp. 18–19).

Can we facilitate with the patient the experiencing of more "emotional elbow room" to be fully who s/he is now, or do we become preoccupied with future goals, prognoses, or outcomes? Or, as the British psychoanalyst, Eric Rhode, writes with regard to Bion's notion of "O":

> As the variable, "O" activates a state of *becoming* unrelated to any claim to therapeutic progress or cure. In the religious vertex [point of view] nothing progresses or is cured. There is either an evasion or a recognition of "O" by way of a *becoming*.
>
> (1998, p. 118, emphasis in original)

This "way of becoming" that Rhode points to, as I see it, relates directly to the ongoing functioning or activity described by the action of *gūjin*. For instance, in a discussion of precursors to Dogen Zen that parallels Rhode's observation, the American Zen scholar, Carl Bielefeldt, notes: "… every sight and every smell is the ultimate middle way, in which ignorance is identical with enlightenment, samsara is identical with nirvana, and there is no religious path leading from one to the other" (1988, p. 87). In this context, "samsara" refers to the cycle of "ongoing oscillation or movement," where beings cycle through six psychophysical realms of existence.

Practice/action

The contemporary Soto Zen priest–scholar, Shohaku Okumura, describes the identity of practice and action in Soto Zen. He locates action at the center of the Zen religious endeavor from Dogen's perspective and observes:

> The characteristic theme of Dogen's teaching is "action rather than thinking is practice" … Dogen encourages us to actively encounter everything in our lives as *prajna*" … [And] Since everything is *prajna paramita*, we should enquire into everything. "To enquire into everything" means to try to see the reality of each and every being.
>
> (2010, pp. 40–41)

Gūjin functions simultaneously to point to the way things are and as a prescription for action. This seemingly paradoxical relationship between presently manifesting reality and action is reconciled by considering our mode of being in the world and in our attitude toward life. This "dual orientation" sets forth, as Kim notes, a "radically non-dualistic mode of living and thinking" (1985, p. 55). Total exertion at once functions as a lived expression of the fundamental antinomy of being and as a Zen response to numerous dialectical relationships and identities of seemingly contradictory pairs, including: non-duality/duality, relative/absolute, same/different, self-limitation/self-liberation, samsara/nirvana, realization/delusion, immanence/transcendence, and original enlightenment/acquired enlightenment. For instance, the term "*kōan*" expresses equality/differentiation. In terms of the identity of the relative and absolute from the *gūjin* perspective, Kim notes that "… every dharma in the world has its unique particularity, yet exists in such a way that it bears absolute significance: while being a single unique dharma, it is at once all dharmas and no-dharma" (1985, p. 58).

As an aside, this view exemplifies the Chilean psychoanalyst, Matte-Blanco's (1988), observation from the psychoanalytic perspective regarding unconscious processes that, when what he describes as "total symmetrization" occurs, everything mysteriously becomes everything else. Negation becomes affirmation and affirmation becomes negation. This raises the question: "How do we live in duality–non-duality, in absolute freedom, in kōan?" I will further elaborate Matte-Blanco's ideas in Chapter 4, "Total exertion as intuition" (see also Cooper, 2010, pp. 123–147).

Kim further amplifies the connection between the radical experiential nature of Zen and total exertion as an active process. He writes:

> The reality of total exertion is thoroughly saturated with the principle of ascesis (namely, practice or discipline), privileging the latter over vision, not in order to deny seeing, but to explicate a deeper meaning, one that seeing itself is fundamentally creating and making. That is to say, seeing presupposes the vow or resolution on the part of the seer to create a new being or a new reality; hence, it concerns itself not only with seeing things as they are but creating things as they are meant to be. This is why total exertion can be understood only against the background of the ascesis of *zazen*. It is to be enacted rather than envisioned.
>
> (1985, p. 59)

Concept/action

We can talk about total exertion or point to it conceptually; however, the actual experiencing in actional terms is required to really penetrate this notion. The idea or concept becomes real through lived practice. In this sense, total exertion is *zazen*; *zazen* is total exertion. The path to studying both Zen and psychoanalysis with the former's emphasis on practice is to study the experience of self. The study of self requires being fully and totally present with one's experience here and now. No other time, place, or vantage point exists except the immediate and present situation. The past is no more than a memory, whether faded or vivid. The future is no more than a wish and a fantasy. Past memories and future fantasies all occur in the present. Dogen elaborates this perspective in the *Uji* (Being Time) fascicle of *Shōbōgenzō* (Treasury of the True Dharma Eye), a collection of Dogen's discourses on Zen delivered or written between 1231 and 1253.

Dogen describes the past, present, and future as all occurring in the present moment. This basic assumption lies behind the intensely experiential, personal, and practice-oriented nature of Zen training. With this orientation in mind, it becomes clear that what is the most distinctive and defining feature of total exertion is its inseparability from each and every situation of daily life. As Kim notes:

> When a single thing exerts itself totally and is cast off (*datsuraku*), it does so by virtue of and in concert with all other things in the universe. Thus a single dharma is "illumined," whereas all other dharmas are "darkened."
> (2007, p. 63)

In Dogen's extensive writing, the notion of total exertion is simultaneously pervasive and illusive: pervasive because it constitutes a major theme implicitly drawn upon throughout his writings; illusive because despite its significance for Dogen's active, in the world, non-dualist religious praxis, he did not write a specific or detailed fascicle devoted exclusively or exhaustively to the concept. Commentators pull on threads throughout Dogen's extensive writings to address total exertion. For example, the notion of total exertion finds indirect and implicit expression in the title of the pivotal "*Genjō-kōan*" fascicle of *Shōbōgenzō*. "*Genjō-kōan*" translates to "spontaneous realization of enlightenment" (Heine, 2012, p. 42), "The Way of Everyday Life" (Maezumi, 1978, unnumbered pages), "The Realized Universe" (Nishijima & Cross, 1996, p. 33), and "Manifesting Suchness" (Waddell & Abe, 2002, p. 39), among many other versions. Despite the variations, immediacy functions as a common and insistent thread in all of the translations. This implicit connection to *gūjin* is evident in Waddell and Abe's introduction to their translation of this important fascicle. They observe that:

> The term *genjō-kōan* is difficult to translate satisfactorily into English … but in *Shōbōgenzō*, Dogen attached a special significance to it, using it as a technical term and an important concept in his thought. *Genjō*, literally something like "becoming manifest" or "immediately manifesting right here and now," does not refer to the manifesting of something previously not manifested but rather to the immediate presence (or presencing) of all things as they truly are in their suchness, untouched by our conscious strivings; their ultimate reality, realized in religious practice.
> (2002, p. 39)

Total exertion also finds implicit expression in Dogen's action-oriented and highly practical *Tenzo-kyokun* (*Instructions to the Cook*). He writes:

Select the rice and prepare the vegetables by yourself with your own hands, watching closely with sincere diligence. You should not attend to some things and neglect or be slack with others for even one moment.
(Translated and quoted by Okumura, 2010, p. 176)

When we focus our full energy and attention on the task at hand, whatever that activity might be – washing dishes, sitting in *zazen*, walking, eating, or working – we become experientially and intuitively aware of the lived, ongoing, total exertion of life. In other words, from the perspective of the individual, life becomes fully exerted; we become totally exerted; the situation becomes totally exerted. From this perspective, Okumura notes that "We do this over and over again with whatever we encounter, one thing at a time, each time …" (2010, p. 176). In terms of realization, Dogen writes: "… the known [which appears limited] is born and practiced simultaneously with the complete penetration of the Buddha Dharma" (translated and quoted by Okumura, 2010, p. 178).

This quote from the classical Japanese poet and literary critic, Tamekane (1254–1332), exemplifies total exertion in terms of creative practice. While Tamekane does not use the term, he provides a working example of how total exertion influences his approach poetry. He writes:

In order to express the true nature of the natural scene, one must focus one's attention and concentrate deeply upon it … Therefore, if you try to harmonize your feelings with the sight of cherry blossoms in spring or with the autumnal scene, and you express them in words without allowing anything to intervene between your feelings and the scene, then your work will become one with the very spirit of heaven and earth.
(Translated and quoted by Miner, 1968, p. 27)

Tamekane points to the interfering impact of abstractions such as concepts, definitions, ideas, dogma, religious beliefs and theories, which can intrude and buffer direct experience. Without such intrusions, the poem becomes a matter of lived experience – no more, no less. My intention here is not to devalue concepts and reasoning processes, a topic I take up in Chapter 6, "Thinking, not thinking, beyond thought." I simply want to demonstrate, at this point, the notion of freedom from obstruction, which is crucial to understanding and living in total exertion.

The following haiku serves to exemplify this point:

the spring breeze pushes
somebody
down the slope
  – Issa (eighteenth century
   translation: Lanoue, no date)
(http://haikuguy.com/issa/search.php)

Note that there is no speculation, no inference – simply the scene itself. The reader who remains open to the experiential dimension of the poem will be placed in the scene and will feel its impact. The objective aspect of the experience presented in the poem evokes the reader's subjective participation. There are no preconceived notions concerning any aspect of this poem. The total situation fully involves both poem and reader. As a result, the reader has the opportunity to fully participate in the scene. As the reader, I am on the slope, pushed by the breeze. Issa does not intrude or impose himself on the reader. He does not have to tell the reader who "somebody" is or what to feel. My psychic space remains unsaturated. I am free to fully feel whatever emerges for me.

We might ask, what is the true nature of any scene? What is the true nature of any moment, sitting in *zazen*, the psychoanalytic encounter, the marketplace, the sound of crows at dawn? What is natural, spontaneous, unnatural, contrived? Can we know these things? How do we know? Do we know through cognition, intuition, or a combination of both? Is one mode privileged at the expense of the other? How do we live in fullness, in emptiness, in the fullness of emptiness and/or the emptiness of fullness? How do we live in transcendence, in transcendent transcendence, in immanent transcendence? Are these questions amenable to answers? From the Zen perspective, the question *is* the answer. In any case, such questions (and answers) serve as loose threads to pull on and to push the edges of our horizons.

Definition

In terms of defining *gūjin*, the philosopher, Joan Stambaugh, writes: "Looked at from the standpoint of the situation itself, the situation is totally manifested or exerted without obstruction or contamination" (1999, p. 6). Stambaugh further notes that, "The person experiencing the situation totally becomes it. He is not thinking *about* it; he *is* it. When he does this, the situation is completely revealed and manifested" (1999, p. 6, emphasis in original).

She continues by noting that total exertion refers to an opening that calls for a response to every situation that "… is never anything passive but can be quite strenuous" (1999, p. 7). In this context, "strenuous" refers to exertion without force or strain. The intention is on opening or presencing as fully and as completely as possible. Total exertion both generates and is the experience of absolute reality as that reality manifests in one's lived experience. Total exertion requires full participation totally with nothing left out for opening to and fully experiencing this manifestation. Kim further describes Dogen's fundamental idea of:

> The total exertion of a single thing (*ippō-gūjin*) … was maintained less in the static mode of emptiness and more in the dynamic and creative mode

in which any single act (dying, eating, what not) was totally exerted contemporaneously, coextensively, and coessentially with total mind – not with a fragment of the mind.

(2004, p. 125)

Heine adds:

... if a person completely comprehends one particular thing and its Buddha Dharma ... they will be able to comprehend completely all things or dharmas in harmonious conjunction with the whole of Buddha Dharma. This view follows the notion of *ippō-gūjin*, or the thorough investigation or total exertion of a single dharma.

(2012, p. 55)

As noted above, *gūjin* is also translated as "total penetration." In this context, penetration has a cognitive connotation in the sense of penetrating into the deep meaning of the subject, whether abstract or concrete. This cognitive connotation is implied in Tamekane's advice to the poet quoted above because he refers to the active exertion by the experiencing subject. Alternatively, as Stambaugh suggests in her definition, one lives totally lived, intuitively felt in the moment of the experiential disclosure of ultimate reality. The Zen scholar, Francis Cook, clarifies this distinction. He notes that:

In the first sense *gūjin* refers to the ability of an individual to totally penetrate the nature of an experience or entity, this ability being the hallmark of authentic selfhood. In the second sense, *gūjin* is the same as *zenki* (total dynamic functioning) and *genjō-kōan*.

(1985, p. 142)

In this regard, *gūjin* refers to the individual self, whereas *zenki* refers to all existence or to what Buddhists describe as the universal Self.

I use the term "total exertion" rather than total manifestation or total penetration for the sake of consistency and because it points to the active involvement of the practitioner that engenders manifestation and realization. In this respect, the emphasis is on the practitioner's participation in an ongoing active process rather than simply with a result, which can become reified and limiting, as well as paradoxically devaluing of the present moment. As an active process, the opportunity for total exertion occurs in each and every moment. Every ordinary moment, every ordinary activity becomes special, sacred, and profound in its ordinariness and simplicity. Total exertion engenders and is an expression of this manifestation of absolute reality when no aspect or part of the self is left out; when one is fully present. This fully lived moment, here, now is *it*!

Anxiety

Cook notes that for Dogen, "... that which is appearing, manifest, or being present as a datum of one's experience is the absolute reality" (1989, p. 22). However, the anxieties that might be stirred up regarding living fully present interfere with this experiential realization and fully lived, "no part of the self left out" awareness. As a result, life becomes difficult and seemingly more of a challenge than we bargained for. We leave ourselves out, perhaps more or less partially present. We daydream, become preoccupied with results, or simply space out. We maintain a naive attachment to and strive toward preferred psychological states and we imagine alternative realities. If there is another transcendent state, reality, or being other than what is present here and now, right before us, then what would that state be? This points to the internal perceptual shifts that enable one to fully realize this reality here and now, in this moment. *Zazen* makes sense through the experience that verifies for the practitioner that such practice engenders the capacity to totally penetrate or exert the sense of wonder, depth, specialness, and spiritual being in the ordinary activities of everyday life. In this respect, total exertion functions as an activity that facilitates intuition and subjective knowing, or what the Japanese philosopher, Shin'ichi Hisamatsu, describes as being "in complete unity with the flow" (1979, p. 2). The ordinariness of this unity and flow is expressed in the Zen tradition through such phrases as "chop wood, carry water," "eat plain boiled rice, drink plain green tea," and "when eating, eat; when drinking, drink!"

Anxiety can create and feed aimless rushing around mindlessly and half-heartedly getting through the many tasks of the day that we are faced with. This rushing unconsciously and unwittingly further increases anxiety. We can get caught in a vicious downward spiral until we burn out. This ongoing mindless recklessness becomes internalized, contributes to an unquestioned way of life, and inadvertently increases anxiety. Mindlessness replaces living in awareness as the full attention to our activities diminishes and, with it, the quality of what we produce suffers, as does the quality of life. Awareness can be co-opted by this anxiety-driven defensive mindlessness by splitting the person into an observing self watching an operating self, but safely split off and removed in the distance from the fullness of being. The British psychoanalyst, Betty Joseph, captures this split-off and emotionally removed type of mindfulness in the psychoanalytic encounter graphically. She writes:

> I believe we can observe a splitting within the personality, so that one part of the ego is kept at a distance from the analyst and the analytic work. Sometimes this is difficult to see since the patient may appear to be working and co-operating with the analyst, but the part of the personality that is available is actually keeping another more needy or potentially responsive and receptive part split off. Sometimes the split takes the

form of one part of the ego standing aside as if observing all that is going on between the analyst and the other part of the patient and destructively preventing real contact being made, using various methods of avoidance and evasion.

(1989, p. 75)

Ouch!

One moment of preoccupation and mindless rushing through some errands and I found myself needing to be picked up off the street after a fall that severely twisted my ankle, fracturing the bone, which left me incapacitated and restricted my movement for the next several months and which still causes me discomfort and serves as an accurate indicator of coming shifts in the weather. Situations like this occur all of the time. Small mindless actions engender unimaginably magnified consequences.

Slowness: a case in point

Over time, meeting the pressures of the day in this anxious, half-hearted way becomes normalized. I am reminded here of a patient who simply could not tolerate as much as a moment of silence or what she perceived as my "slowness" during our sessions. She complained to me that "this is not moving fast enough for me; you keep stopping; I don't have time for stopping." She found my suggestion to "sit back and give yourself a chance to see what comes to mind" to be quite offensive and a waste of her time. She simply wanted a laundry list of tasks from me. This would have only added more to her manic approach to life. She left after our second meeting. Psychically, she might never have arrived in the first place.

Practice

black coffee,
steam swirls rising:
silent morning.
   (Cooper, 2014c, p. 2)

Zazen expands the moment and diminishes the need to rush. I can sip my morning coffee with full awareness, savor its aroma and flavor, feel it warming my chest, and enjoy a sense of satisfaction when it is brewed well. Alternatively, I can gulp it down, possibly scald my tongue and quickly run out the door. The choice is mine. Practice expands each moment into infinity, which spreads out in infinite directions. This expansion and presencing of each moment can contribute to a feeling of well-being. The experience itself takes one beyond any cognitive notions dichotomized as "mindfulness/mindlessness." We simply sip coffee – no more, no less. On this point, Hisamatsu observes, "In the present there is stability and composure. Since in ordinariness there is the quality of the present, man, in his ordinariness, can feel at ease and live his life" (1979, p. 3).

In this regard, total exertion reflects the fundamentally subjective nature of Buddhist experience and engenders living a fully unified and subjective life. Our anxiety-driven preconceptions engender less than full participation in each moment and can also limit the flow and direction that the moment takes. Over time, practice makes this experientially clear. It is a basic human habit to follow well-worn streams of thoughts, feelings, or moods. Like a river, mind currents forge channels in the riverbed and create the conditions of the flow. The work of total exertion can alter this flow by creating new channels and altering or softening old ones. The following clinical example expands and clarifies this point.

Bena

During silent moments, Bena typically experiences me as viewing her in a critical and negative light. Among the infinite possibilities that the moment presents, she would always find herself flowing down this particular thought stream. This stereotypical response to the moment and to my silence was set a long time ago as a result of her mother's cold and silent expression of negativity toward her. Bena has understood this cognitively for quite some time. Still, the depths of her emotional experience continued to pull her in this direction, as if caught in a riptide of currents too strong to swim against and that foreclose any other possibilities or potentials of the moment. For example, she could not consider the possibility that my silent attention to her narrative might be motivated by my interest in uninterruptedly hearing what she has to say; by my intention to understand her experience; by my genuine curiosity about her life, feelings, beliefs, thoughts, and values; by providing her the time and space that would allow her own experience to evolve and become manifest. The coloration of Bena's past would repeatedly spill over into the present and operate as forms of obstruction that would prevent her whole self from becoming totally exerted with a lived, "no part left out" presence.

Francis Cook's comment regarding *gūjin* finds clinical relevance here. He writes, "Looked at from the person who experiences the situation, it means that one is identified with it utterly. Looked at from the standpoint of the situation itself, the situation is totally manifested or exerted without obstruction" (2002, p. 43).

Bena was not able to allow this process of awareness to unfold. Her attachment to past influences was safely familiar, albeit limiting and painful. She found herself in the grip of the human tendency to grasp on to the familiar, even though the familiar is noticeably dysfunctional, especially during times of increased anxiety. As a result, her experience of the situation was obstructed and colored by the past and the limiting streams that channeled her present perceptions of the other – in this case, me. She was not able to take in or respond to my wonder, curiosity, or interest. This utter and complete manifestation from a Zen kōan, "Dongshan's Hot and Cold," from *Shoyo Roku* (*The Book of Serenity*), a thirteenth century collection of Zen kōans, which Cook refers to finds expression in such statements as "when it is hot, be completely hot; when it is cold, be completely cold" (2002, p. 43). In terms of relationships, for Bena, perhaps a suitable translation of this Zen expression as it relates to the psychoanalytic encounter might be "with a listener or witness, simply be listened to and be witnessed," or "when talking, talk!"

The potential for freedom resides in our capacity for exercising total exertion. This freedom derives from embracing or being the situation. In this respect, total exertion simultaneously becomes an affirmation of the situation itself, an expression of the situation itself – ultimately, of life. Zen practice thus becomes a full expression and affirmation of life manifesting as it is, which is the fundamental message of "*Genjō-kōan*" mentioned above.

Practice engenders a radically realistic solution to suffering. Rather than becoming removed from the seemingly mundane, ordinary, everyday world and its problems, the Zen practitioner experiences a shift in perception. This sudden and radical alteration of perception occurs instantly upon what Dogen describes as "body and mind dropping off." Infinity radiates from the nodal point of the lived moment. As this moment expands into infinity – or rather, as infinity becomes realized – expressive possibilities expand. New creative expressions evolve into form. For instance, for the writer, to draw on Matte-Blanco's notion of symmetrization that I mentioned above, the blank page – so full of blankness, blankness totally exerted – becomes the fullness of blankness and the matrix of expression. Blankness is fullness; fullness is blankness. Can a writer, for instance, write from blankness or only from fullness? Can our momentary options expand? From this expanded vantage point, the world comes to be viewed differently, priorities change, relationships change, and life becomes revitalized.

> *drifting*
> *in and out of dreams*
> *this blank page*
>   (Cooper, 2014c, p. 5)

Through total exertion, the practitioner experiences reality being just as it is and, through the simultaneous movement away from limiting self-reference, can respond to that reality selflessly as needed. From this perspective, compassion is automatic, spontaneous, and selfless and consists of a sincere and heartfelt action or response to that reality.

Implications

Total exertion holds profound implications for every area of our lives, how we relate to ourselves, how we respond to others, and how we deal with work and with play. The activities of everyday living become expressions of compassion, wisdom, and realization. Realization becomes an ongoing active participation in a magnified life, not a static end point. Buddha-nature becomes expressed in all activities "... and frees one from compulsive self-serving motives and deeds, anxiety, fear, hatred and illusion" (Cook, 1989, p. 39). In short, when the energy of the Zen impulse becomes totally exerted, we can have an impact and life has an impact. Bena begins to feel listened to non-judgmentally and taken seriously, and her relationship with her experience broadens as new channels in the psychic streambed become forged. These internal changes manifest externally in shifting relationships with her family and friends.

This impact includes how we approach religious practice and how we use or misuse scriptures or how we understand notions of spirituality, most particularly the notion of transcendence, which I will unpack in Chapter 5, "Realization and delusion."

Living by total exertion demands that the practitioner goes beyond the bounds of what can be defined as formal aspects of practice, in addition to *zazen*, ritual performance, prayer, and work practice. Total exertion as practice encompasses all activity. It is inclusive, not exclusive. Sitting on the toilet, sitting on the *zafu*, sitting on or behind the couch – no difference! It is in this ordinariness of simple, everyday activities that self-realization truly takes place. Dogen observes "... that enlightenment is just eating rice and drinking tea, that simple acts like these are indeed marvelous ..." (Cook, 2002, p. 54).

Uniqueness of the moment

The actuality of each and every particular moment cannot be devalued, judged, neglected, or dismissed as irrelevant to realization. Rather, each moment emerges as unique, totally exerted, manifesting infinite freedom and possibility. This makes every ordinary situation significant and important. We can say that each situation is unique in its ordinariness, ordinary in its uniqueness. We will return to this topic in order to spell out the implications with regard to discussions on meditation and psychoanalytic listening in Chapter 8, "Two arrows meeting: Zen insight, psychoanalytic action."

Can total exertion be applied in all situations? Can we exercise the same sense of attention to washing a dish as we do to saying a prayer? For me, this teaching becomes real through this challenge. Can I bring the same relaxed and focused attention to walking through New York City's bustling Grand

Central Station between the commuter rail line and the downtown bus in the morning rush hour as I negotiate throngs of rushing commuters that I exert during *kinhin* (walking meditation) in between periods of *zazen* in the *zendo*? Do we get caught up in preoccupations with "Will I catch my bus and get to the office on time?" or, "Do I have time to grab some breakfast?" Do we get caught up in all sorts of mini-dramas and struggles that we encounter as we negotiate this vast sea of humanity flowing in and out of harmony that we call "rush hour"? The "marketplace" can be thought of as the super-luxury model – over-saturated, overstimulated modern-day reality that is embellished with all sorts of add-ons and unexpected challenges or surprises. Formal Zen practices function as the stripped-down prototype model – a bare-bones version of life conducted in an environment that is structured, predictable, and provides the experience of our enlightened being that can be generalized into the way we relate to the unstructured and unpredictable "marketplace" of human interaction.

Do we really tend to the moment fully and totally? A simple moment of observation can be instructive. When rising from the *zafu* (round meditation cushion) at the end of a period of *zazen*, is the mind already rushing ahead to a preoccupation, to the next task at hand? Are we fully present with stretching out our legs, rising to our feet, and bowing, or do we simply go through the motions blindly and absent-mindedly? When rising from the chair at the close of an analytic session, do our thoughts rush ahead to the next patient, to who left a phone message or e-mail? Can we stay with the experience of the moment-to-moment beginnings and endings in the transitional spaces that separate activities?

A simple exercise

Ask yourself the following:

> When brushing my teeth in the morning, am I already thinking ahead to coffee or hair-brushing or picking out my clothing for the day? Am I fully and totally aware of the sound of the toothbrush, the taste of the toothpaste, the sensation of the brush against my teeth and gums, with no part of me left out? If I can't do that when I am alone, how can I expect to be fully present with the complexities of being with others: a group, a friend, a partner, or a patient? When with a patient, am I truly present with that experience and its impact or am I preoccupied with a wish for cure, which, not unlike a wish for transcendence, is really an abstraction about the future and not at all about the concrete, lived present? Is there something intolerable about the present or about the impact of a friend, a partner, or a patient that keeps me focused on the future, dreaming cure, change, or outcome?

What feelings reside beneath this "thinking ahead mind"? What stirs up from within and needs to be defended against: anxiety, resentment, humiliation, boredom, anger or feeling exploited, inadequate, deprived, or embarrassed? What happens to our sense of self-importance when we need to scrub the toilet? How do external factors influence our feelings and behaviors?

The options and variations are infinite and endless. Can we take them up one by one?

Chapter 2

Simply sitting: origins

"*Zazen* is good for nothing!"
Kodo Sawaki, Roshi (Uchiyama & Okumura, 2014, p. 138)

"Psychoanalysis tells you nothing; it is an instrument, like the blind man's stick …"
W.R. Bion (1992, p. 356)

Introduction

This chapter explicates differences in style and intention of *zazen* – Zen sitting meditation – beginning with a discussion of the limits of the typical etymological definition of *zazen* as simply derivative of the Indian *dhyāna* (meditation). Despite the fact that *zazen* holds a central position across various Zen sects, there are diverse descriptions regarding its form, function, goals, and practices. Given this diversity, an etymological definition does not address the tremendous variation between Buddhist sects and within individual sects in terms of definition, technique, ideology, or the soteriological function of any given form for a particular sect. This diversity also permeates various contemporary Zen sects as well.

The specificity of the particular form *shikantaza* – the central practice promulgated by Dogen that I will discuss in greater detail in the next chapter – first demands a re-examination and elaboration of how Zen and *zazen* come to be defined and how any specific practice influences the individual practitioner.

With this foundation in place, we will explicate and explore the relationship between *shikantaza* (just sitting, only sitting), the core Soto Zen meditation practice, in terms of understanding Dogen's radical orientation toward Zen practice with attention to how *shikantaza* functions as an active expression of basic assumptions of the Soto Zen system. Brief comments will demonstrate how sitting and related instructions dovetail and parallel Bion's psychoanalytic orientation and associated technical recommendations to relinquish memory, desire, and understanding (1967, 1970).

Transformations

While the transliteration of *dhyāna* to Ch'an and then to Zen is linguistically accurate and functions as a basic definition of Zen (e.g. Loori, 2002), complex and important if not radical distinctions exist between Indian meditation styles and the resulting transmission and transformation of Indian Buddhism's transmutation into evolving Chinese Ch'an and the resulting development of Soto Zen imported from China to Japan and advocated by Dogen in the thirteenth century. Additionally, a further complication not covered by the simple etymological definition stems from the great diversity of meditation styles within Chinese Ch'an and Japanese Zen. For example, within Zen itself, various approaches to *zazen* might include choiceless awareness, following the breath, counting the breath either on inhalations, exhalations or both, concentrating on the *wato* (head word) of a kōan such as "*Mu*," or some combination of any of these methods.

For example, carrying this radical shift to a highly practical form of Ch'an Buddhism to Japan, Dogen (1244) writes in the *Zanmai O Zanmai* fascicle of the *Shōbōgenzō* ("King of Samadhis" or "Honorable Samadhi"): "To practice [za]zen is to get free of body and mind. Just to sit is to have attainment from the beginning" (Nishijima & Cross, 1996, p. 372). "*Zanmai*" is the Japanese translation of the Sanskrit term *samadhi* and is usually translated into English as "concentration" or "absorption."

As will be discussed in the next chapter, Dogen's *shikantaza* in this regard derives from the Ch'an subitist or "sudden" understanding of realization (Gregory, 1987). From the sudden perspective, enlightenment is immediate. Immediate, in addition to sudden in the temporal sense, also means without mediation, without concepts, or what Thomas Kasulis describes as "pre-reflective" (1981, p. 75) or, in Bion's terms, without memory, desire, or understanding. This orientation originates in Chinese Ch'an Buddhism and Japanese Zen Buddhism, and as the Ch'an scholar, Bernard Faure, notes, "It seems to represent the Chinese reaction – particularly clear-cut in the Chan school – against Indian dhyana and the abhidharmic maps of the path" (1991, p. 34).

Zazen

In the Zen tradition, the term *zazen* refers to meditation. The use of the term "sitting" in this discussion is intended to distinguish this specific form of Zen practice from the more general and abstract idea of "meditation." Meditation, as I hope to demonstrate, is an inaccurate and vague term, as well as misleading in the array of associations that it typically stirs up, such as exclusively a "relaxation response" (Benson, 1975). On this point, Peter Gregory notes that "… although we use a word like 'meditation' without a second thought in our discussions of Buddhism, our word does not correspond to any specific term or general concept within Buddhism" (1986, p. 4). He bases this distinction on the teachings of the influential Sixth Patriarch of Ch'an, Hui-neng's (638–713) description of meditation:

> When he defines seated meditation (*tso ch'an, zazen*), the Sixth Patriarch makes no reference to any physical activity: Sitting (*tso*) means not activating thoughts in regard to external objects, and meditation (*ch'an*) means seeing one's original nature and not being confused.
> (Translated and quoted by Yampolsky, 2012, p. 3)

Despite the enormous diversity between the various Zen Buddhist schools and sects noted above, there is no question that sitting, regardless of the countless ways it is defined and practiced, forms the consistent and common core of Zen Buddhism. For each tradition, sitting serves as the central expression of its belief system as well as its primary realizational method. With regard to the distinctive development of Chinese Buddhism from its Indian origins, the Buddhist scholar, Robert Buswell, notes that it is not possible to separate "the ontology of Buddhism for its soteriological schemata and meditative practices" (1987, p. 326). Therefore, any concrete description of sitting is at once both a practical guide to Zen technique and a religious statement reflecting a particular sect's core beliefs. On this point, in the following discussion, it is important to keep in mind the Dogen scholar Hee-Jin Kim's caution: "Although meditation is the common core of Buddhism, there are many different conceptions and interpretations of it, and these differences have pervaded the history of Buddhism" (2004, p. 58).

Historical shift

With *zazen* at the core of religious practice, a shift occurred historically in Zen religious orientation away from abstract philosophy and doctrine to lived experience and action. For this reason, Zen (and *zazen*) is tough to understand with the depth and nuance that it demands. Zen's highly experiential base makes it hard to approach intellectually. In fact, the intellect is often viewed as an obstacle to a real depth of understanding.

Contemporary scholarship indicates that the Chinese reaction to the highly esoteric and hierarchically organized Indian Buddhism resulted in a uniquely Chinese version of Buddhism. Additionally, the development of Ch'an functioned as a reaction to the highly rigidified and intellectualized Buddhism that was prevalent in China and limited to the educated. As a result, what emerged was at once highly practical, experiential, non-exclusive, and non-hierarchical. Most importantly, the Ch'an orientation functioned in sharp contrast to teleologically-oriented traditions in which at-one-ment represents the experiential nodal point of the religion's soteriological goal and that define a gradual path that leads to such goals. The sudden approach to meditation described above evokes *prajna*, or intuited experiential knowing (See Chapter 4), described as "immediate," "not-mediate," or "sudden" (Gregory, 1987), or, in Buswell's words, functions soteriologically "… as an abrupt approach to spiritual attainment that involved nothing more than direct vision of the enlightened nature of the human mind" (1987, p. 322).

Jōshū's "Wash Your Bowls"

This orientation toward cultivating in the moment lived, experiential, intuited knowing advocated by Ch'an teachers and that intersects with Bion's teachings finds expression in many Zen encounter dialogues and kōans. Kōan Seven, from the *Gateless Gate* (1228) collection of forty-eight Zen kōans compiled in the early thirteenth century by the Chinese Zen master, Wumen Huikai (Japanese: Mumon Ekai; 1183–1260), Jōshū's "Wash Your Bowls" exemplifies this point:

> A monk asked Jōshū in all earnestness, "I have just entered this monastery, I beg you, Master, please give me instructions?" Jōshū asked, "Have you eaten your rice gruel yet?" The monk answered, "Yes I have." Jōshū said, "Then wash your bowls." The monk attained some realization.
> (Yamada, 1979, p. 45)

This kōan is one among many that critiques and negates the need to understand obscure doctrines and philosophical treatises. The kōan addresses the prioritization of direct experience as well as the interference of cognition.

Wumen comments on the encounter between Jōshū and the monk in verse:

> Just because it is so clear,
> It takes us longer to realize it.
> (Yamada, 1979, p. 45)

It was customary for monks to maintain a meditative awareness in all activities on and off the meditation cushion. Dogen emphasizes this orientation in the *Zazenshin* (1242a) fascicle of his *Shōbōgenzō*. He advises the student to not be attached to the form of sitting. Rather, he admonishes the student to maintain the mind of *zazen* in the four basic postures of sitting, standing, walking, and lying down. These four postures are metaphors for all activities. This admonishment demonstrates the continuity from Ch'an to Zen and derives directly from Hui-neng's Platform Sutra: "The samādhi of oneness is straightforward mind at all times, walking, staying, sitting, and lying" (Yampolsky, 2012, p. 59).

Jōshū is asking if the monk was able to maintain meditative absorption throughout the meal. The monk answers "yes." He also realizes that Jōshū's question is the teaching. With this background in place, we will now turn to the standard definition of Zen meditation and its limitations, followed by explication of an alternative view informed by the Soto Zen perspective.

Standard definition

I briefly noted above that the term "Zen" etymologically derives from the Chinese term "Ch'an," which is a transliteration of the Sanskrit term *dhyāna*. *Dhyāna* refers, in general, to "meditation," "meditative concentration," or "meditative practice" (Yen, 2001, p. 1). I also noted that Zen as a name for a diverse array of religious groups points directly to the radical practice orientation of the Zen religious system as a whole. This definition, based on etymological transliterations as Buddhism spread eastward, is standard and typical. However, it is not quite an accurate depiction of *shikantaza*, which will be discussed in detail in the next chapter, or for that matter of its roots in Chinese Ch'an, which departed from its Indian roots by developing what Buswell describes as "an autonomous sectarian identity for itself" (1987, p. 321). In this process, over a period of centuries, meditation practices evolved that were unique to Chinese Ch'an and were in turn imported, modified, and assimilated into the developing Japanese Zen.

Many religious and spiritual systems describe and teach meditations that entail concentration on particular objects such as sounds; focus on visual images such as geometric shapes or deities; involve attention to body processes such as breathing or posture; or provide stories such as kōans or specific phrases from kōans. The brief text of the first kōan in the *Gateless Gate* collection, "Jōshū's Dog," serves as an example: "A monk asked Jōshū in all earnestness, 'Has a dog Buddha nature or not?' Jōshū said, 'Mu!'" (Yamada, 1979, p. 13).

In the kōan collection compiler Mumon's commentary following this terse dialogue, we find the following advice:

> Then concentrate your whole self, with its 360 bones and joints and 80,000 pores, into Mu making your whole body a solid lump of doubt. Day and night, without ceasing, keep digging into it ... It must be like a red-hot iron ball which you have gulped down and which you try to vomit up, but you cannot.
>
> (Yamada, 1979, p. 14)

Mumon's dramatic admonishment for intense and committed practice clearly points toward deep and exclusive concentration on Mu. These practices are intended to engender magnified and rarified states of awareness referred to as *samadhis* or absorptions and a resulting dramatic and sudden breakthrough into self-realization referred to as *kensho*. The Tibetan Buddhist commentator, David Komito (1987), describes eight such absorptions or what he refers to as "stages of *dhyāna*," each increasingly more concentrated and rarified (pp. 59–60). Komito notes that these stages of *dhyāna* represent "… a progressive concentration of the attention and detachment from both physical sense and mental sense experience" (p. 59).

An alternative entry into definition

The Chinese term *"dun"* (Faure, 1991, p. 34) or *"tun"* (Buswell, 1987, p. 321), meaning "all at once" (Gregory, 1987, p. 3), provides an alternative to the problematic, strictly etymological definition of *zazen* as simply a transliteration of the Sanskrit *dhyāna*. Additionally, but no less importantly, *dun* serves as a direct and clear connection to tracing the relation between core assumptions within Zen Buddhism. For instance, drawing from Masao Abe's elaboration and explication of Dogen's reframing of Buddha nature from the original "All beings have Buddha nature" to "Whole being is Buddha nature" (1985, pp. 25–68), the activity of *zazen* – in this case, *shikantaza* – becomes an expression of Buddha nature, which is sudden, imminent, and without mediation.

Dun holds several levels of meaning, including sudden in the temporal sense and immediate in the perceptual sense (i.e. without mediation) or absolute, as in the radical non-dualism in the sense of "that which works, arises or is reached without intermediary" (Faure, 1991, p. 36). From a practice orientation, this form is free from contrivances, either intentional such as desiring a goal or technical such as breath counting, reciting a mantra, or focusing exclusively on an object of concentration such as a candle flame or an image.

Three marks of existence

Many of the meditation techniques promoted by various contemplative religious traditions are intended to engender the experience of oneness with the world, the universe, the cosmos, or a deity. The influence of Indian Hindu religious beliefs on Bion's thinking exemplifies this point. Gerard Bleandonu, Bion's biographer, notes, "India made an indelible impression on the young Bion" (1999, p. 13). These impressions become vividly clear with the significance Bion places on "at-one-ment" (1967, 1970). His conversations regarding technique frequently address the importance of the experience of "at-one-ment" (1967, 1970). For instance, regarding the realization of "O," he notes, "No psycho-analytic discovery is possible without recognition of its existence, at-one-ment with it and evolution" (1970, p. 30); the distinction between memories evoked by sensuous greed and possessiveness and the spontaneous arising that occurs through what he refers to as evolution: "The evocation of that which provided a container for possessions, and of the sensuous gratifications with which to fill it, will differ from an evocation stimulated by at-one-ment" (1970, p. 33). Similarly, with regard to "O," a seminal aspect of his theory and technique, he writes:

> We can be at one with "O" but we cannot know "O." It is possible to be at one with it. That it exists is an essential postulate of science but it cannot be scientifically discovered. No psycho-analytic discovery is possible without recognition of its existence, at-one-ment with it and evolution.
>
> (1970, p. 30)

We will return to a discussion of Bion's "O" and "K" from a Zen perspective in Chapter 7, "Zen musings on Bion's 'O' and 'K'." In closing, with respect to the present discussion, Bion's comments exemplify a specific approach to Indian *dhyāna*. With this background, we now turn to an alternative approach to defining and understanding *zazen* practice.

While at-one-ment and bliss constitute desirable outcomes for many practitioners with diverse religious orientations – states that sudden practice can produce – such experiences are not prioritized, sought out, or held on to by Ch'an practitioners. Rather, continued practice engenders a lived experiential awareness of what Buddhists describe as the "three marks of existence." That is, from the Buddhist perspective, life is characterized by emptiness, impermanence and the lack of any inherently existing, permanent, separate self. All phenomena, including but not limited to self-experience, arise and fall contextually, subject to causes and conditions.

It is from this orientation that all-inclusive practices, in contrast to traditions that view at-one-ment, the shutting out of sensory input, or the eradication of thought processes as desirable realizational goals, involve a choiceless, non-judgmental awareness of the ongoing rising and falling of all experience without attachment or aversion or, as Bion asserts, "without memory, desire or understanding," or, "without irritable reaching after facts" (1967, 1970).

Dan Leighton describes the purpose of this practice in a discussion of silent illumination, a Ch'an forerunner of *shikantaza*, as to:

> allow intent apprehension of all phenomena as a unified totality. This objectless meditation aims at a radical, refined nondualism that does not grasp at any of the highly subtle distinctions to which our familiar mental workings are prone and which estranges us from our experience.
>
> (2000, p. 1)

Quietist and insight orientations: false dichotomies, real distinctions

There are several ways to describe and distinguish various meditation practices. Typically, they are divided into "quietist" or concentration techniques and wisdom or "insight" techniques. For example, Tibetan Buddhists, various Ch'an teachers, and Japanese Tendai Buddhists describe *shamatha* or calm abiding and *vipasyana* or insight meditations as distinct forms that serve different purposes. In some systems, they are practiced sequentially, beginning with the former and culminating in the latter. For example, Tibetans describe and elaborate Lam Rim or a gradual path to enlightenment (Dhargyey, 1974). Japanese Tendai Buddhists speak of "step-by-step" or *shuzen* meditation.

In this way, they are considered as stages in a sequence culminating in enlightenment. In the Rinzai Zen tradition, concentration techniques, such as counting the breath, often serve to prepare the practitioner for *kanna-zen* or kōan introspection, which, through increasingly intensified concentration on the *wato*, such as Mu, described above, the practitioner will have a sudden breakthrough to enlightenment. In this way, practice and realization are viewed as separate.

These distinctions and an individual's perception and understanding of meditation practices exert an influence on the therapeutic situation in terms of the contemporary therapeutic uses of meditation. For example, on the one hand, psychologists recommend meditation prescriptively to reduce symptoms such as anxiety (Pollak & Pedulla, 2014; Wolf & Serpa, 2015), while on the other hand psychoanalysts and psychoanalytically informed therapists practice and promote the use of meditation to increase psychoanalytic listening and insight (Epstein, 1984, 1988; Rubin, 1985).

The operation of *avidya* (primary ignorance, active not-knowing) reifies and polarizes these positions and implies a general sectarian allegiance to an entire set of principles, doctrines, and associated techniques while simultaneously devaluing whole-cloth principles and practices promulgated and promoted by what is now viewed as an opposing sect (or school of psychotherapy). For instance, in reality, both Soto and Rinzai sects support dynamic, actualized realization and both view static, quietist approaches as inadequate.

This whole problem seems to be exacerbated by such contemporary trends in "pop" psychology and in "New Age" spirituality that often view these complex traditions as simplistic, polarized, and monolithic, rigidly defined structures. It seems to me that we could more accurately view these traditions as equivalence classes with similarities, differences, and identities, which are in a constant state of flux as they continue to evolve in a particular culture. For example, the symptom relief and evidence-based culture of behavioral psychology differs radically from the insight-oriented culture of psychoanalysis. Therefore, their response to, adaptation, and integration of Buddhist practices and principles reveal radical differences. Further, what presents in the foreground at any given moment within the general parameters of a genuine religious system can be mediated by the emphasis, interests, and personality of a given teacher.

Instrumental and expressive orientations: identities, similarities, and differences

The distinction between "instrumental" or facilitative or "practice prior to enlightenment" (*shōzen no shu*) on the one hand and expressive or enactment approaches or "practice based on enlightenment" (*shōjō no shu*) on the other regarding meditation practices provides an alternative view to the distinction between quietist and insight meditation described in the preceding section. This alternative view addresses the complexity of such practices in relation to core religious assumptions that simultaneously acknowledge distinctions while accounting for similarities and identities. This classification emphasizes the intention that drives the process in terms of what is actually in motion at any given moment of practice. This is in contrast to the quietist/insight distinctions, which are articulated in terms of outcomes or states of mind such as mental stasis, at-one-ment, or *satori* (enlightenment). The distinction between instrumental and expressive orientations makes clear the connection between basic and differing soteriological orientations of the traditions despite the shared Mahayana orientation expressed in the Bodhisattva Vow "to save all beings" (Yakai, 2010, p. 8). Both approaches are dynamic in terms of technique. They are not completely mutually exclusive, which diminishes exaggerated and distorted sectarian polarizations.

By facilitative or instrumental I mean that, as Bielefeldt notes, *zazen* functions as a "utilitarian approach to religious practice, based on the generation of sudden insight through the practice of *k'an-hua*, or contemplation of the *kung-an*" (1985, p. 25). The instrumentalist or facilitative view inadvertently devalues *zazen* and kōan study because the interest is explicated in terms of its function merely to accomplish a higher future goal. This orientation posits meditation as a tool or instrument that facilitates realization as a final state of intuited illumination such as Tibetan Lam Rim, Tendai *shuzen*, and Rinzai *kanna-zen* described above, which are tossed aside when no longer needed.

The expressive or enactment ritual orientation expresses or "enacts" a posited already present enlightenment, which is enacted ritually through the activity of meditation and can be described as an ongoing, in the moment "actional realization." For this reason, we say, "practice begins with enlightenment!" That is, practice is realized and enlightenment is expressed or enacted through *zazen* and through our everyday activities in the world. From this viewpoint, *zazen* is not an instrument or tool for engendering mental stasis or a state of perfect enlightenment as a static state of being. Rather, *zazen* is conceptualized as the expression of the basic perfection that is already present in all beings.

Despite these distinctions, a radically non-dualistic realizational view integrates both orientations. The one traditional metaphor compares this type of practice with the use of a boat to cross a river. The traveler leaves the boat behind upon reaching the other shore. The realizational or expressive view integrates both. From the realizational perspective, each experiential moment when totally exerted requires full acceptance, not judgment, not dismissal, not devaluation, nor a utilitarian, goal-oriented attitude. Kim observes that, "All in all, total exertion is Dogen's appropriation of the traditional Mahayana principle of non-duality/absolute emptiness; it is the core of the realization-kōan and for that matter, of *single-minded sitting*" (1985, p. 59, emphasis added).

Differing kōan interpretations exemplify the distinction between facilitative and expressive approaches. For example, these differences are exemplified in "Nan-chuan Sweeping on a Mountain" (Heine, 2002), "Polishing a Tile to Make a Mirror" (Nishijima & Cross, 1996), and "Tai-yuan Fans Himself" (Loori, 2011). They were originally interpreted as criticisms of meditation. However, Dogen radically reinterprets them in support of the unity of practice and realization. Here is one example that Dogen elaborates in *Zazenshin* (1242a) and in *Kokyo* (1241).

"Polishing a Tile to Make a Mirror"

In this story, while practicing *zazen*, Baso and his teacher, Nangaku, discuss the relationship between meditation practice and realization. Nangaku compares Baso's practice of *zazen* "to become a buddha" as useless and as futile as polishing a tile to make a mirror. In the Zen tradition, the mirror serves as a symbol of the enlightened mind. This story is paraphrased as follows:

> Nangaku one day goes to Baso's hut, where Baso stands waiting.
> Nangaku asks, "What are you doing these days?"
> Baso says, "These days Dōitsu just sits."
> Nangaku says, "What is the aim of sitting in *zazen*?"
> Baso says, "The aim of sitting in *zazen* is to become a Buddha."
> Nangaku promptly fetches a tile and polishes it on a rock near Baso's hut.
> Baso, on seeing this, asks, "What is the master doing?"
> Nangaku says, "Polishing a tile."
> Baso says, "What is the use of polishing a tile?"
> Nangaku says, "I am polishing it into a mirror."
> Baso says, "How can polishing a tile make it into a mirror?"
> Nangaku says, "How can sitting in *zazen* make you into a buddha?"
> (Adapted from *Zazenshin* in Nishijima & Cross, 1996, pp. 93–95)

This kōan can be taken in two radically different ways. A popular view reflecting a facilitative approach interprets the dialogue as critical of *zazen* practice, at most a temporary tool. Viewed from this perspective, this conversation between Nangaku and Baso seems to imply that Baso is wasting his time practicing *zazen*. However, Dogen turns the meaning of the story around to support his radical non-dualism. He shifts the tile polishing metaphor around and characterizes both Baso's *zazen* and Nangaku's tile polishing as expressive of "practice in realization (*shōjō no shu*)" (Heine, 1994, p. 216). In this manner, he verifies and validates Baso's *zazen* as expressive of realization' that is, polishing a tile and *zazen* both become the activity of realization.

Dogen's interpretation is radically different from the popular view. He upholds the centrality of *zazen* and the necessity of continued practice. Dogen notes that Nangaku is cautioning Baso against waiting for realization, but not against continued *zazen* practice. Thus, for Dogen, becoming a buddha by sitting in meditation is impossible because buddhahood is not the end result, but the starting point of spiritual endeavor. In this regard, Dogen points to the dynamic here and now of tile polishing (and sitting), not a final result. The mirror *is* the act of polishing; Buddha *is* the act of sitting. Viewed in this light, doing *zazen* becomes indispensable not so much as a means of seeking personal experiential verification of realization, but as an enactment and lived, in the moment expression of our already enlightened being. Further, we express this basic Buddha nature by being who we are. Hence, as Dogen notes in his commentary: "Clearly, in truth, when polishing a tile becomes a mirror, Baso becomes buddha. When Baso becomes buddha, Baso immediately becomes Baso. When Baso becomes Baso, *zazen* immediately becomes *zazen*" (1241, p. 259). In this regard, *zazen* becomes the prototype expression of realized being. Kim summarizes Dogen's position as follows: "Here the nonduality of tile and mirror, of sentient beings and Buddha, of practice and verification, is elucidated" (Kim, 1985, p. 223). In other words, the tile cannot become the mirror because it already is the mirror. "The practice of *zazen* has absolute significance in itself" (Kim, 1985, pp. 164–165).

Intention

From Dogen's perspective, realization can be described as being driven by an ongoing intention to make a buddha. In short, making is being. In terms of total exertion, the issue of whether to meditate or not, for example, shifts away from this either–or dichotomy and toward an emphasis on the *intention* that an individual brings to practice, both in the world at large and through formal structured religious practice. Suzuki (1970) addresses the issue of intention in his notion of "beginner's mind." Following Dogen, he writes: "In the beginner's mind there are many possibilities; in the expert's mind there are few" (1970, p. 21). He raises the question of how one keeps the practice fresh and alive over time. In this respect, Suzuki mirrors Dogen's concern with the authenticity and quality of practice.

This concern cuts through debates regarding whether or not practice has a role or any value in Zen training. We can ask: "What is the intention of any act?" I am reminded of a busy medical doctor. His waiting room was full and his time in the office was limited; however, while not wasting a moment, he conveyed a sense of full, personable attentiveness, presence, and sensitivity in his interactions with all of his patients. His caring attitude left me feeling fully attended to and with a sense of confidence in terms of his response to my medical concerns, even though we only spent a few minutes together.

With regard to *zazen* practice, techniques in terms of one's physical posture and mind-set are easy enough to master; however, what becomes crucial over time, in terms of Suzuki's caution to keep the practice fresh for the long term, centers on the levels of energy, determination, and authenticity one brings to practice. On this point, Kim notes that "the real issue was not whether to meditate but how to meditate; the how was obviously not a matter of technique so much as a matter of authenticity" (2004, p. 68).

In practice, activity becomes totally exerted and penetrates the reality of the situation, beyond self, doctrine, and beliefs, and becomes, from the Soto perspective, an expression of being Buddha-nature. Total exertion *is* total expression. *Zazen* is both action and expression and so is every act that might occur in human relations, when totally exerted with authenticity, presence, and wholeheartedness. Rituals, *zazen*, prayer – when considered holistically – represent a significant, important, but small portion of the spiritual aspect of all phenomena. *Zazen* and total exertion are inextricably intertwined.

From the perspective of total exertion, one single dharma is simultaneously all dharmas. It is the one and the many. *Zazen* as one dharma moment is all dharmas. Its particularity cannot be reduced to nothing more than an instrument in the service of some higher plane or, as noted above, simply a boat that the traveler leaves behind upon reaching the other shore. *Zazen* practice as one totally exerted dharma is, to use Suzuki's term "being as-it-is," not a separate vantage point split off from reality, observing as if from a distance. Reality is ultimately one indivisible whole, which includes the action, thought, feelings, and experience of *zazen*. At the same time, reality is "the many." Everyone who comes for psychotherapy, for instance, is a unique individual, and presents him or herself to us as such. It would be a disservice to ignore each person's uniqueness through the use of dogmatic, preconceived interpretations and formulaic responses. As we witness each individual's unique story, that individual will provide us with the essentials of their particular story and the clues of how to respond effectively with freshness, aliveness, and compassion, respectfully honoring that individual's being. I will elaborate on this point through extended case studies in Chapters 9 and 10.

Reality

Zazen does not change experience or provide an entry into a separate or different reality. Rather, practicing *zazen* actualizes an ongoing and continuous realization of reality. Reality becomes magnified and deepened. Change occurs naturally because that is the nature of all experience in the phenomenal world.

Similarly, from Bion's fresh and unique perspective on psychoanalysis with regard to his mandate to relinquish memory, desire, and understanding, he concludes by noting the analysis remains alive, fresh, unique, and new because we are relating to a unique individual and not to poorly remembered theories, fixed ideas, preconceptions, or rigid beliefs.

This neutral, goal-free stance in *zazen* constitutes the containing function and facilitates the disengagement from reactive states, for example, of intellectualization, suppression, avoidance, splitting, denial, or projection. Non-reactive, choiceless awareness remains open to what is typically split off in an unconscious endeavor to maintain self-esteem through a positive self-image.

Zazen exerts a direct deconstruction of unconscious, habitual chain reactions that engender stereotypical thoughts, feelings, and attitudes by disrupting deeply ingrained thought trains. The Theravada Buddhist teacher, Analayo, describes this process succinctly in the context of mindfulness meditation as follows: "One of the central tasks of sati is the de-automatization of habitual reactions and perceptual evaluations" (2004, p. 267). As a result, perceptual alterations engender experiencing reality simply as it is; that is, an awareness of all phenomena exactly as they are without conceptual interference or mediation.

Ironically, with the attitude of *mushotoku* or "no gaining mind" (Deshimaru, 2012, p. 96), change does occur. Often, the awareness of change occurs retrospectively, such as when a tense situation emerges in which we respond out of wisdom and compassion rather than react through aggression, attachment, fear, or aversion. In this regard, we become highly polished river stones. The stones in the river have no intention of becoming smooth and polished and the river does not flow over the stones with the intention to polish them. Yet, the polishing occurs. For instance, a young woman whom I worked with for many years in analysis entered treatment with a rather serious stuttering problem. Intensive speech therapy proved ineffective. While no interpretation was offered and the issue rarely came up in her narrative, over time, the stuttering disappeared. How did this happen? Perhaps the experience of being listened to and taken seriously over the many years that we worked together gradually softened and smoothed out the difficulty. Unlike her parents, I exerted no pressure for her to change. She often spoke about a consistent lack of feeling heard, listened to, or taken seriously in her family. In fact, quite the contrary, she was constantly reminded that her feelings were basically "a waste of time." However, over time, her experience changed and her stuttering no longer interrupted her narratives.

Chapter 3

Dogen Zen: radical reformulation

The Ch'an evolution described in Chapter 2 that engendered a distancing from Indian Buddhism and accompanying practices is clearly carried forward into Japanese Zen and articulated by Dogen, who writes, for example, in *Fukanzazengi* that: "The *zazen* I speak of is not learning meditation. It is simply the Dharma gate of repose and bliss, the practice-realization of totally culminated enlightenment" (Waddell & Abe, 2002, p. 4). The technique alluded to in the above quote that Dogen advocates, and that will be described in detail below, falls into the expressive or enactment approach to practice described in the previous chapter.

Paraphrasing and expanding Dogen's description, Leighton (2002) notes: "This just sitting is not a meditation technique or practice, or anything at all [It] is the dynamic activity of being fully present ... Just sitting, one simply meets the immediate present" (pp. 3–5). In terms of the Soto Zen tradition, this orientation refers specifically to the expression of realization from the radical non-dualistic perspective promulgated by Dogen as "the unity of practice-enlightenment" (*shushō-ittō*) (Kim, 2004, p. 63) and "simply the Dharma gate of repose and bliss" (Waddell & Abe, 2002, p. 4). It should be noted here that by "repose and bliss" (also translated as "ease and joy"; Bielefeldt, 1988, p. 135) Dogen is not referring to physical and/or psychological benefits, although they are not excluded. Rather, he is directing attention to the soteriological aim of realization in the religious sense. Despite any ancillary psychophysical benefits, from the Soto perspective, sitting functions as the practice of ongoing enlightenment and "transcends the mere cultivation of trance" (Bielefeldt, 1988, p. 135). The consistent critique of both quietist and facilitative practices becomes a central thread that weaves its way throughout Dogen's writings. For instance, in *Zazenshin*, he refers to quietists as "stupid illiterates" (Bielefeldt, 1988, p. 190).

Two wings: meditation and wisdom

Zen Buddhist traditions place meditation and wisdom in a position of mutual interrelatedness. They can be described as simultaneously separate in their unique identities and connected in their interpenetration. The image of the two wings of one bird depicts this connection and relationship. In the Zen Buddhist school, they are always conceived of as together in both structure and function. Dogen expresses this inseparability from a non-dualistic perspective as *shushō-ichinyo* or *shushō-ittō*, "the oneness of practice/realization" or "realization/practice one." No matter how wisdom and meditation are defined, understood, or experienced, this inseparability of practice and wisdom distinguishes Buddhist thought from most Western religious, philosophical, and psychological systems.

Perhaps the most radical expression of this core principle is in the Soto Zen School – as I mentioned in the previous paragraph – as Dogen's notion of the oneness of practice and realization. While a great diversity of interpretations and practices exist among and between the various schools, including various Zen sects, this inseparability and core teaching of practice/realization has led Hee-Jin Kim to note that no matter how their relation and function are understood, meditation and wisdom "… serve as the primary structural elements of the Buddhist symbolic model" (2004, p. 51).

Understanding and expression

How these relationships are understood and expressed in practice hover at the center of a long-standing controversy between Zen and other Buddhist sects regarding the role of formal *zazen* practice in terms of how different traditions view religious development and its obstacles. The differences in viewpoint – some subtle, some more obvious – have been the cause of confusion with regard to the Western reception of Zen, especially when various readings are taken out of their socio-historical context; when hagiographical accounts of various leaders are taken at face value as historical fact; when basic principles are highly skewed in a particular direction to meet sectarian agendas; or when the ongoing linear development of Zen thought and practice are not considered. Between various Buddhist sects, throughout Zen's development, different viewpoints have emerged regarding the role of practice, insight, original purity of the mind, and sitting practice, to name a few.

For example, from the Japanese Soto Zen perspective, which is practice oriented, the primary obstacle to liberation is articulated in terms of action and non-action. Either an individual practices or does not practice; responds to others compassionately or selfishly.

In contrast to the Soto Zen emphasis on action and inaction, the Pure Land or Amida Buddhism, which was established by Hōnen in the twelfth century and continues to be a major sect in Japan, views sin as the primary obstacle to salvation. Pure Land Buddhists hold a sense of hope in a heaven and an afterlife.

The Japanese Zen teacher, Kosho Uchiyama, describes the difference between Pure Land and Zen through the use of the term *goshō o negau*, which in the Pure Land tradition expresses hope. Speaking from the Soto Zen standpoint, in contrast, the Zen emphasis on action is clearly asserted by Uchiyama, who notes:

> But that's not a very good understanding of the expression. What *goshō*, or "afterlife," refers to is the life that arises when one clarifies this matter of death. It means knowing clearly just what death is, and then really living out one's life.
>
> (2004, p. 8)

From this non-dualist orientation, in addition to his severe critiques of quietism, Dogen was equally quite critical of instrumental or facilitative practices. In sharp contrast to the "stages" approach, described in the previous chapter, Dogen asserts an insistent critique of any practice that entails or elaborates a linear progression of stages. Following Ch'an Buddhism's subitist orientation, consistent with the notion of *gūjin*, Dogen asserts an immediate realization based on active engagement with the present moment. For instance, he states: "Not accompanied by the ten thousand things [a metaphor for relative reality], what stages could there be?" (In: Leighton & Okumura, 2004, p. 281). For example, consider this quote from *Bendowa* (1231):

> To think that practice and enlightenment are not one is a non-Buddhist view. In the Buddha-dharma they are one. Inasmuch as practice now is based on enlightenment, the practice of a beginner is itself the whole of original enlightenment. Therefore, in giving the instruction for practice, a Zen teacher advises his/her disciples not to seek enlightenment apart from practice, for practice points directly to original enlightenment.
>
> (Translated and quoted by Kim, 2004, p. 63)

With respect to practice based on enlightenment, Dogen notes in *Fukanzazengi* that: "It is activity beyond human hearing and seeing, a principle prior to human knowledge or perception. This being the case, intelligence, or lack of it does not matter, No distinction exists between the dull and sharp-witted" (Waddell & Abe, 2002, pp. 4–5). As we can see by his comments above, Dogen emphasizes the uniquely East Asian meditation as distinct from the gradualism of step-by-step Indian forms. This is where Ch'an (Zen) Buddhist practice departs from Indian Buddhism as well as traditional non-Buddhist contemplative practices.

Dogen therefore characterizes the sequential steps posited by Buddhist stage-oriented approaches that I mentioned as "qualities of enlightenment" or "aspects of enlightenment" rather than as progressive stages. He conceptualizes each stage as a different quality of enlightenment rather than as increasingly advanced steps that approach enlightenment. Further, he argues that practice and realization are not separate and characterizes the sequence of practice to enlightenment as dualistic thinking and "defiled" or "impure." It is important here to note that by "pure and defiled" Dogen means not characterized by dualistic thinking such as using meditation simply as a means to an end, such as enlightenment as characterized in facilitative or instrumental approaches.

Zen teachers speaking from this stage orientation often caution that the separations between stages can be arbitrary and are not always so clear-cut. For example, they often note that calming techniques and insight-oriented techniques are ultimately inseparable, like water poured into water. For example, with regard to silent illumination, which functioned as a forerunner to Dogen's *shikantaza*, the Ch'an teacher Sheng Yen (2008) notes that the notion of stages functions as a "natural way" to understand (p. 42) the teachings and the practice. For instance, with respect to emptiness, he advises the student:

> It is possible to contemplate emptiness and selflessness at any stage in Silent Illumination; it is also possible to experience enlightenment at any stage of this practice. It is not necessary to progress stage by stage.
>
> (pp. 42–43)

Yen further notes:

> I repeat and emphasize that you should not take these stages of Silent Illumination as a spiritual ladder to be ascended stage by stage. Each stage is complete and a possible entry point for genuine Silent Illumination. So please do not anticipate a presumably better stage than where you are now.
>
> (p. 43)

However, it is also important to note that the unity of practice and enlightenment does not wipe out the distinction between the two; tension between them always exists, yet each remains pure. It is this tension that drives practice. Dogen often approvingly quoted Nan-yüeh Huai-jang's (677–744) answer to Hui-nêng, the sixth ancestor of Zen in China (638–713). For instance, in the *Bendowa* fascicle of *Shōbōgenzō*, he asserts: "Practice and enlightenment are not obliterated but undefiled" (Kim, 2004, p. 64).

This ongoing expression of realization is not a rigidified belief system, a seeking out or a collection of experiences, an absolute or a fixed dogma or a static end point or state. Rather, it's a fluid and constantly moving, ongoing, fluctuating experience that the Zen philosopher, Shin'itchi Hisamatsu (1979), describes as "flux," "flow," or *Heijoshin*, often translated into English as "Ordinary Mind." This approach orients the practitioner toward openness and spaciousness; away from habit formations and toward spontaneous arising of all experience, what Bion would describe from the psychoanalytic perspective as "O" or the infinite openness of unsaturated psychic space; an ongoing "becoming."

Shikantaza: simply sitting

As we can see from the background material discussed in Chapter 2 and the above comments, Dogen's Zen departs radically from the traditional approach to meditation.

For instance, Dogen consistently distances his teachings and his practice of *shikantaza* from Indian *dhyāna* through intense and repeated critical remarks, describing *dhyāna* as inducing "trance states," advocated by quietists who misunderstand the true Buddhist teachings. For example, in the *Butsudo* fascicle of the *Shōbōgenzō*, he asserts "... this practice is not exhaustive of the enlightenment of the Seven Buddhas and the Twenty-eight Indian Patriarchs, nor is it by any means the essence of the *buddha-dharma*" (Bielefeldt, 1988, p. 136).

Regarding quietist implication, in the *Tashin-tsu*, "The Power to Know Others" (1245), he warns against "cutting off considerations and forgetting objects" (p. 136). The implication extends to the fundamental Mahayana Buddhist principle articulated in the Bodhisattva Vow to save all beings. Preoccupations with mental stasis, preferred psychological states, chasing after and accumulating experiences, or inner bliss states while remaining oblivious to the suffering of others function as personal agendas that are antithetical to the Mahayana position.

Current scholarship further supports this view that meditation is not an accurate term to describe the process of *shikantaza*. For instance, the contemporary Soto Zen teacher and Dogen scholar, Shohaku Okumura, writes:

> *Shikantaza, zazen* as Dogen Zenji teaches it, is a unique practice – even compared to other meditation practices within the various traditions of Buddhism. When we practice *shikantaza*, we do nothing but sit with the whole body and mind. We do nothing with the mind, so this is actually not a meditation practice. ... we simply sit in an upright posture and breathe deeply, quietly and smoothly through the nose and from the abdomen.
> (2010, p. 80)

In this regard, *shikantaza*, from the Soto perspective, refers to just sitting, only sitting, resolute sitting, sitting fixedly, and nothing else. Hence, realization finds immediate expression.

This expressed realization functions as the heart of Soto Zen wisdom and realizational practice. The clinical implications of this central Soto Zen notion of fully realized ongoing presence are exemplified and elaborated through an extended case study in Chapter 7, "Zen musings on Bion's 'O' and 'K'." Dogen offers this description of *zazen*: "Sitting itself is the practice of the Buddha. Sitting is non-doing. It is nothing but the true form of the Self. Apart from sitting there is nothing to seek as the Buddha Dharma" (Okumura, 2010, p. 85).

Dogen describes this practice as *shikantaza*, which translates as simply sitting, just sitting, only sitting, or wholehearted sitting. Katagiri breaks the term down from an absolutist perspective as follows:

> *Shikan* is translated as wholeheartedness, which seems to be sort of a psychological state or pattern. But *Shikan* is not a psychological pattern. *Shikan* is exactly becoming one with the process itself. Literally, *za* of *taza* is *zazen*, and *ta* means to hit; so, from moment-to-moment, we have to hit the bulls-eye of *zazen* itself. This is not a technique.
>
> (2002, p. 103)

Shikantaza was refined and elaborated by Dogen in a series of writings including *Bendowa* (1231), *Fukanzazengi* (1227), *Zazenshin* (1242a), *Zazengi* (1243), and *Zanmai-o-zanmai* (1244). *Shikantaza* functions as the specific form of *zazen* that serves as the core ritual "enactment" (Leighton, 2008) or expression of the Soto Zen ethos and religious belief system. In this context, "wholeheartedness" directly relates to *gūjin* (total exertion) and exemplifies in practice the core teaching that wholeheartedness is expressive of ongoing realization, totally exerted. The notion of practice as expressive relies on the notion of Buddha-nature being imminent, or innate, not something that must be developed or an object to be discovered or uncovered; not something at all. This notion of Buddha-nature as activity is central to the sudden school teaching. In this manner, *shikantaza* functions as the prototypical and ultimate expression or ritual enactment of the foundation or core teachings of the Soto School. When internalized through continued practice, *shikantaza* creates a deeper experiential intuited understanding and appreciation of the present moment that will, in turn, exert an influence on therapeutic work.

In contrast to the detachment and depth of concentration described in the previous chapter by Komito that exemplifies linear, progressive, stage approaches to realization, Dogen describes *shikantaza* as panoramic, inclusive of all rising and falling experiences without judgment, grasping, or pushing away.

Dogen, through the core teaching of the unity of practice-enlightenment, maintains his link to the orthodox Buddhist tradition, while simultaneously and paradoxically making *shikantaza* uniquely and exclusively his own. He thus follows the general East Asian Sinification of Buddhism through a radical separation from and rejection of Indian Buddhism both in theory and practice. In this manner, Dogen also distances himself from quietist practices that attempt to erase all thoughts, the induction of trance states, instrumental practices that posit future breakthroughs, or evaluative practices that function to replace afflictive mental states with "preferred psychological states" (Diane Martin, personal conversation). He reinforces this distance and thus the uniqueness of his offering, with the notion of totally culminated enlightenment. In other words, realization is already present at the beginning. Hence, *shikantaza* functions as an expression of enlightenment, as noted above. Dogen further reinforces this radically non-dualistic orientation with the comment in the *Bendowa* (1231) fascicle of *Shōbōgenzō*: "As it is from the very first realization in practice, realization is endless. As it is the practice of realization, practice is beginningless. ... enlightenment is beginningless; practice is endless" (Waddell & Abe, 2002, p. 19). Ultimately, what Dogen offers to Kamakura-era (1185–1383) Japan finds its roots in the Ch'an Sudden School of Zen described in the previous chapter.

The resulting technique, *shikantaza*, is not simply a recycled version of Indian *dhyāna*, as the etymological definition might inadvertently suggest. On the contrary, *shikantaza* functions as a unique form of practice that emerged within the Chinese cultural and religious context and that became further revisioned through Dogen's unique and creative expression and his importation of the practice to Japan. For Dogen's flock, this meant that the religious notion of the oneness of practice and enlightenment makes a direct means of realization amenable to the lay community. He offers a simplified vehicle of a direct and simple practice not complicated by the complexities of steps intended exclusively for Indian monastic practice. Ordinary folks living in an everyday world now had access to religious salvation while not needing to be cloistered away far apart from family life and social responsibilities. This orientation finds expression in the title of *Fukanzazengi*, which translates as "Universal Principles of Meditation." Universal in this context renders the practice appropriate for everyone. On this point, in the opening paragraph of *Fukanzazengi*, Dogen writes: "It is never apart from you right where you are. What use is there going off here and there to practice?" (Waddell & Abe, 2002, p. 2).

Impact

Through continuous *shikantaza* practice, the extent to which external factors that influence and determine what we experience and reify as "my own mind" become revealed as dependently arising empty mind moments. In this regard, the intent of *shikantaza* as "just sitting" is non-facilitative, reflecting an ethos that is free from any teleological agendas. As a technical method of religious practice, *shikantaza* reflects and activates the basic philosophical tenets of Soto Zen through the very process of non-attachment to goals, desirable minds states, at-one-ment with the divine, or to reified, habitually generated versions of self.

From the Buddhist perspective that Dogen draws on and is aligned with, *shikantaza* as practice-realization expresses the historical Buddha's spirituality; that is, an expression of his enlightenment. As an expression of the inherent nature of the enlightened mind, *shikantaza* functions, by definition, as the activity of such a mind. Bielefeldt provides this description:

> *Zazen* is the orthodox practice of Buddhism. At the same time this *zazen* is not merely a utilitarian device for producing the perfected state of enlightenment (*sabutsu*) but the expression of a more fundamental perfection inherent in all things (*gyōbutsu*).
>
> (1988, p. 140)

Intention, attitude, relationship

One question that applies to any religious system or associated practices centers on the intention, attitude, and relationship that the practitioner or sect brings to a particular form. For instance, while the actual form and process of a particular technique might appear identical with another, one sect might include that practice as one among many alternative forms prescribed by the teacher's evaluation of the student's needs and "level" of practice. In contrast, for Dogen, *shikantaza* is considered to be *the* practice par excellence. In other words, the interpretation of a particular practice can differ considerably from one sect to another. However, as I will discuss below, this does not mean that the sects promulgate radically opposing religious goals or that there are no areas of overlap or identity between the sects. Sectarian differences do not necessarily imply dispute or mutually exclusive practices.

However, any set of instructions, no matter how concrete, practical, or seemingly non-sectarian, serve as a religious statement and reflect the underlying foundational principles of the particular sect's belief system and its historical roots that can be traced back for generations of lineage. For example, with regard to Dogen's *Fukanzazengi* quoted above, Bielefeldt notes that:

> [I]t is by no means merely a practical manual on the technique of contemplation: it is also – and perhaps more conspicuously – a theological statement of the Zen approach to Buddhism and a literary appreciation of Zen training ... [and] the tendency of his [Dogen's] writings to link the technique of meditation to its theory and to embed the practice of meditation in its sectarian tradition.
>
> (1988, pp. 109 and 114)

Despite the many differences noted between sects, Dogen was also extremely sensitive to divisive tendencies. Ironically, while promulgating his *zazen* as the truly transmitted dharma that can be traced back to the historical Buddha Shakyamuni, Dogen was highly critical of sectarian distinctions, despite the fact that they do in fact exist and have done so for centuries. For example, he writes in the *Butsudo* fascicle of *Shōbōgenzō*: "Remember, the name 'Zen Sect' has been devised by demons and devils" (Dogen, 1243c, p. 87).

Shikantaza: the practice

Fukanzazengi exemplifies in a most brief, terse, and condensed form the specifics and details of practice and the connection between practice and core principles. The mechanics of *shikantaza* are quite straightforward and easy to describe. However, despite the practical simplicity of *shikantaza*, the practice, as I have noted repeatedly, is saturated with religious meaning. For example, Bielefeldt writes, "avoidance of the extremes of self-indulgence and deprivation is, of course, a basic principle of the Buddhist ethic of the middle way, but it is also common Buddhist practical advice to the meditator" (1988, p. 110).

Shikantaza constitutes the structural core of the Soto Zen belief system and practice. Whether on the cushion or off, the principles of meditative awareness and insight guide our mode of being in the world.

For instance, Dogen's radical non-dualism as reflected and enacted in *shikantaza* successfully excised all elements of "stages of enlightenment" at once, both from his teachings and from his practices. For example, we find this orientation in his approach to realization/practice oneness, as mentioned above, and in his writings in terms of his radical revisioning of traditional kōans.

Returning to the notion of sitting as an enactment ritual that instantly expresses fully realized enlightenment, or the Buddha's mind, s*hikantaza* actualizes the non-dualistic orientation described above. Bielefeldt notes that "… the meditation of just sitting, in which the practitioner, by abandoning his conscious efforts to acquire Buddhahood 'sloughs off,' as he said, 'body and mind' (*shinjin datsuraku*) and abides in his inherent enlightenment" (1988, p. 26). Leighton describes the core of Dogen's approach as follows:

> Buddhas do not think like that. They do not wait for awakening. The actual lively performing Buddhas know that awakening does not happen later as a result of spiritual practice. Practice is not about getting something later. This is a very central teaching of Dogen.
>
> (2011, pp. 77–78)

Benefits of the expressive orientation

Practically and experientially speaking, it has been my experience that this practice takes pressure off those individuals who have been using an instrumental approach either in attempts to silence the mind, to achieve some type of rarified or transcendent state of mind, or to facilitate a dramatic breakthrough to enlightenment. Briefly stated, Dogen argues cogently and convincingly that *shikantaza* functions realizationally, not transcendentally. The practice is objectless, subjectless, formless, goalless, and purposeless. Further, this practice does not rely on any external or internal supports such as a mantra, visualization, or object of attention and is non-concentrative and non-directive. But it was not void of intellectual content as in a vacuum. Kim notes, "What *zazen*-only did was to not eliminate reason and intellect, but to realize them" (2004, pp. 62–63). Again, Dogen's *shikantaza* finds its roots in Ch'an beliefs and practices. Consider the following:

> Chan implies a negation of conventional truth [which is based on dualistic thinking, cognitive processes and perception] from the standpoint of ultimate truth [which "evolves" (to use Bion's term) through intuited experiencing]: it emphasizes the ineffable, nonrepresentational, nonsensational, nonfactual nature of awakening. But awakening itself soon becomes a mere referent, an alibi, and apophatic discourse turns into a rhetorical technique that may at times mask the superficiality of the experience.
>
> (Faure, 1991, p. 39)

The non-facilitative orientation of *shikantaza* negotiates a middle way that embraces the total exertion of all experience while simultaneously and non-reactively letting go.

When experiencing a projection, it should be considered without taking it as "I" or "mine." It simply should be experienced or "intuited," as Bion (1970) would say. In the psychoanalytic context, the projection serves as a crucial aspect of the patient's communication of what cannot be known by the patient at the moment for whatever reason. The patient needs to be able to "speak" to us through projective identification, not unlike *shikantaza*, without the intrusion of theory, hypothesis, or as a reaction. Authentic and useful response to the patient's narrative requires a neutral witnessing, so while internally there can be an intense emotional reaction, it is observed from a non-reactive standpoint. In other words, it is simply noted (Bion, 1970) like a motion-sensitive light switch. When there is motion, the light goes on. It doesn't matter how it was triggered – by a person, vehicle, animal, whatever – it simply goes on. Similarly, the patient's projection triggers a reaction in me, but it's simultaneously not mine, not me. In *shikantaza*, breathing happens; not I am breathing. In the therapeutic situation, projections and their accompanying reactions happen, but they are not mine.

Dogen addresses the importance of intuition in *Fukanzazengi*. He asserts, "You should therefore cease from practice based on intellectual understanding, pursuing words and following after speech, and learn the backward step that turns your light inward to illuminate yourself" (Waddell & Abe, 2002, p. 3). Dogen's advice dovetails with Bion's comment with regard to putting his technical instructions into practice. He writes: "His interpretations should gain in force and conviction – both for himself and his patient – because they derive from the emotional experience with a unique individual and not from generalised theories imperfectly 'remembered'" (1967, In: Aguayo & Malin, 2013, p. 138). For Bion, intuition supersedes intellectual understanding, which engenders an experiential realization of intuited reality that is not "sensuous reality" (1970, p. 26). Along with Dogen, he points to the interference engendered by "... awareness of the sensuous accompaniments of emotional experience are a hindrance to the psychoanalyst's intuition of the reality with which he must be at one" (1967, In: Aguayo & Malin, 2013, p. 136). From the Zen perspective, this orientation finds expression simply as "only nonseeing is true seeing" (Faure, 1991, p. 34).

Further, in terms of realizing "O," Bion's term for ultimate reality, he observes that "O does not fall in the domain of knowledge or learning save incidentally; it can be 'become', but it cannot be 'known'" (1970, p. 26). For instance, if, during the psychoanalytic encounter, one is thinking about theory, a possible intervention, or an outcome, then one is not, as Bion would say, attuned or in "at-one-ment" with the evolution of "O" (1970, p. 30). Similarly, Dogen warns, "No traps or snares can ever reach it" (Waddell & Abe, 2002, p. 4). For Dogen, "traps and snares" function as metaphors for the intellect and discursive reasoning.

Zen describes this prioritizing of intuition as the functioning of *prajna*, which operates as the primary, "pre-reflective" (Kasulis, 1981, p. 56) mode of understanding. Various definitions of *prajna* include awareness, wisdom, intuition, "quick knowing" (Evans-Wentz, 1954), intimate knowing, and "flash-like intuition" (Abe, 1985, p. 3). This is why Abe, among others, emphatically notes, "For the realisation of Zen, practice is absolutely necessary" (1985, p. 3). Intuition will be further defined and elaborated in Chapter 4, "Total exertion as intuition." Bion's "O" from the Zen perspective is further elaborated in Chapter 7, "Zen musings on Bion's 'O' and 'K'."

Mechanics of *zazen*

With this background in mind, we now turn to a set of simple practice instructions from Dogen's (1227) *Fukanzazengi*:

> For *sanzen* (*zazen*), a quiet room is suitable. Eat and drink moderately. Cast aside all involvements and cease all affairs. Do not think good or bad. Do not administer pros and cons. Cease all the movements of the conscious mind, the gauging of all thoughts and views. Have no designs on becoming a Buddha. *Sanzen* has nothing whatever to do with sitting or lying down.
> At the site of your regular sitting, spread out thick matting and place a cushion above it. Sit either in the full-lotus or half-lotus position. In the full-lotus position, you first place your right foot on your left thigh and your left foot on your right thigh. In the half-lotus, you simply press your left foot against your right thigh. You should have your robes and belt

loosely bound and arranged in order. Then place your right hand on your left leg and your left palm (facing upwards) on your right palm, thumb-tips touching. Thus sit upright in correct bodily posture, neither inclining to the left nor to the right, neither leaning forward nor backward. Be sure your ears are on a plane with your shoulders and your nose in line with your navel. Place your tongue against the front roof of your mouth, with teeth and lips both shut. Your eyes should always remain open, and you should breathe gently through your nose.

Once you have adjusted your posture, take a deep breath, inhale and exhale, rock your body right and left and settle into a steady, immobile sitting position. Think not-thinking. How do you think not-thinking? Non-thinking. This in itself is the essential art of *zazen*.

(Waddell & Abe, 2002, pp. 3–4)

This final instruction regarding thinking, not-thinking and non-thinking will be taken up in detail in Chapter 6, "Thinking, not thinking, beyond thought." With these simple instructions in mind, I close this discussion of *shikantaza* with a direct and simple instruction that I received from my first teacher in response to my question regarding the relationship between practice and study. He responded: "Read and study all you want, but *just keep practicing no matter what!*"

Chapter 4

Total exertion as intuition

Introduction

In this chapter, I will explore total exertion in terms Dogen's notion of "sensing" and Wilfred Bion's explication of intuition of "O" derived out of dreaming the analytic session along with the patient as the primary tool of the psychoanalyst (1965, 1970). Bion's point will be further elaborated in relation to the Kyoto school Zen philosopher Shin'ichi Hisamatsu's (1979) use and understanding of intuition in terms of his discussion of *heijoshin* (quelled, constant, or tranquil mind and translated into English as "ordinary mind"). I will weave these themes together by pulling on threads in the writings of the Chilean psychoanalyst Ignacio Matte-Blanco's work on "Bi-logic" (1975, 1988) and his notion of symmetrization, which I mentioned briefly in Chapter 1.

The Japanese psychiatrist, Zen practitioner, and student of Karen Horney, Akihisa Kondo's (1952) overlooked work on intuition will serve as an entry point for the ensuing discussion. From the common ground shared by this diverse group of thinkers, total exertion comes into focus as the action that facilitates the awareness of the evolution or ongoing operation of intuition. Simultaneously, intuition functions as the natural, pure dynamic expression of total exertion. Implications for the psychoanalytic encounter and for Zen practice are also considered. Before proceeding, we will first examine the Sanskrit term *"prajna,"* which will add clarity to the ensuing discussion on intuition.

Prajna wisdom

The Sanskrit term for wisdom, *prajna*, central to Buddhist philosophy and practice and frequently encountered in the Buddhist literature, literally means "fundamental knowing," "intuitive knowing," "inherent knowing," "intimate knowing" (Heine, 2012) or "quick knowing" (Evans-Wentz, 1954) and "flash-like intuition" (Abe 1985, p. 3). The term consists of two parts: *"pra,"* which means "before," and *"jna,"* which means "wisdom." The Canadian

Zen teacher, Albert Low, further elaborates the meaning of *jna* and writes that "*jna*" as wisdom "... is variously translated as 'intelligence,' 'knowing,' 'awareness,' or to be responsive and spontaneous" (2006, p. 18).

When combined, *prajna* means "what comes before wisdom." In this sense, *prajna* functions as an intuitive, "pre-reflective" (Kasulis, 1981) knowing. Reflective knowing, by contrast, is retrospective, cognitive, and discursive. It is important to keep in mind that both forms of knowing are necessary and contribute to "binocular vision" (Bion, 1970).

The highly influential Soto Zen treatise, *Goshō*, the first *Shōbōgenzō* commentary, was composed in 1308 by Senne, a disciple of Dogen, and his student, Kyogo. They note that "... when a person intimately perceives things by engaging whole body and mind ... he will realize the truth of the Dharma of the object" (In: Heine, 2012, p. 55). In his commentary, Heine makes the point that "intimate knowing is identified with intuition as a higher form or spiritual insight" (2012, p. 55).

The contemporary American Zen teacher, Enkyo O'Hara, differentiates intuitive knowing and cognitive knowing and points to the non-discursive, non-categorical experiential nature of *prajna*. She writes: "If I call it 'The Wisdom of Non-Duality', 'The Wisdom of Unknowing', 'The Wisdom of the Source', then you have a handy shelf to put it on and it's no longer *Prajna*; it's another concept, another idea" (2011, p. 12). Similarly, drawing from the American Zen teacher, John Buksbazen (2002), Alfano writes that he "suggests that the word 'reverie' is unfortunately classified as a noun" (2005, p. 229). She further comments:

> Unfortunately, because in its reification it becomes something static, fixed, a thing to be defined. Perhaps reverie should be a verb, a gesture, an act of allowing oneself to float freely in a psychic sea, acted upon by currents unseen to the knowing eye. It is through this floating that the analyst comes to know viscerally and intimately the movements that carry her into a state of transcendent attunement.
>
> (2005, p. 229)

Regarding the intrusion of reification processes that engender reflective knowing in contrast to the active and instantaneous intuitive pre-reflective nature of *prajna*, Low notes that:

> When we think of wisdom, we tend to think of something that is acquired and static, a repository of wise sayings; very often we think of an old woman or an old man with a beard, with a long history and rich experience to draw on. This is not the way of *prajna*; *prajna* is the ability to *respond* spontaneously.
>
> (2006, p. 18, my emphasis)

In this regard, rather than elaborating a static state of mind, Low points the student toward the *activity* of spontaneously arising, intuitive wisdom as practice. The American Buddhist scholar, Sallie King, amplifies this point and notes that "... it cannot be interpreted as representing any kind of static or substantial basis of subjectivity (such as pure mind or self)" (1991, pp. 51–52). *Prajna* as wisdom in this context represents the cultivation of active subjectivity through Zen practice. In terms of the shift in the process of perception as the activity of *prajna*, the Buddhist philosopher, Yoshifumi Ueda, describes the relationship with objects as follows: "This mind does not know an object through conception, but rather it knows directly the object as it really exists" (1967, pp. 162–163). Ueda points to the pre-reflective, active, ongoing, intuitive "knowing" before thinking.

Knowledge and truth

The definitions of *prajna* outlined above point to implications for psychoanalysis by describing a fundamental difference between Freud's agenda of making the unconscious conscious, which derives from a positivist knowledge-based model, and Bion's truth-based model. That is, from the Freudian perspective, once a "something" is brought into awareness, it is discovered and then will always be known. This is in contrast to the ongoing evolution of truth described by Bion (1970), Rhode (1994, 1998), and others who prioritize an experiential truth-based approach to psychoanalysis. We are always at the presencing and ever-changing horizon of ever-evolving awareness. Experience constantly changes, rising and falling in and out of form without any fixed end point. Each moment engenders an opportunity to respond compassionately, which is the activity of *prajna*. Alternatively, the individual can react on the basis of old, deeply embedded karmic formations, which color perception of the present. Low qualifies the difference between response and reaction and notes: "But this response is not a blind impulsive mindless response, a knee-jerk response, or quick repartee" (2006, p. 18). Despite the different areas of interest that the above authors bring to the discussion, notice that the emphasis in discussing and defining *prajna* is on the *activity* of *prajna* as an ongoing, experiencing activity and not on "wisdom" as the result of gathering and accumulating static and discrete pieces of information.

Zen practice and *prajna*

For the Zen practitioner, the process of *zazen* creates the possibility to feel and experience the ongoing activity of *prajna* in this moment where we are right now. This vantage point provided by *shikantaza,* described in Chapter 3, functions as the activity of the total exertion of knowing. The activity of intuitive knowing manifests in the ability to respond spontaneously and with clarity. As the expression of knowing in action, *prajna* functions as the ongoing operation of the "Zen impulse" (Cooper, 2010). This is the activity that keeps on going no matter what. *Prajna* finds representation in the iconic swing of the Buddhist Bodhisattva of Wisdom, Manjushri's sword, which is in constant motion, cutting through delusion more rapidly than we can see.

Akihisa Kondo on intuition

Kondo (1952) provides a very basic and straightforward discussion of intuition in one of the first integrative studies of Zen and psychoanalysis to appear in a psychoanalytic journal. Kondo anticipates both Bion's and Matte-Blanco's work on intuition and unitive experience by decades. He describes intuition as "one of the deepest functions of the human mind" (1952, pp. 10–14). Kondo defines intuition as "a means of perceiving reality directly, not by means of logic and reasoning" (p. 10). He comments on the ineffable nature of intuition and notes that "This experience is so spontaneous and so direct that one cannot describe it" (p. 12). He adds that "We call it an intuitive experience, in its genuineness, its wholeness and its oneness" (p. 12).

Similarly, in a radical shift away from the positivist paradigm, Bion acknowledges the elusive nature of description by referring to the awareness or realization engendered by intuition simply as "O." He writes:

> I shall use the sign O to denote that which is the ultimate reality represented by terms such as ultimate reality, absolute truth, the godhead, the infinite, the thing-in-itself. O does not fall in the domain of knowledge or learning save incidentally; it can be "become," but it cannot be "known." It is darkness and formlessness but it enters the domain K when it has evolved to a point where it can be known, through knowledge gained by experience, and formulated in terms derived from sensuous experience; its existence is conjectured phenomenologically.
>
> (1970, p. 26)

Bion uses this vague descriptor for what he describes as "emotional Truth" in order to keep psychic space free, open, and not saturated by meanings derived from other sources such as sense perceptions. He views psychoanalytic data as not being available through sensory perceptions and argues that language serves to articulate sensory-based experience. This is the experience that Bion describes as "at-one-ment" (1970, p. 30) as the result of the intuitive awareness of "Truth evolution" (p. 27). Implicit in this description is the relationship between intuitive experiential knowing and cognitive knowing. His notion of evolution describes the process by which pre-reflective awareness is followed by retrospective knowing, which he describes simply as "K." Following Bion, Stitzman describes intuition as one of the senses that "make it possible to perceive emotional experience" (2004, p. 1137). However, he limits his definition to the psychoanalytic encounter.

Dogen's "sensing"

Bion's position parallels Dogen's discussion of non-sensuous intuition. In the *Zazenshin* ("A Needle for *Zazen*," 1242a) fascicle of *Shōbōgenzō*, Dogen describes the total exertion of intuition as "not touching but sensing," by which he means not through sensuous experience or cognition, but through intuition. Dogen writes: "This sensing is naturally subtle: there has been no discriminating thought. The state in which 'thought' is 'sensing' is not always reliant on external assistance" (translated and quoted by Nishijima & Cross, 1996, p. 103).

He further describes sensing as follows:

> "Not touching things, yet sensing." Sensing is not sense perception; sense perception is small-scale. Neither is it intellectual recognition; intellectual recognition is intentional doing. Therefore, "sensing" is "beyond touching things," and that which is "beyond touching things" is "sensing."
>
> (p. 102)

Dogen continues by speaking of "not opposing circumstances" (p. 102). I understand Dogen's comments with regard to intuition in psychoanalysis in terms of working with what is presented right in front of us, both internally and externally; by what spontaneously stirs up in our bodies and minds and by what the analysand says or does not say. In this sense, the analyst fully witnesses and contains the analysand's experience and the inner experience of the analysand without judgment, evaluation, or discrimination. For example, if the analysand's mind is in chaos and that chaos is projected, then the analyst will experience the chaos and needs to work with it by containment, introspection, notation, or interpretation. The analyst who attempts to meditate oneself out of the chaos or prescribes meditation as a palliative defeats the emerging infinite possibilities by shutting down the operation of intuitive knowing.

Dogen's observations parallel Bion's discussion of what he describes as the "non-sensuous" domain of psychoanalysis, which finds clear expression in his comments on the distinctions that he draws between medicine and psychoanalysis. Bion writes:

> The point that demonstrates the divergence most clearly is that the physician is dependent on realization of sensuous experience in contrast with the psycho-analyst whose dependence is on experience that is not sensuous. The physician can see and touch and smell. The realizations with which a psycho-analyst deals cannot be seen or touched; anxiety

has no shape or colour, smell or sound. For convenience, I propose to use the term "intuit" as a parallel in the psychoanalyst's domain to the physician's use of "see," "touch," "smell," and "hear."

(1970, p. 7)

Dogen continues:

We should not consider speculatively that it is universal awareness, and we should not think narrowly that it is self-awareness. This "not touching things" means "When a clear head comes, a clear head does. When a dull head comes, a dull head does."

(Nishijima & Cross, 1996, p. 102)

From the psychoanalytic perspective, we can add: when a cluttered mind comes, a cluttered mind does; when a chattering mind comes, a chattering mind does; when a blank mind comes, a blank mind does. In other words, from Dogen's radically non-dualistic perspective, all moments of mind consciousness are considered the reality of the moment and are part of the psychoanalytic field not to be ignored, judged, dismissed, or actively eradicated (if that were possible) through the active application of palliative meditation techniques. The latter operation would be considered, as Dogen notes, "intentional doing" and would require judgment, which is based on intellectual recognition, and dualistic thinking (splitting).

The centrality of intuition

Despite radical theoretical differences between the various psychoanalytic theories, some form of intuition serves as the central experiential tool for psychoanalytic listening. Zen and this particular strand of psychoanalytic thought both endeavor to engender an awareness beyond discursive thinking, which Kondo notes "is not fully equipped to deal with the dynamic reality or the living totality of the human mind" (1952, p. 10). Kondo goes on to note that *prajna* as intuitive knowing is the "crucial point of Zen" (p. 10). In line with Dogen, Kondo contrasts intuition and intellect by pointing out: "The intuitive experience is an awakening from intellectual somnolescence" (p. 12).

Zen achieves realization through intuitive experience. In line with Karen Horney, who draws from the Zen scholar D.T. Suzuki's (1960, p. 53) notion of "sincerity of spirit" or "wholeheartedness," Kondo associates intuitive experience with "wholeness" or "oneness" (1952, p. 12). Previously, I have described the striving toward wholeness as the common ground and goal of all psychoanalytic theories and legitimate religious belief systems (Cooper, 1998).

Ignacio Matte-Blanco on symmetrization

In a similar move, Matte-Blanco (1975, 1988) draws the psychoanalyst's attention to what he describes as "bi-logic," which takes into perspective the range and function of intuition and discursive linear thinking that operate to varying degrees depending on the extent of what he describes as symmetrization processes. He does not deny or negate ordinary logic or reasoning processes; rather, in line with Kondo, as the latter puts it in terms of Buddhist thought, "... Buddhism wishes to draw our attention to something beyond mere intellectualism" (Kondo, 1952, p. 10). For Matte-Blanco, the experience of oneness is the experience of total symmetrization. As a result of total symmetrization, Matte-Blanco observes that in an "indivisable mode" (1988, pp. 77–81) everything mysteriously becomes everything else. Linear logic and ordinary reasoning processes fail to capture this experience, which is only accessible through intuition.

One of the problems with classical psychoanalysis, as I see it, is the all too common tendency to over-idealize logic and thinking in an attempt to understand the irrational; a misguided use of discursive dualistic thinking to attempt to understand the unitive; devaluing intuition of unitive experiencing and confusing such experiences as exclusively "regressive"; over-reliance and exclusive use or misuse of discursive thinking; and using the wrong functions of mind (i.e. rational discursive rather than the intuitive faculties that are inherent in all of us whether we are aware of our capacity for intuition or not and whether that capacity is developed or not). James Grotstein emphasizes the defensive function of this over-reliance on discursive processes with regard to psychoanalytic theory with reference to Bion's truth-based formulation of O. He writes:

> I believe that the concept of O transforms all existing psychoanalytic theories (e.g. the pleasure principle, the death instinct, and the paranoid–schizoid and depressive positions) into veritable psychoanalytic manic defenses against the unknown, unknowable, ineffable, inscrutable, ontological experience of ultimate being ...
>
> (2007, p. 121)

In an article on Zen and psychoanalysis, Zoltan Morvay emphasizes this point and he observes that "Freud's model for mental health idealized the rationality and logic of the ego" (1999, p. 25). This attitude is exemplified in Freud's famous and oft-quoted dictum, "Where id was shall ego be."

One outcome of this orientation has been the opinion that the ascendance of primary process reflects an exclusively "regressive" situation without any consideration for the possibility that something progressive might be occurring. This position finds expression, for example, in Franz Alexander's critique of Buddhist meditation, which he views exclusively through a pathologizing lens and which he describes as an "artificial catatonia" (1931, p. 131).

Drawing from Zen teachings that are consistent with Matte-Blanco's notion of symmetrization, I have endeavored to articulate a non-pathologizing view of what has been traditionally characterized as regressive merger through the notion of "unitive experience" (Cooper, 2010). This notion finds support in the experiential arena and has been described variously, such as by Freud as a "bending toward," by Kohut as "empathic attunement" or "vicarious introspection," by Bion as "reverie" or "intuition," by Reik as "listening with the third ear," and by Winnicott as "maternal preoccupation" and by "self forgetting." Horney (1945), as I noted above, for example, draws from Zen and she speaks of "wholehearted self-forgetting." She quotes D.T. Suzuki (1960), who exemplifies this self forgetting in his approach to understanding a flower. He writes that the process

> ... is to become the flower, to be the flower, to bloom as the flower blooms and to enjoy the sunlight as well as the rainfall. When this is done the flower speaks to me and I know all of its secrets, all its joys, all its sufferings, that is all its life vibrating within itself.
>
> (p. 11)

Commenting on this quote in a discussion of intuitive knowing and Karen Horney's notion of wholeheartedness of spirit, Morvay further notes that:

> A wholehearted understanding is an intuitive grasp of the other, a compassionate communal of being with the other. ... For the psychoanalyst this means developing the ability to lose oneself in knowing the client without preconceptualizations. Compassion automatically follows from this understanding.
>
> (1999, p. 33)

Bion describes this experience with regard to what he refers to as "emotional turbulence" engendered in the psychoanalytic setting as "storm-tossed, but not shaken" (1980, p. 77). By emotional turbulence, Bion means that all psychic change is catastrophic and engenders an emotional turbulence. From the Zen perspective, we might more accurately regard mergers into unitive experience as neither progressive nor regressive. On this point, Magid argues that "Perhaps it is finally time for psychoanalysis to stop thinking that experiencing 'oneness' means momentarily returning to the way things *were* and to recognize that it means seeing things as they *are*" (2000, p. 519, emphasis in original). In this regard, both "progressions" and "regressions" reflect an evaluative judgment of some sort or another, such as the emphasis on evaluating whether or not a psychotherapy patient is meeting standardized and/or predetermined treatment goals. Such a model and related expectations reflect hidden teleological assumptions typical of most religious systems, as I describe in Chapter 5, "Realization and delusion" conceptually and that

I further elaborate experientially in Chapter 9, "Taste the strawberries" through an extended case presentation and through a discussion of a dream.

Bion's intuition of "O"

Similar to the Buddhist notion of *prajna* as "quick knowing," Wilfred Bion observes that through intuition, "It becomes increasingly possible to arrive at conclusions instantaneously which at first are the fruits of laborious intellectualization" (1963, p. 73).

As I noted above, Bion describes this Truth simply as "O." He distinguishes O from what he notes as "K" (knowledge). For Bion, O is the reality of life prior to definition, prior to the intrusion of K. That is why he asserts that O can be intuited, but not known. It can only be known through evolution into K. However, K derived through memory, desire, or understanding occludes the totally exerted flow of this evolution; it prevents one from "becoming and being the flower," as D.T. Suzuki notes (see above quote). To continue with Suzuki's flower image, forcibly drawing from memory would be like looking up the image of a flower in a botany book. Bion strives for something more direct, more lived, multi-dimensional, felt, and experienced through intuition. By grasping at forced memories or at preconceptions of cure (desires), for instance, we are trying to make what Hisamatsu describes as "constant" what is, as he notes, "inconstant" (1979, p. 1). This natural human tendency toward the illusion of constancy emphasizes what Hisamatsu describes as the synthesizing function of mind and ignores the fundamental impermanence or tendency toward the antithesis of all phenomena.

This natural human tendency engenders an over-emphasis and over-reliance on secondary process functioning or what in Zen parlance is often described as discursive mind or what the Tibetan teacher Chogyam Trungpa describes as "dualistic fixation" (1976, p. 25), to the point where the basic human capacity for intuition becomes occluded or obliterated. This is at the expense of our intuitive capacities that derive, according to Bion, through evolution, which relies on processes that are primary and not solely rooted in asymmetrical, logical, everyday linear thinking and sense perceptions.

Nishiari Bokusan's advice for developing a deep understanding of Zen teachings exemplifies the place of intuition, which is engendered through the practice of *zazen*. He notes that: "First of all, you should get right down to your *hara* [energy center just below the navel]. This cannot be done solely by thinking" (2011, p. 12). On the other hand, he does not disregard or devalue thinking, which is a common misunderstanding regarding Zen that was addressed in Chapters 2 and 6. He writes, "On the other hand, you cannot grasp it without knowing the basic principle. So first, I will explain it for the moment in an analytical fashion" (p. 12). In this regard, Bokusan, closely following Dogen, sets up a balance that integrates intuitive knowing and cognitive understanding. Analytical understanding functions as a structure for the containment and emergence of intuition.

Dreaming psychoanalysis

Similarly, as I noted above, Bion describes a binocular vision that integrates rigorous thinking with deep reverie. As Bion notes:

> But I believe that the analyst may have to cultivate a capacity for dreaming while awake, and that this capacity must somehow be reconcilable with what we ordinarily conceive of as an ability for logical thought of a mathematical kind.
>
> (1992, p. 215)

Bion describes the earliest modes of infant and mother intuited communication in terms of internal reverie and notes that

> ... reverie is that state of mind which is open to the reception of any "objects" from the loved object and is therefore capable of reception of the infant's projective identifications whether they are felt by the infant to be good or bad. In short, reverie is a factor of the mother's alpha-function.
>
> (1962, p. 37)

"State of mind" implies and exemplifies Buksbazen's concern with reification. However, Bion points to the fluid nature of reverie in terms of his notion of evolution, which he describes as a fluid moving process of ongoing non-sensory awareness of the emotional truth of any session.

From a perspective that weaves together threads between Bion's psychoanalytic notion of intuition and Zen intuition, Bobrow offers the following:

> Intuition means direct, unmediated knowing. O cannot be "been" by chasing out through the senses, yet it is embodied in birdsong, the flavor of dark chocolate, the smell and touch of a loved one, and the scowl of an adversary. This is difficult to "wrap our mind around." Why? It is our mind.
>
> (2002, p. 67)

Bion renders his notion of intuition of "O" clinically applicable through the use of reverie, which he describes as taking the form of wide-awake dreaming. He (1992) observes that the analyst needs to dream the analytic session. Freedom from memory, desire, and understanding has been interpreted in the negative, which is understandable if the reader relies exclusively on Bion's stated mandate taken out of the larger context of his theory and its influence on this related technique (1967, 1970). That is, according to this misguided view, Bion is simply asserting what the analyst should not do without giving the analyst a clue as to what s/he might do and that his recommendation is simply technical and not related to his theoretical position. However, Bion's point that the analyst must dream the session is firmly rooted in his theoretical thinking and reflects a positive spin on the matter. That is, "dreaming the session" means to allow reverie to become manifest in the foreground of the analyst's intuited experience of the session. Bion's point is that forced and active intrusions of memory and desire can occlude the experiential intuition of reverie.

Not unlike *prajna*, reverie is always active, but it is not always accessible to the analyst's awareness. Reverie is the action of wide-awake dreaming in the session, which, according to Bion, relies on "negative capability," elaborated in Chapter 8, to unfold. Grotstein offers a reasonable rationale. He writes: "... dreaming [reverie] functions as a filter that sorts, categorizes, and prioritizes emotional facts that are stimulated by this incoming data" (2007, p. 264). This process engenders that action of "selected fact." However, it demands "negative capability." This whole process exemplifies operationally what Bion describes as "binocular vision." That is, as Grotstein notes, "... in which any and all phenomena can be observed from two or more vertices to achieve a stereoscopic perspective" (p. 265) – in this case, intuition of "O" and cognition, which from the Zen perspective would be described as *prajna* and discursive thought.

One significant problem with understanding the relationship between relinquishing memory, desire, and understanding in relation to Zen meditation is the confusing misunderstanding regarding the supposed devaluation of thought. What Zen teachers and psychoanalysts who take this approach are calling for is developing an altered *relationship* to thought. I emphasize relationship here because that is a point of significance for both Zen and Bion's version of psychoanalysis. The misunderstanding regarding Zen might stem from a literal reading or misreading of the aphorism "No reliance on words and letters." This point will be further elaborated in Chapter 6.

Through the process of projective identification, the analyst's reverie (dream function) completes and complements the patient's dream function and, through the patient's introjection process, the actual capacity to dream. In this manner, ultimately, the patient's ability to dream one's own dreams as alpha function is built, rebuilt, or restored. From this perspective, it is not only the process of conscious listening that is important, but also the *function* of listening, which has a dual purpose. Listening functions in order to engender an understanding of the patient's emotional Truth while simultaneously influencing the patient's alpha function through ongoing unconscious communicative cycles of projection and introjection by which the patient experiences being understood consciously and develops alpha function (capacity to dream) unconsciously. This is why, in my opinion, interpretation takes on diminished importance in contemporary psychoanalysis when viewed from this perspective.

Religion and spirituality

One external and disturbing social and cultural manifestation of this tendency to shut down intuition is the increasingly common and widespread breakdown of religious institutions and the increasingly widespread alienation from religious organizations by its congregants. This phenomenon has engendered an ever-widening gap between religion and spirituality because meaning and self-fulfillment are drained out of religious structures to the point that dead, brittle lifelessness (manifested as secondary process) predominates and shuts down access to spiritually enriching insights and experiences accessible through intuition. On the other hand, spiritual searching operates without the benefit of structure that secondary process and the capacity for discursive thinking or the binocular vision that both Bokusan and Bion seek provides. Bi-logic fails because symmetrical and asymmetrical processes are thrown out of balance.

Self-engendered structures that guide active and authentic spiritual searching are often influenced by unconscious forces in ways that simultaneously support and reflect character structures that can be less than optimal. This "pick and choose" from a seeming over-abundance of choices approach to spirituality that has been described, for example, as "shopping in the spiritual supermarket" exemplifies Bion's caution with respect to the distortion of memory "by the influence of unconscious forces" (1967, p. 17).

Here is an important distinction and caution. Psychoanalytic experience as it evolves into form produces diagnostic definitions. This reflects a natural human tendency and wish that everything makes sense, even if the result of sense making ultimately turns out to be an illusion. In this manner, all diagnostic categories are also reflections of psychoanalytic experience. The point to keep firmly in mind is that psychoanalytic (or religious) experience cannot be "bottled up" in diagnostic definitions (or simplistic dogmatic pronouncements) and neatly boxed and stored in secondary process categories for future use. We need to be aware of the tendency to be led around by definitions rather than using them as secondary tools that facilitate working with the primary experience of the total exertion of O evolutions known through intuition. I think that this point can be summed up in the old expression: "Does the man ride on the donkey's back or does the man carry the donkey on his back?"

Hisamatsu's ordinary mind

I mentioned Hisamatsu's (1979) notion of "ordinary mind" in relation to synthesis and antithesis above. Let's take a closer look at his ideas and their relevance to intuition. Bion's intuition of O through evolutions to K that I described above addresses what Hisamatsu (1979, p. 2) describes as "flux" or "flow." He uses these two terms interchangeably. Hisamatsu describes intuition of flow or flux as a subjective process, which he distinguishes from the objectivity of scientific observation. Bion notes, as I described above, that psychoanalytic data cannot be known through the senses, but must be "intuited." For intuition to occur, the psychoanalyst must become one with the evolution or perhaps, more accurately, realize the ever-present oneness with evolution. As noted above, he uses the term "at-one-ment" to point toward this process and he argues that this is a requirement for a complete and thorough analysis. Similarly, Hisamatsu writes, "Things which are in 'flux' cannot be perceived. It is impossible to know those things which are in flux, while they are in flux, unless flux is arrested without disturbing the flux" (1979, p. 2). He adds, "The flow, while flowing, must at the same time be in a state of arrest" (p. 2). This simultaneous flow and arrest rests on and serves as an expression of the basic Zen principle of the identity of the relative and the absolute. Bion notes that the analyst must "suffer" or permit this experience. His notion of evolution acknowledges and parallels Hisamatsu's point that we *are* the flow. (We *are* the evolution; we *are* "O" in evolution.) Harris and Bick comment on Bion's awareness of the ephemeral quality of this experience:

> His attitude would be that truth can never be attained, or possessed; it is never static. Glimpses of aspects of truth occur fleetingly, on the way to becoming more experienced. This entails the ability to live in the present, bringing one's experiences from the past constantly into the present to link up with the perceptions of the present. The Self grows in experience and in the ability to express itself.
>
> (1980, p. 49)

In the context of the role that perception plays in relation to delusion and realization, Heine writes, "When one opposes the flux by wishfully seeking a state of immutability or stagnation ... the result tends just the reverse – heightened frustration ..." (2012, p. 51).

In a radically non-dualistic critique of scientific method, Hisamatsu notes that:

> It might be supposed that "intuition" means to enter the flow from without and to unite oneself with it. But that which arrests the flow is not something which enters the flow from outside, and further, intuition must be that which already exists within the flow itself. ... In other words, that which intuits must not be something which enters the flow from outside; instead it must have arrested the flow within the flow itself, and done so in complete unity with the flow.
>
> (1979, p. 2)

This means that on the one-to-one level, the psychoanalyst needs to relinquish his or her role as an outside observer and acknowledge the full involvement in the unfolding of the emotional Truth of the session without resisting deepening symmetrization processes. We need to realize that we are "in the soup," sometimes as an additional mild flavoring, at other times strong and pungent, still at other times – as the notions of transference and countertransference point to – as a "main ingredient." On an existential level, as Heine notes, "The self must continuously lose itself in the shadowy world of impermanence to ultimately realize itself liberated from yet still involved in the unceasing process of continual change" (2012, p.73).

Bion acknowledges this "arresting" that Hisamatsu speaks about through his grid category "notation." In other words, flow becomes at once subject, verb, and object. The Zen teacher, Kosho Uchiyama, expresses this radical non-dualism in a manner that mirrors Matte-Blanco's notion of total symmetrization, Bion's notion of at-one-ment, Suzuki's "blossoming as the flower," and Hisamatsu's depiction of unity with the flow in terms of practice. He writes, "*Zazen* is the self doing itself by itself" (2004, p. 22).

This emphasis on subjectivity and its relation to unitive, experientially intuited reality is clearly articulated by the psychoanalyst, Lou Andreas-Salomé. She voices a strong argument for psychoanalysis as a subjective discipline and delineation from the called for objectivity of the scientific method and observes that:

> There is an unalterable contradiction in the application of a method derived from science – the logical analysis by which we gain control of the outer world – to the immediate data of our innermost experiences. It is not simply a question of inspecting psychic life from the outside, a matter of "psychology" so to speak, but rather an invasion and a definition of its spontaneous flow *in vivo*; the analyst participates actively, not just by understanding.
>
> (Translated by Leavy, 1964, p. 73)

Past, present, future

Intuition of flow or evolution from the perspective of the identity of the relative and the absolute, according to Hisamitsu, identifies "... that the present resides in the arrest of the flow even as it continues to flow" (1979, pp. 2–3). In other words, the evolution of O to K is intuited or experienced without grasping. This non-grasping stance is what Bion advocates when he makes a call for freedom from memory, desire, and understanding. As I noted above, Bion is advocating that the psychoanalyst resists the forcing of memories. His stance is intended to clear the psychic space for spontaneously emerging memories. He distinguishes between the two by describing the latter as "evolutions." Thus, Bion maintains an open non-dualistic stance. The K articulated by the analyst through interpretation, notation, or observation functions as an artifact or reified representation of the experience of the ongoing activity of intuited evolution; an experienced "presencing," if you will, which we artificially divide up into what we refer to as "moments." It would be a misunderstanding to argue that Bion advocates the total elimination of memories and desires. It would be more accurate, as I see it, to note spontaneously arising memories and wishes, which in the form of reverie are part of the present evolution of any given psychoanalytic encounter. Not unlike all thoughts, as the influential Indian Buddhist sage Nagarjuna notes, they emerge, crystallize into form, and dissolve. Bion is asking the psychoanalyst to relinquish forced memories, wishes, or preconceived categories of understanding such as diagnoses. He is attempting to free the analyst from the imprisoning grip of an over-domination of secondary process. Hisamatsu, following Dogen's notion of "*Uji*" or "being time," points out that

> ... it is not that the present is cut off from the past and the future, but that the present must be without distinction of past, "present" and future. The present must be none other than the time wherein the distinction of before, during and after has ceased.
>
> (1979, p. 3)

We can see the role of intuition asserted in Dogen's *Fukanzazengi* ("Universal Principles of Meditation," 1227), his first written piece upon his return from his four-year sojourn in China. He writes:

> You should therefore cease from practice based on intellectual understanding, pursuing words and following after speech, and learn the backward step that turns your light inward to illuminate your self. Body and mind will drop away of themselves, and your original face will manifest itself.
>
> (Translated by Waddell & Abe, 2002, p. 3)

In this context, realizing or realization, derived from the Japanese *shō*, refers to making real, verifying, confirming, and proving to oneself through the activity of one's own intuitive awareness, which is experientially and personally derived for each of us as individuals. Again, Dogen informs the student that realization occurs through non-perceptual intuitive awareness in *Bendowa* (1234). He writes, "Any such mingling with perceptions is not the mark of realization, for the mark of true realization is beyond such illusion" (translated by Waddell & Abe 2002, p. 13).

Intuition: instrumental and realizational

Intuition at once points to the way things are and functions as a prescription for wholehearted action. This seemingly paradoxical relationship between reality manifesting – "being-as-it-is" (Suzuki, 1970); "beening" (Bion, 1970), and as a call for action – are reconciled in our mode of being in the world; in our attitude toward life; in our response to others; in how we view ourselves. Kim describes this manner of living and thinking as set forth by Dogen as "radically non-dualistic" (1985, p. 55). Total exertion functions at once as a lived expression of this seemingly contradictory relationship between one/many, relative/absolute, same/different, or self-limiting/self-liberating.

The way things are and as a prescription for action as *gūjin* come together at once in *zazen* through the exertion and spontaneously arising expression and experience of intuition. *Zazen* is expressive of Buddha-nature, which becomes enacted and realized when we sit. *Zazen* is also instrumental in that it renders realization available into awareness. How do we live in duality/non-duality, in absolute freedom? How do we relate this to *zazen* practice or to psychoanalytic practice? Do we need to make these distinctions? What do you think? What is your experience?

Chapter 5

Realization and delusion

> *Our present walking, staying, sitting, and lying, every response to opportunities, and contact with others – these are all the way.*
>
> – Baso Dōitsu, eighth century

Introduction

This chapter examines the relationship between realization and delusion as expressed in notions of transcendence and immanence to illustrate the functioning of *gūjin* with regard to Dogen's radical non-dualism, which he expresses in his notion of the oneness of practice and realization (*shūshō itto*). That is, as noted in the previous chapter, Dogen views practice as an enactment or an expression of realization. From this perspective, practice does not facilitate a movement from an inferior deluded state to a superior enlightened state. This latter view of practice as instrumental, to reiterate, engenders and implies a devaluation of the experiential present moment.

One example that demonstrates the duality/oneness of the realization/delusion is the idea that sacred scriptures and the world at large both "speak" the truth of being. It is up to the individual to cultivate this awareness. This reality, which is constantly in flux, is totally exerted always as it is. It is our perception or awareness and hence our relationship to this fluid reality that changes. The influential Zen master, Nishiari Bokusan (1821–1910), who takes an absolutist position that emphasizes oneness, describes it this way: "When you are deluded you are a sentient being. When you are enlightened you are invariably a Buddha" (2011, p. 46). Okumura adds:

> Though we are deluded as individual karmic beings, we are still living within this absolute reality that is Buddha Dharma, and even though we are living within this universal reality, we are still deluded as individual karmic selves.
>
> (2010, p. 60)

Bokusan and Okumura both point to the reality of human beings in the world in a typical Zen fashion. As individuals we are living deluded within realization. On the other hand, practice enables us to experience the reality of our delusion. From this perspective, realization is clear, simple, ineffable, and not acquired from outside of personal experience. In this regard, as Gomez notes in his discussion of the distinctions between sudden and gradual realization writes from the sudden perspective, "states of bondage and suffering are seen as mere delusion, the result of an error in perception or conception; liberation is therefore similar in nature to opening the eyes" (1987, p. 71).

Consistent with this subitist orientation, Dogen compares realization as waking up from a dream. When asleep we think that the dream is real until we wake up. We are no longer ignorant of our delusion. This orientation expresses Dogen's radical non-dualism, as Kim notes: "Dogen inevitably (and quite consistently) returned to the non-dualistic soteriology of Buddha-nature, radically conceived with the logic of realization rather than the logic of transcendence" (2004, p. 203).

The point is that reality is reality, regardless of how we perceive it or what words we use to describe it. We are an integral part of reality in delusion *and* in realization. In this sense, reality doesn't care what we call it. The labels that we ascribe to reality are abstractions about reality. As Dogen, who covers all possibilities, notes in *Genjōkoan* (1233):

> Those who greatly enlighten illusion are Buddhas. Those greatly deluded amid enlightenment are sentient beings. Some people continue to realize enlightenment beyond enlightenment. Some proceed amid their illusion deeper into further illusion.
> (Translated by Waddell & Abe, 2002, p. 40)

From the Mahayana Buddhist perspective, as Sallie King notes in her discussion of the Buddha-nature treatise, "There is only one world, the world of interdependent phenomena, which can be experienced in an entirely delusory, partially delusory, or enlightened fashion" (1991, p. 47).

Not unlike *zazen* as a prototype model that I described in Chapter 2, scriptures can serve as a prototype for learning to hear the world sutra in the sound of rustling leaves, the wind, the morning dove, the busy market place, or passing traffic. Whether or not any of these aspects of the material world brings delusion or realization into the perceptual foreground depends on our subjectivity. This point requires further clarification. From the Soto perspective, as prototype, sutra recitation, study, and work practice are all expressive and demonstrative in that they contribute to and express realization simultaneously. In this respect, both the practitioner's discriminative and intuitive functions are active. I will elaborate this point later and will further discuss this relationship in terms of thinking, not thinking and beyond thought in Chapter 6.

In the present context, the question becomes one not of classification and judgment, but of how one integrates and uses one's discriminative and intuitive capacities in response to all experiences. The following vignette from psychoanalytic case supervision exemplifies this point.

A psychoanalytic candidate described her policy of charging her patients a fee for missed sessions. After explaining her policy to a new patient who had failed to show up for her previous session, she asked: "How is that for you?" The patient was silent for a moment, but after some consideration she said, "That's fine. I totally understand." She then proceeded to pay for the missed session. However, the therapist experienced a sense of discomfort in the patient. This was intuitively communicated. That is, while on the one hand she expressed a conscious and cognitive understanding and acted accordingly, on the other hand, emotionally, unconsciously, and silently, she was not fine. The therapist intuited the patient's silent and private experience, which enabled her to open up an exploration of the patient's deeper feelings and her need to comply with the therapist's policy without question.

This example demonstrates that from an objective, external, cognitive/discursive perspective, the patient was seemingly fine. However, from a subjective, internal, non-verbal, intuitive perspective, we "hear" a very different story.

Both intuitive and cognitive capacities are part of the equipment of the human mind. They require acknowledgment and need to be brought into an integrated balance. This inclusive stance with respect to all experience holds implications with regard to how Zen views religious goals. I will turn now to the relationship between transcendence and immanence to illustrate this point.

Transcendence

There are many ways to discuss transcendence. This discussion emphasizes the ongoing realization that comprises Zen's religious function. One way that religious intention is activated and maintained is through the ritual recitation of the Four Universal Vows:

> Beings are numberless; I vow to save them.
> Afflictions are inexhaustible; I vow to end them.
> Dharma gates are boundless; I vow to enter them.
> Buddha's Way is unsurpassable; I vow to become it.
> (Yakai, 2010, p. 8)

Let's take a look at the Third Vow, which clearly expresses the ongoing nature of realization: "Dharma gates are boundless; I vow to enter them." From this perspective, transcendence refers to our capacity to identify and step beyond self-oriented limiting views and to respond to life (our own and others) from the broader realization of compassionate action. Each moment presents us with the opportunity to express realization or delusion. Each moment functions as a dharma gate. This demonstrates and expresses the Zen view that freedom and realization occur in the here and now and that *zazen* is an expression of that realization. In this regard, as Abe notes, "Practice as such is a manifestation of realization" (1985, p. 59).

Basically, different religious belief systems espouse one of two positions. They can be loosely described as oriented toward a "transcendent, other worldly transcendence" or as an "immanent, here and now transcendence." The former goal-oriented, dualistic teleological notion of transcendence points toward an end point typically described as an afterlife in terms of eternal rewards and punishments usually characterized as heavens and hells. The latter process-oriented radical non-dualism espoused in Zen soteriology emphasizes realization in immanence through full awareness of being in the moment and living out the reality of our life. This position emphasizes our relationship to self, other, and inner and outer experience as beings in the world.

From the Zen perspective, liberation refers to freedom from the bondage and suffering engendered by ignorance – a failure to realize the impermanence of life and the fundamental insubstantiality of what we experience in a relative way as "self." As noted in the previous paragraph, the present moment is the nexus of all experience. The present moment is the dharma gate. This here and now emphasis that I outlined in Chapter 1 reflects in the notion of *gūjin* or total exertion. It is important to keep in mind that the here and now emphasis is not intended as a negation of the past or the future. Rather, what becomes crucial is our relationship to our past experiences and our future wishes. Memories and wishes spontaneously arising and dissolving are aspects of the lived present. Kasulis writes, "To negate the past and future is to negate the basis of the distinction by which the word *present* has any meaning" (1981, p. 79). Further, negation of a sense of the past and the future as they spontaneously arise in the present would constitute a negation of totally lived experience.

Zen teaches that through our own experience we come to realize all existence in the here and now as potentially imprisoning or liberating. In this regard, the realization that liberation is lived in the present moment replaces notions of otherworldly transcendence. This realization requires that we overcome the exclusivity of the subject/object split and that we actualize our wider self that is all-inclusive of everything. This is the intention behind Dogen's translation of the traditional Buddhist statement "all beings *have* Buddha nature" as "whole being *is* Buddha nature." This non-dualist orientation views transcendence in immanence and immanence in transcendence. From this perspective, Uchiyama notes that:

> Fundamentally, no matter what kind of circumstances we may have fallen into, we are always in the midst of enlightenment. To the extent that we

live in the world of letting go of all our own puny ideas, we live in the middle of enlightenment. As soon as we open the hand of thought and let go of our own insignificant ideas, we begin to see that this is so.

(2004, p. 19)

This subject/object split, as noted in the introduction, functions to maintain a sense of separate, permanent, and individual self, which serves to defend against the fundamental anxiety engendered by the truth of the impermanence and ultimate insubstantiality or evanescence of life. In this regard, letting go of the "puny ideas" that Uchiyama speaks of becomes transcendence and stems from the realization of the defensive and illusory nature of this "small self." In this regard, transcendence is a self-transcendence that requires a shift in one's orientation away from preoccupations with the negative behaviors of seemingly split-off and separate others. From the perspective of the "small self" and "puny ideas," our responses to others are exclusively bound to whether or not we will benefit from our interactions. As a result of the perceptual shift that occurs through practice, this exclusive self-orientation dissolves. This complex notion requires further elaboration.

When the universe as self becomes clear to the individual, one relates to other as self. We become aware of the simultaneity of separateness and connectedness. As compassion develops out of this awareness, negative feelings toward others can be resolved by attending to one's inner responses to the behaviors of others. Here is an illustrative example.

Adam

During a routine doctor's examination, Adam was advised to undergo a test that was only administered in the local hospital. The doctor's assistant phoned the hospital and arranged for Adam to have the test immediately. However, when he arrived at the hospital, Adam was kept waiting for the examination because it was scheduled at the last minute as an "add-on" squeezed into the hospital radiology department's already full schedule of appointments. The longer Adam waited, the more annoyed he became. The annoyance turned into anger and then into a negative response to the hospital staff and to the situation. He was not able to take in the apology of the radiologist when she finally greeted him to prepare for the test. He simply said, "You people have no regard for other people's time." As Adam sat back and reflected on his doctor's urgent insistence that he take the test immediately and, upon self-reflection, on his own emerging feelings of hurt around what seemed to be neglect, he became aware of an increasing anxiety that he felt lingering in the background of his thoughts regarding what the outcome of the test would be. His doctor's urgency conveyed for Adam that this might be a matter of life and death. As he began to sit with the anxiety, he began to feel a sense of gratitude for the radiologist's willingness to fit him in for the exam in her already over-booked schedule. Adam also realized that the time that he waited presented a good opportunity to do some reading in a cool and comfortable environment in the middle of an intense New York City August heat wave. He began to reflect on a verse of a seventh century Chinese Zen poem, *Hsin Hsin Ming*, or Faith in Mind, attributed to the third patriarch of Zen Seng-ts'an that he had been reading:

> Indeed, it is due to your grasping and repelling
> That you do not see things as they are.
>
> (Clark, 1973, p. 1)

This situation required a shift in Adam's orientation away from the initial negative perception and an accompanying negatively tinged, judgmental stance toward the hospital staff and toward the underlying self-states and accompanying feelings of hurt and anxiety. Adam's initial vitriolic, judgmental stance served to protect him from his deeper, more vulnerable feelings; feelings of fear and hurt that he would not permit into awareness. However, his willingness to sit with his experience and accompanying feelings engendered a shift, which in turn facilitated an altered perception of the radiologist and a feeling of gratitude for her concern for Adam, a total stranger.

The here and now, action-oriented emphasis of total exertion that I described in Chapter 1 renders every situation new, fresh, unique, and holding the potential for freedom through experiential realization. Adam's practice facilitated a movement from being trapped in a seemingly endless loop permeated by rage and anxiety to an open and receptive internal space characterized by gratitude and understanding. His relationship to the hospital staff and to himself shifted dramatically. He was able to *respond* rather than *react* to the situation with authenticity and express both his fear and his gratitude. On this point, Hisamatsu notes:

> Everyday actuality is not a stage in the process of the realization of an ideal state, or a means directed toward an end. Everyday actuality itself, in and of itself, is the ideal, the end. This is not mere realism or naturalism. It is of that nature that, "each and every being is perfect as it is."
>
> (1979, p. 23)

Not unlike the practice of *zazen*, when Adam was able to catch himself in the midst of being caught in a negative thought pattern, he was able to return to the immediacy of the moment with a renewed sense of clarity. This sense of immediacy engendered through practice holds important implications for how transcendence is viewed from this perspective, as well as how the relationships between transcendence, immanence, realization, and delusion are understood as aspects of ordinary everyday life that can occur in rapid, moment-to-moment oscillations.

As noted above, one way to view the realizational process entails healing the split that occurs through erroneously objectifying internal and external experience. Judgment, for instance, kept Adam split off from both the internal and external reality of the situation. Introspection resulted in his awareness of the split between his fear and his rage. His false perception of the external situation – the reality of the doctor's schedule and offer to squeeze him in – maintained his rage. His rage, in turn, served to keep his fear completely split off and out of awareness. In other words, the judgmental, raging aspect of his self-experience kept his vulnerable self and associated fear protected from exposure. As a result, he remained protected from the fundamental anxiety of impermanence engendered by the urgent need for the medical test. In this state, he could not exercise compassion toward himself or toward the radiologist. When he cut through the split, his attitude softened and changed.

Drawing from Hisamatsu, Joan Stambaugh amplifies the point that realization is rooted in our ordinary here and now existence, as exemplified in the case of Adam. She writes: "Hisamatsu brings out the unique feature of Zen that seeks to overcome the view of the holy or divine as something transcendental and objective completely outside of human being" (1999, p. 27). She quotes Hisamatsu, who notes that: "The crucial position of Zen is to affirm the 'sacred in man' by retrieving the sacred from the reaches of transcendent views or objective forms and returning it to the fold of human subjectivity" (Hisamatsu, quoted in Stambaugh, 1999, p. 27).

Transcendence and dehumanization

The notion of transcendence as an other-worldly state divorced from the material aspect of being – spirituality as separate from the physical – is actually dehumanizing, because the fullness of our human existence, which, by definition includes the physical, material, as well as the subtle or spiritual, is denied, ignored, disregarded, or completely split off. This approach, whether conscious or unconscious, maintains the subject–object split. The effort to heal this split results in a humanizing process that Zen offers the participant and ultimately engenders compassion. This points to the humanness of Zen and makes no effort to create distractions from the total exertion of the reality of the lived moment. No future promises of eternal salvation (or damnation) separate and free from the human condition are on the table. Rather, as in the case of Adam, Zen demands that we develop clarity with respect to the reality of our lives. Adam, for instance, experienced freedom right in the center of his life. On this point, Cook notes that "Buddhism demands that we abandon all self-deception, all myths and daydreams, all beguiling fairy stories that prevent us from truly understanding the nature of our lives" (2002, p. 41).

Elsewhere in his writings, Cook further explicates this point by articulating a strong and useful distinction between transcendence and realization, which further clarifies this point. He prefers the term "realization" and notes:

> Realization is the way of thoroughly comprehending or penetrating (*gūjin*) the true nature of some situation such as impermanence or death in such a way that it is not transcended, or evaded, or denied but rather radically affirmed and accepted. The condition does not vanish, nor does the individual literally escape involvement in it. The freedom to be had in the midst of conditions comes from the absolute, unequivocal affirmation and acceptance of the condition through comprehension.
>
> (1989, p. 27)

Reification and associated splitting and projective processes transform the notion of transcendence into something imagined as other-worldly, such as a heaven or a pure land. This model supports the belief that suffering is ameliorated by leaving the present, conditioned, impermanent *samsaric* world for something else conceptualized as a permanent *nirvana* that is free from all suffering and conditioning. However, as depicted in the Buddhist Wheel of Life as the God Realm, this state is characterized by self-absorption, complacency, stagnation, and a lack of sensitivity or awareness for the suffering of others. This promise of an other-worldly, suffering-free existence generated a compelling attraction to Indian Buddhism that articulated such goals.

In contrast, Dogen advocates an in-the-world, action-oriented practice that actualizes in relationship to self and others. This firmly rooted in reality transcendence (e.g. with respect to the individual) finds clear expression in Kasulis' depiction of the Zen Master who

> ... is not schizophrenically detached from the historical situation. The Zen Master does not speak in tongues ... he does not cease to eat – he eats the same food as the other monks. He does not transcend the world – he is firmly implanted in it.
>
> (1981, p. 134)

From the teleological frame of reference, which is the basis for most Western religions, an end point – such as heaven or hell – becomes an idealized, objectified, mythologized conceptualization of what is posited as a goal. For Buddhism, this would include nirvana/enlightenment when posited as distinct from samsara/delusion. This appears as a seemingly inescapable conundrum of most religious endeavors, which, to repeat, Dogen articulates as the totally exerted "oneness of practice/realization" (*shūshō itto*).

The teleological perspective creates a problem because it denudes the present of any meaning or significance in and of itself. Religious practice becomes reduced to nothing more than a means to an end. This conceptualization engenders alienation from the present and from those we come into contact with. People become objectified in terms of whether or not they will serve our agenda. Psychotherapy patients become conceptualized and pigeonholed in terms of diagnosis, prognosis, and cure, and in this manner they can become dehumanized. Meditation techniques become reduced to palliative prescriptions to reach future goals and to engender preferred psychological states (Cooper, 2010). The hyper-manic need for constant stimulation is symptomatic of this process. People, places, events, and objects all become passing aspects of our agenda on our way to some abstracted someplace else that we ironically never reach. In the long run, manic hyper-stimulation does not satisfy our basic restlessness. Dogen supplies an antidote, which Abe elaborates as follows:

> In contrast to the aim-seeking approach, the oneness of means and ends implied in Dogen's idea of the oneness of practice and attainment provides an entirely different view of the present and future. In the realization of the oneness of means and end, each and every step of the present is fully realized as the end itself, not as a means to reach the end. And yet, at the same time, each and every step of the present is totally realized as a means toward a future goal because we are living at the dynamic intersection of the temporal–spatial dimension and the transtemporal–transpatial dimension. In this way, firmly grounding ourselves in reality, we can live our lives creatively and constructively toward the future.
> (1985, p. 109)

Emptiness perspective

From the perspective of the Heart Sutra, which is a primary expression of the "emptiness tradition," there are no fixed or permanent states or conditions such as "samsara" or "nirvana," "delusion" or "realization," "ignorance" or "enlightenment," "illusion" or "truth." The belief in such fixed states supports facilitative or instrumental practices that function as resistances to the truth of reality. Such beliefs in what appear as "things," whether in the form of tangible objects, thoughts, feelings, wishes, or memories, are actually transient, impermanent, and in a constant state of "flow" (Hisamatsu, 1979, p. 1).

Belief in permanence and transcendent states serves to support dualistic thinking and, conversely, are engendered and maintained by dualistic thinking, thus perpetuating ignorance through the reification of experience and a self–object dichotomy. As reified objects, our habitual thought trains, our internal narratives, become fixed. This condition drives the desire to permanently substitute undesirable psychological states with preferred psychological states and results, as Bion notes, in a failure to suffer our experience. In this regard, even our dysfunctional, limiting, self-defeating, and negative narratives are cherished and held on to rigidly and tightly. Transformations might constitute radical disruptions to the psyche and engender what Bion describes as "catastrophic" (1965, p. 8) states of emotional turbulence. On this point, Hisamatsu observes that "Ordinary things, though they may be called 'constant,' are in fact inconstant, mutually limiting, and contradictory" (1979, p. 1). Okumura observes, "In this situation we cannot be released from samsara and delusion, because in trying to escape them we actually create them" (2010, p. 40).

The Heart Sutra supports realization and freedom by describing delusion and realization, samsara and nirvana as identical. Commenting on Dogen's *Genjōkoan*, Nishiari Bokusan asks: "What is it that you realize? You realize delusion ... Look. When you are deluded, what are you deluded about? You are deluded about enlightenment" (2011, p. 47). From this perspective, all phenomena become sources of awareness of reality and therefore of freedom.

Practice

Realization, not unlike all phenomena, is fundamentally empty and impermanent and therefore cannot be objectified, possessed, or remain fixed. In fact, we really cannot experience enlightenment. If, for instance, we observe an experience and, as a result, say, "I am enlightened," we have already split off and objectified the experience. We have made it into something separate that we then examine and judge. From a practice point of view, Okumura advises that:

> Rather than striving for a particular experience or goal, we should simply keep practicing without judgment or evaluation. This means approaching all that we do without selfish desire, without even the desire for enlightenment; to practice in this way is to manifest universal reality.
> (2010, p.71)

Dogen teaches that realization emerges as a penetrating experiential awareness that self is not a personal, fixed, or permanent possession. With this in mind, rather than getting caught by or preoccupied with concepts such as immanence or transcendence, we should simply practice right here and right now. If here and now is not the time and place to practice, then where and when is?

If we look for heaven, nirvana, or the pure land outside of ourselves or outside of the present moment or as something somewhere else, not now, something to fill ourselves up with – enlightenment, realization, insight, or wisdom – of course we will feel hollow, empty, or depressed. We will find ourselves in conflict between empty/full, enlightened/ignorant, etc. These erroneous views and associated states will leave us continuously grasping, discontented, dissatisfied, and caught by desire. This grasping motivated by desire is no different than grasping after material things. Both are perceived as an internal lack. However, until we come to terms with this process through the activity of *prajna*, we continue to view outside as the location of the solution. We then devalue our immediate experience and miss the full impact of being in the moment.

The implication for practice engendered by notions of other-worldly transcendence is that it encourages and supports an exclusively functional instrumentalist view accompanied by a goal-oriented approach to practice that overlooks practice as the coincidence of realization/expression, as a "manifestation of realization" (Abe, 1985, p. 59), or what Leighton describes in sharp contrast to an exclusively instrumentalist view as "performance art" (2011, p. 7) or as a "ritual enactment and expression of awakened awareness" (2008, p. 167). From a similar position, Kim speaks of practice as "at once metaphor and reality" (2004, p. 67). In this way, from an exclusively instrumentalist orientation, *zazen* becomes diminished and the moment becomes diminished. We diminish ourselves. We could say that duality/unity manifests functionally at once in *shikantaza*: instrumental as an expression of reality; realizational as the total exertion of the unitive nature of reality that engenders realization.

In contrast, freedom from suffering paradoxically emerges through a radical acceptance of the ultimate impermanence of human life. This is central to the Zen salvational endeavor, as Heine notes: "Genuine spiritual realization must be found by embracing – rather than eliminating – one's emotional response to variability and inevitable loss" (1997, p. 29). He further elaborates this point as central to Dogen's thinking:

> It is the emotional identification with the plight of evanescent things, and the consequent anguish and outrage, that awakens the need for release from suffering. Enlightenment is attained as empathetic grief is transformed into a realization of the nonsubstantive basis of human existence … Impermanence as the very structure of reality must not be resisted but embraced through a sustained awareness of the formlessness of all forms.
>
> (pp. 41, 47)

If everyday life in the material world is the problem, then following this line of thought, the solution is not found in some mystical somewhere else, but is also found in everyday life in here and now situations that occur in the material world and that challenge us to push our edges in each and every situation.

Realization requires full acceptance. Such acceptance requires practice. Practice becomes continuous because every discrete situation that we encounter requires total exertion with no aspect of self left out or by not participating in order to fully reveal the situation's reality. As Abe notes, "It involves a recognition that people are immersed in the midst of delusion and suffering in this floating world and that there is no self-existing Reality apart from this fact" (1985, p. 59). True reality in this context is not meant to imply that there are two or more separate realities; one or some realities being true and the other realities false. Reality is always reality. Dogen reminds us that there is nothing to worry about, but if you are worried, that is reality, too! Action becomes free from discrimination, evaluation, self-reference, or self-serving qualities; there is simply free, clear, unobstructed action. However, it must be clearly understood that non-judgmental acceptance does not imply passivity, inaction, denial, or withdrawal from social reality. On the contrary, action, when required, becomes decisive and thorough.

From the Soto Zen perspective, religious fulfillment is not deferred to an after-death heavenly afterlife beyond body and mind. Nor is it the transcendence of a soul or a consciousness to another plane of existence divorced from the body and physical existence in the here and now. Rather, realization is the here and now as it becomes manifest in an ongoing rising and falling of manifestation. As Kim notes, "Hence, this present birth-and-death is the only absolute locus – discrete from before and after – in which we can speak of religion, that is, our liberation" (2004, pp. 167–168). Kim continues:

> In short, birth-and-death is the very locus in which the two possibilities of enlightenment and delusion are offered to every one of us. Thus, "in the midst of birth and death, an ordinary person wanders around in delusion, whereas the great sage is liberated in enlightenment." Life can either be a blessing or a curse; hence we must choose either enlightenment or delusion, but not both. Dogen's view of religious life bore strictly on this life – no more, no less.
>
> (p. 168)

From this perspective, total exertion is full, whole, and self-sufficient. There is nothing concealed that needs to be revealed. There is no final outcome. On the contrary, what is presented here is not a teleological model. Rather, Kim suggests:

> ... that self-realization of Buddha-nature in its myriad forms of existence defies the model of processes, degrees, and levels of potentiality to actuality, from the hidden to the manifest, from the lower to the higher, from the imperfect to the perfect. In contrast, it is the realization that each form of existence is whole and self-sufficient in its "total exertion" (*gūjin*) in the Dharma-position (*hōi*), which amounts to the total actualization of Buddha-nature.
>
> (p. 131)

Realization derives through the activity of *gūjin*. Insight, both cognitive and intuitive, demands the active participation of one's whole being with, as

I noted above, no part left out. Intuition occurs as action is exerted. Action occurs as intuition is activated.

On this point, Cook notes that "Dogen presents enlightenment as the way in which one encounters an event authentically by penetrating thoroughly (*gūjin*) to its true reality, which is variously symbolized as Buddha, emptiness, and absolute nothingness" (1989, p. 31).

This ties in to notions of transcendence, which requires unpacking. If anything is transcended, it's the false perception of reality that engenders and maintains a split between such dualities, such as when separation in opposites occur like inner/outer; material/spiritual; immanence/transcendence; ordinary/special; self/other; good/evil; now/later; means/ends; pathology/cure; self-benefit/other benefit; internal/external; ignorance/enlightenment.

As a constantly evolving, shifting, and mediating constant conjunction, *gūjin* functions at the subjective/objective interface of the moment-to-moment evolution of life and death (birth and extinction). In this regard, realization and delusion turn on our subjective response to the objective reality of life and death. For the individual, the question might be asserted as follows: does the fundamental anxiety of being human in a transient world mobilize *avidya* (ignorance, active not-knowing) or does the individual, through practice, fully penetrate each evolving moment in its budding, blossoming, and perishing? How does any individual respond to the ongoing life- and-death oscillation rising and falling in each and every passing moment of before, now, and after?

This split between what is evaluated as either "spiritual" or "material" derives, at least in part, from an over-idealization of mind that operates as part of the defensive structure mobilized to cope with the fundamental anxiety engendered by impermanence and mortality. Mind becomes self-endowed with metaphysical and various all-encompassing qualities, such as an immortal soul. Simultaneously, there is a devaluation of the body and the material aspects of being, which becomes the repository of what is vile, defiled, decomposing, and impermanent.

In contrast, Dogen emphasized a radical non-dualist stance. This stance finds expression in a complex and minutely detailed sets of instructions for conducting all of the basic activities of life (see Leighton & Okamura, 1996). Teaching is simply hearsay until the practitioner makes it personally real through experience, which derives from practice. Simply stated, everything becomes practice. Washing dishes and taking out the garbage hold the same meaning and are equally important activities as sitting *zazen* and other formal religious practices. They require the same moment-to-moment awareness and the same attitude of reverence and are carried out with the same intention. All activities become expressions of and create opportunities to further bring out the realization of our Buddha-nature; that is, "making real" presencing in each moment. *Zazen* creates a defined and structured space of this "real-making." It serves as a model that generalizes and influences our everyday life. A movement occurs, over time, from self-centered desire to compassion.

This movement applies to internal states as well, which we tend to think of as only self-oriented (desire based). For the psychoanalyst, this means that all of the patient's productions deserve equal attention (and non-attention), whether judged as superficial, concrete, deep, abstract, petty, or profound.

Battling demons

Suppose an individual has a profound belief and faith in God as Supreme Being. Suppose this individual undergoes an experience of the divine that engenders joy, ecstasy, a deep sense of peace, and a sense of oneness with all creation. Can such an individual who has truly experienced a transformational realization and experiences, for example, divine love express that love and realization through a full, non-critical acceptance of the experiences and beliefs of others, even if such beliefs and reports of experiences contrast or contradict their own? If this is not possible, then the validity of such so-called "transcendental experiences" demands serious questioning regarding the validity of the reported experience. Can we exert the honesty necessary to question and challenge our own beliefs? In the ideal, Zen remains non-dogmatic, "Advocating a mode of relating to others rather than a set of doctrines, [as a result] its applicability is virtually limitless" (Kasulis, 1981, p. 133). However, this questioning does not mean non-acceptance. I am not talking about agreement. I am talking simply about acceptance. S/he sees it differently from me. S/he believes in God – I don't. S/he believes in reincarnation – I don't.

Consider this example:

> A young man consulted with me upon urging from his wife. He had been arrested and hospitalized for indecent exposure and disturbing the peace in a public place. He insisted that he was "the Chosen One and was doing battle with demons" at the time. He wanted spiritual direction from me so that he could continue his mission as the Chosen One and, as he put it, "rid the world of Satan." I informed him that I was not trained to deal with his religious needs and that he could benefit through contact from a religiously trained person qualified to provide spiritual direction within the context of his own belief system. However, I did offer to assist him with dealing with the emotional needs that he was struggling with in carrying out what he saw as his mission, but that if he felt a need for spiritual direction, he would need to work with someone more qualified than I. This is acceptance of another's beliefs and experiences without subscribing to the same beliefs. I am not referring to a naive, anything-goes acceptance. Such a view would in effect be a denial of this suffering young man's serious psychological problems that landed him in the hospital. This calls attention to the need to maintain a simultaneous sense of connectedness and separateness (Cooper, 2010). One way to formulate

this orientation would be through the question: can I maintain my own center of balance without rigid dogmatic clinging and simultaneously, to use a Zen term, "take a backward step" and meet the individual where s/he is without attachment or aversion? That is, in essence, the Middle Way in action.

The Zen teacher, Taizan Maezumi, summarizes this point regarding spiritual experience clearly in his comments on Dogen's writing. He notes: "Perhaps most cogently, as a body of religious work we see in these [Dogen's] writings that excellent state of well-accomplished enlightenment that transcends the duality of good and evil" (In: Cook, 2002, p. ix).

The non-duality of transcendence and immanence renders all situations as opportunities for practice and to manifest and express realization. This means *all* activities *are* practice, not just activities typically associated with spirituality such as meditation, prayer, or rituals. There is no judgment and no splitting. Simultaneously, all activities *are* Buddha-nature manifesting here and now. When the situation is totally exerted, there is no judgment and no splitting. This sense of non-discrimination is precisely what Zen practice demands – no splitting between "sacred and profane."

Chapter 6

Thinking, not thinking, beyond thought

Dogen concludes the practice section of *Fukanzazengi* (1227) with the comment: "Think not-thinking. How do you think not-thinking? Non-thinking. This in itself is the essential art of *zazen*" (Translated by Waddell & Abe, 2002, p. 4).

This comment is a condensed version of a Zen encounter dialogue that serves as the most direct and clear expression of the function of mind while practicing *shikantaza*. Dogen is insistent and consistent that this dialogue expresses with complete clarity the practice of *shikantaza*, as the title suggests: "Universal Promotion of the Principles of *Zazen*," (Waddell & Abe, 2002, p. 1) or, alternatively, "Principles of Seated Meditation" (Bielefeldt, 1988, p. 174). Dogen's instruction comes from the dialogue, "Yüeh shan's Not Thinking." This brief and terse interaction holds extremely important practice implications that reflect Dogen's radical non-dualism. It is a primary source for Dogen's teachings on seated meditation. He quotes this interaction along with his terse and concise interpretation a number of times in his writings, including *Fukanzazengi* (1227), *Zazenshin* (1242a), and *Zazengi* (1243a). The full text quoted in *Zazenshin* is as follows:

> Once, when the Great Master Hung-tao of Yüeh shan was sitting [in meditation], a monk asked him, "What are you thinking of, [sitting there] so fixedly?"
> The master answered, "I'm thinking of not thinking."
> The monk asked, "How do you think of not thinking?"
> The master answered, "Non-thinking."
> (Translated and quoted in Bielefeldt, 1988, pp. 188–189)

Thinking, not thinking, beyond thought

Dogen resolves the question "how do you think of not-thinking?" by positing a triadic relationship based on his elaboration of the encounter dialogue. Drawing from the encounter dialogue, he posits a third position, *hishiryo* (non-thinking, beyond thinking, beyond thought), as an alteration in perception and relationship to thought processes that simultaneously deconstructs and realizes both *shiryo* (thinking) and *fushiryo* (not-thinking). This triadic relationship functions as a basic structure for understanding Dogen's point of view and his recommendations for *shikantaza*. The three terms in this brief encounter dialogue require elaboration. In Japanese, to repeat, they are: *shiryo* "thinking," *fushiryo* "not-thinking," and *hishiryo* "beyond thought" ("beyond thinking" or "non-thinking," depending on the translation).

Here is the rub: "*fu*" and "*hi*" both mean "no" or "not." However, in the Japanese language, *shiryo* functions both as a verb and as a noun. The prefixes, in this case *fu* or *hi*, determine whether *shiryo* functions as a verb or a noun. The prefix "*fu*" is used with the verb form of *shiryo*; hence, "not-thinking." "*Hi*" is used with the noun form; hence, "non-thought" or "beyond thought." So a good working translation for *hishiryo*, which I will use as we proceed, is "beyond thought." Okumura notes that *hishiryo* at once negates and includes both thinking and not thinking. For this reason, he prefers the term "beyond thought" over "non-thinking" (personal conversation). However, it is important to keep in mind that "beyond" does not imply transcendence or absence of thought. Rather, from Dogen's point of view, *hishiryo* points to *Genjōkoan* or presently manifesting realization and actualization. In other words, "What is happening now?" Kim clarifies this distinction:

> The function of nonthinking was not just to transcend both thinking and not-thinking, but to realize both, in the absolutely simple and singular act of resolute sitting itself. Ultimately, there is nothing but the resolute act of sitting ... Thus in Dogen's conception of *zazen*-only, nonthinking was used not transcendentally, so much as realizationally; it was objectless, subjectless, formless, goalless, and purposeless. But it was not void of intellectual content as in a vacuum.
>
> (2004, pp. 62–63).

Thinking occurs and not thinking occurs, often in barely perceptible, rapid oscillations. Every single thought is separate, but the separations can be so microscopic that we don't notice the gap between them. Bion's approach leaves open space for this movement to occur without bias or saturation of the psychic space until one can "observe a constant conjunction" (1970, p. 11). Additionally, the experience that is neither thinking nor not thinking and yet is both thinking and not thinking also occurs and becomes obvious in realizational moments.

Thinking and not thinking are mutually exclusive. In any given moment, you are either thinking or not thinking. Rather than getting caught in a dualistic tension or struggle between the two, from Dogen's perspective, *hishiryo* "holds," if you will, both in equanimity. Thus, *hishiryo* becomes an experiential and operational expression or "ritual enactment" (Leighton & Okumura, 2004) of the Middle Way Buddhist orientation rooted in the notion of no attachment, no aversion. This is the psychic realizational space of *hishiryo*.

Let's keep in mind that thinking is the function of the mind. Thinking is what the mind does. Insight-oriented Zen teachers speaking from the Middle Way perspective teach, "a still mind is a dead mind." So the process of *shikantaza* is not intended to defeat thinking. The practitioner simply forms a different *relationship* to both thinking and not thinking through the all-encompassing realizational awareness of beyond thought that can develop between the two. No labeling, no reaction – just sitting. The intuited wisdom that is thoroughly free from judgment or discrimination operates beyond the tensions between thinking and not thinking. The point is that there is no judgment or devaluation of thoughts, associated feelings, wishes, or memories, of the so-called "endless chatter" or thinking process itself. Rather, the practice clarifies what actually is. That is, we don't confuse our projections based on our thoughts with what is real.

It is also important to keep in mind that, from the Zen perspective, the term *shiryo* not only includes thoughts, but also wishes, dreams, fantasies, reveries, memories, desires, and emotions. Nothing is evaluated or excluded. This approach reflects and expresses Dogen's radical non-dualism, which I addressed in terms of psychoanalytic reverie in Chapter 4, "Total exertion as intuition," and will elaborate further in terms of psychoanalytic listening in Chapter 8, "Two arrows meeting: Zen insight, psychoanalytic action."

Fushiryo refers to the blank spaces between thoughts. Sometimes they can be pleasant, quiet spaces. Sometimes they can be terrifying because a sense of the ego dropping away and an accompanying loss of old reference points that serve as psychic anchors might occur, which typically activates thinking almost instantly.

Interrogatives/declaratives

From the traditional Soto Zen perspective, the dialogue describes a series of declarative statements. They are not treated simply as questions and answers. Each statement expresses the Truth of *zazen*. For example, the monk's initial statement through reversal in perspective can be expressed as an assertion rather than as an interrogative somewhat as follows: Monk: "Sitting fixedly and thinking can only be described as 'What!'" From Dogen's radical non-dualistic perspective, both the monk and the master together are expressing the realizational truth of just sitting. This realizational truth finds active expression through thinking, not thinking, and non-thinking in the practice of resolute, fixed, upright sitting.

Dogen's take on this dialogue from his non-dualistic perspective advises that the practitioner should neither think nor not think in an ordinary sense. He refers to "beyond thought" as "thinking of not thinking," which differs from ordinary thinking and/or not thinking. If one thinks of enlightenment as a goal of practice, then one will not get it. In this regard, the notion of enlightenment is just another thought or concept, just as the notion of cure is, from Bion's perspective, simply another thought or "desire," and not the evolving reality or "O" of the moment. Dogen's viewpoint exemplifies the radical non-dualism central to the realizational perspective. He places equal weight on whatever emerges without judgment or evaluation. It will not do if one does not think anything at all. In this regard, he warns against falling into inertia when activity is required. Dogen repeatedly and cogently advises the student that the authentic practice of *zazen* functions as essential instrument or instrumental essence, which has been correctly transmitted through the patriarchs directly from Sakyamuni, the historical Buddha. For Dogen, however, *zazen* is not merely a means by which enlightenment is attained. Dogen maintains that the actual practice of *shikantaza* itself is a manifestation and expression of enlightenment.

Penetrating the meaning of this dialogue between Master Hung-tao and the monk clears up a huge misunderstanding that has permeated Western culture's reception of Zen meditation in general and regarding *shikantaza* in particular. I have noticed that when people understand and internalize this orientation, they often report feeling more relaxed and less pressured about their approach to practice. As a result, their meditation experience becomes more precise and clear – relaxed, but not lax; firm, but not rigid. Similarly, the psychoanalyst who, to use a Zen phrase, takes a step back and doesn't force listening, being present or remembering, and remains openly relaxed, without desire, finds insights and responses to be deeper, freely arising and more accessible, along with reports of higher degrees of sensitivity as experience becomes magnified.

The context of the historical emergence of Zen in America will help further tease out this point. Based on D.T. Suzuki's Rinzai-influenced, intensely intuitional orientation and strong impact on the early American reception of Zen, thinking has come to be believed as antithetical to religious realization. Dogen, however, describes a dynamic relationship between thinking, not thinking, and beyond thought that neither privileges nor devalues either. He views both thinking and not thinking as equally valid and relevant. Realization thus comes to be actualized through both thinking and not thinking, as the moment requires. Further, Dogen criticizes what he describes as a false separation between thinking and not thinking. In this framework, not thinking is prioritized. The practitioner actively attempts to enter a state of not thinking, non-differentiation. However, from the realizational perspective, when thinking is fully exerted, it serves as an expression of realization. Consider the following passage from *Zazenshin*:

> Yüeh-shan's [Hung-tao] utterances are the very best because of his "thinking through not-thinking." [Thus] thinking is the skin, flesh, bones, and marrow [of *zazen*]; likewise, not-thinking is the skin, flesh, bones, and marrow [of *zazen*].
>
> (Translated and quoted by Kim, 2007, p. 81)

In this regard, Dogen places both squarely in the concrete actional reality of everyday life, freed up from the confines of abstraction and conceptual thought.

One problem is pitting thinking and not thinking against each other and prioritizing not thinking as a religious goal. The viable alternative advocated by Dogen posits that, along with beyond thought, both become equal and valid vertices or focal points that engender the possibility for realizational opportunities without applying nihilist or substantialist reductionist tendencies to either. He cuts through nihilist and substantialist extremism and associated quietist practices by giving equal weight to both thinking and not thinking. He writes in the *Hossho* ("Dharma Nature") (1243b) fascicle of the *Shōbōgenzō*: "thinking and not-thinking *alike* are of dharma-nature" (translated and quoted by Kim, 2007, p. 88). This abstract philosophical notion finds lived, concrete expression in the relation between thinking, not thinking, and beyond thought as operationalized in *shikantaza* practice. *Hishiryo* simultaneously negates and validates both. We can experience and verify this for ourselves through practice. Rather than viewing not thinking as a negation or transcendence of thinking, I take the position that not thinking is simply the momentary space that simultaneously connects and separates thoughts, regardless of the duration. Similarly and simultaneously, *shiryo* separates and connects the empty spaces. In this regard, both Dogen and Bion emphasize the evolving processes involved in being rather than static states of mind. For instance, with regard to Freud's use of the archeological metaphor to describe psychoanalysis, Bion writes:

> The value of the analogy is lessened because in the analysis we are confronted not so much with a static situation that permits leisurely study, but with a catastrophe that remains at one and the same moment actively vital and yet incapable of resolution into quiescence.
>
> (1959, p. 311)

Similarly, with regard to concrete images and part objects, the emphasis clearly falls on relationships, activity, and function. Evolution implies that everything is in motion and impermanent. Bion describes this dynamic relationship as follows:

> The conception of the part-object as analogous to an anatomical structure, encouraged by the patient's employment of concrete images as units of thought, is misleading because the part-object relationship is not with the anatomical structures only but with function, not with anatomy but with physiology, not with the breast but with feeding, poisoning, loving, hating. This contributes to the impression of a disaster that is dynamic and not static.
>
> (p. 312)

Quietist influences

In addition to the misconception of Zen practice due to D.T. Suzuki's intuitionistic orientation described above, another significant problem that interferes with understanding the mutually beneficial roles that both thinking and not thinking play in Zen soteriology stems from factors related to the emergence of Eastern wisdom traditions in North America. Historically, many quietist-oriented Buddhist and yoga meditation-based, practice-oriented traditions place a high value on the cessation of all thought processes. For instance, the second verse of Patanjali's Yoga Sutras (tenth century) is "Yoga is the restriction of the fluctuations of the mind-stuff" (translated by Woods, 1914, p. 8). Commentators note that the entire collection of Patanjali's sutras is geared toward explicating this one point. This thought eradication notion has seeped into the psychoanalytic reception of meditation through a devaluation of natural and normal mental processes, such as in Alexander's (1931) depiction of Buddhist meditation as an intentionally induced "artificial catatonia" or viewing the flow of mental processes as "endless chatter" (Rubin, 2009, p. 96). In the former case, meditation practices and accompanying states of mind becomes pathologized. In the latter case, the subjective experience of a still and empty mind becomes idealized without questioning the objective therapeutic value of such mental contents that might inform the therapist about unconscious aspects of the patient's inner life through a psychoanalytic understanding of the non-pathological aspects of projective and introjective processes. This latter orientation derives from a shift between subjectivity and objectivity that finds expression through a shift from the abstract notion of projective identification to the experiential sense of "reverie" articulated by Bion (1970) and elaborated by Ogden (1997a, 1997b), which I discuss in more detail in Chapter 8. The pathologizing of meditative mind states and the dismissal and devaluation of thought processes has engendered an anti-intellectual, non-cognitive attitude toward Zen in many quarters and has resulted in an unfortunate misunderstanding of such foundational Zen principles, such as in the commonly expressed admonition "no reliance on words and letters" and the orientation "direct teaching beyond the scriptures." From this perspective, this Zen admonition does not mean abandoning the use of language and discriminative thinking processes. Alternatively, we use them as potential tools advantageously rather than being imprisoned by them. Rather, this mandate addresses an over-dependence that negates the experiential potential for realization in all reality. Further, this is limiting because the mind becomes closed to the limitless opportunities to penetrate each moment of experience that is presented. So the idea here, to summarize this important point, is not to transcend or negate experience, whether seemingly profound or mundane, but to totally exert experience in order to engender a radical shift in our own relation to these experiences.

The mandate that Hung-tao addresses in the encounter dialogue quoted above points to and cautions against an over-dependence that negates the experiential potential for realization in all reality.

Without negating the primary significance of direct experience, contemporary scholarship has questioned this anti-academic, anti-intellectual, anti-linguistic attitude and correctly and consistently points to the historical/cultural origins and purposes of such statements that served as a critique and a warning cautioning against rigid adhesive clinging to dogmatism (e.g. see Heine, 1994).

In *shikantaza*, we disengage our *usual* involvement – not all involvement – in the ongoing operation of the mind. The shift, as Ogden notes, is from being subjectively caught in mental processes to taking a step back into objective neutrality, or as Zen teachers observe, we simply stay in the middle without attachment or aversion; without grasping or pushing away. From the vantage point of this perceptual shift, we can easily observe that the mind continues to function as usual by itself. As Okumura notes: "The stream of consciousness is like a waterfall. It constantly flows, but has no permanent nature or self" (2002, p. 18).

Not only the "waterfall" of thoughts, but also so much else happens: digesting breakfast, circulating blood, respiration, and heartbeat, to name a few. We sit in *shikantaza*, as I noted above, without an object of concentration: no candle flame, no mantra, no visualization, no breath counting. This is the experientially intuited space of Bion's "O" that I discuss in more detail in Chapter 7. This is the realizational space of no object of "memory, desire, or understanding" that Bion describes (1967, 1970). Or, quoting the poet John Keats, as Bion does, exercising "negative capability" with "no irritable reaching after facts" (Bion, 1970, p. 125). This is the psychological and experiential space of *hishiryo*, but it is not free from thought or from spontaneously arising memories or wishes, which Bion distinguishes from preconceived notions or forced memories by referring to their spontaneous emergence as "evolutions" (1967, 1970).

We just sit. True thoughts, perceptions, sensations, memories, and concerns rise and fall on their own, and we just sit without clinging, without pursuing, and without aversion. However, we are human and we continuously find ourselves caught in all of these processes, and we continue to just sit in the moment without judgment; we simply "open the hand of thought," as Uchiyama (2004, p. xxxiii) reminds the student. This activity is the meaning of the encounter dialogue between Master Hung-tao and the monk quoted above: "thinking of not thinking." Of course there is thinking and of course there is not thinking, and all of this mind activity rises and falls in *shikantaza* and is realized through *hishiryo*.

Here is a concrete example: you start up your car in the morning. Before you engage the gearshift to drive, the gear is in neutral. The engine is running, but the car is not moving. Despite the rising and falling of thoughts, we don't take action, we don't engage. We remain in neutral and just sit. The mind is simply idling and we are simply sitting. One distinction between practicing *shikantaza* and psychoanalytic listening, following Bion's point of view, is that we sit exercising negative capability until a pattern emerges, a constant conjunction, then we might say something.

It should be noted at this point that, from this orientation, a constant conjunction joins together and connects two seemingly unrelated facts experientially through intuition, not through logic (Lopez-Corvo, 2005, pp. 67–68).

Bion describes this process experientially as follows in an earlier writing prior to fully developing what Bleandonu (1999) describes as his "epistemological period." Bion writes:

> For an appreciable time my attention dwelt on this parade of associations to the exclusion of a peculiar accompaniment of running commentary on how he was feeling. As this obtruded, I became aware of a pattern which went like this: association, association, association, "definitely a bit anxious," association, association, "yes, slightly depressed," associations, "a bit anxious now," and so on. His behaviour was striking, but the session came to an end without my being able to formulate any clear idea of what was going on. I said that we did not know why all his analytic intuition and understanding had disappeared. He said "Yes" commiseratingly, and if one word can be made to express "and I think that your intuition must have gone too," then his "Yes" did so on this occasion.
>
> (1958, p. 346)

Ignorance: active not knowing

This whole process reflects and expresses the primary soteriological concern of Zen, which is the practical liberation of all beings from the suffering caused by *avidya* (ignorance, an active, unconscious not knowing). Masao Abe describes this fundamental ignorance as "innate in human existence"

(1990, p. 35). With regard to the present discussion of *shiryo*, *fushiryo*, and *hishiryo*, he attributes *avidya* to "the conceptual, dualistic way of thinking peculiar to reason" (p. 35). Abe further argues that "Buddhism insists that only by completely overcoming rational and conceptual thinking can one awaken to suchness, as-it-is-ness, or the original 'nature' of everything in the universe, which is fundamentally unanalysable, unconceptualizable, and unobjectifiable" (p. 35). Further, Abe defines *hishiryo* as "Nondiscriminating Wisdom" (p. 35) through which "everything in the universe is fully realized" (p. 35). Bion captures this same sense through his notion of "O." He captures the ongoing, ever-evolving, ineffable movement with his notion of evolution described above.

However, it must be kept firmly in mind that the "overcoming" that Abe addresses is clearly not a negation of thinking or an absence of thinking. Rather, it is the realization of thinking. The mind is supposed to think, as I noted above – thinking is its function. Abe notes: "Due to its dynamic character, nondiscriminating wisdom does not exclude thinking. Instead being beyond both thinking and not-thinking, it includes both" (1990, p. 35).

The wisdom of beyond thought is referred to in Sanskrit as *nirvikalpajnana* (non-discriminating wisdom). Abe notes that:

> Wisdom that is truly nondiscriminating is free even from the discrimination between "thinking" and "not-thinking," between discrimination and nondiscrimination. Accordingly, nondiscriminating Wisdom is called *hishiryo*, that is, beyond-thought awareness, beyond *shiryo*, thinking and *fushiryo*, not-thinking. Unlike not-thinking (*fushiryo*), non-thought awareness (*hishiryo*) is not an absence of thinking, but rather primordial thinking prior to the distinction and opposition between thinking and not-thinking. Traditional Zen teachings describe this awareness as "Illuminated Mirror." From this perspective thoughts are not the mind. They are reflections in the Illuminated Mirror, which reflects, without bias, whatever is presented to it.
>
> (1990, p. 35)

Consider this example expressed by the Ch'an monk, Shen-Hui (684–758): consistent with Dogen's notion of *hishiryo* as beyond the duality of thinking and not thinking, Shen-hui cogently argues that the illuminated mirror is neither being nor not being. However, when pressed for a response to the issue and its ineffability, not unlike the shift between question and assertion described above in the encounter dialogue – "Sitting fixedly thinking can only be described as 'What!'" – Shen-Hui responds by noting that:

> It is nothing at all. This is why no-mind (*wu-nien*) is ineffable. If one talks about it, it is only in order to reply to the questions [of others]. If one did not respond to questions, then one would have nothing to say about

it. It is like a mirror: if it does not reflect an image, nothing appears on its surface. If one speaks of an image appearing in the mirror, it is [only with reference to] the object standing before the [mirror], which produced the image.

(Translated and quoted by Gomez, 1987, p. 84)

Shen-hui makes a subtle distinction. He notes that in realization, no image exists in the mirror. Gomez notes:

> If someone asks for an explanation of what this enlightened mind is, the enlightened person will have to speak up; then it is as if the mirror were reflecting an image – the image is not the mirror. Whether there is an image or not, the reflecting nature ("illuminating capacity") of the mirror remains. The metaphoric referent of the mirror's inherent capacity to reflect is the mind's innate "luminosity." Here once more Shen-hui separates the fundamental from the superficial or adventitious – mirror from image.
>
> (1987, p. 84)

The significance with respect to Bion's negative capability, Dogen's *hishiryo*, and Ogden's perceptual shift from subjective to objective regards the individual's ability to loosen identifications with thought processes and how one comes to identify with a sense of self.

In my experience, *hishiryo* functions as an alternative perceptual orientation that takes in the larger field that contains both *shiryo* and *fushiryo* and is experienced as an awareness of whatever is being experienced, which at the most expanded level functions in what the psychoanalyst Matte-Blanco describes as "total symmetrization" as the deepest level of the unconscious, where, as he notes, "everything becomes everything else" (1988, p. 181). The question becomes not one of classification and judgment, but of how one uses one's discriminative and intuitive capacities in response to all experiences. Both capacities are part of the equipment of the human mind. The pathologizing or dismissive orientations mentioned above obscure full functioning of intuitive capacities, which become activated through *shikantaza* practice.

Dualistic thinking is not the problem. Dogen advocates the use of reason and intellect throughout his writings. The problem stems from an over-reliance on cognitive processes to the exclusion or total disregard for our potential intuitive capacity. Both capacities need to be integrated to operate synergistically. On this point, the Buddhist philosopher, Joan Stambaugh, observes that "Our customary mode of experiencing has nothing to do with realization. Not only is it not a help; it is a direct hindrance" (1999, p. 49).

Similarly, to negate the significance of scripture, prayer, ritual, or *zazen* reflects the very same dualism exerted from the opposite direction and can represent, from either extreme, a radical religious fundamentalism. So the idea here, to summarize this important point, is not to transcend or negate experience, whether seemingly profound or mundane, but to totally exert experience in order to engender a spontaneously arising realizational process in our own relation to these experiences. It is from the perspective of this foundational principle that my psychoanalytic stance derives from with regard to my caution to not privilege seemingly spiritual from non-spiritual aspects of the therapeutic narrative that I described above.

On this point, Kim notes: "Often in conventional thought, knowledge and truth are ascribed solely to the functions of sensation and reason, while the functions of feeling and intuition are considered merely subjective" (2004, p. 100). One reactionary reversal of this attitude in academic/scientific scholarship derives from a misunderstanding of Bion's emphasis on intuition, which overlooks the value he placed on cognition and scientific precision in his writing. Not unlike Dogen, he advocates a balance between these two functions.

Kim elaborates this point concerning the value of language with regard to the false dichotomy that can get established between thinking and not thinking. Reification processes result in splitting into sides, which become absolutized and polarized. This misguided dualistic misunderstanding in turn creates an unnecessary pressure on the practitioner. The ensuing judgment engenders an idealization of one and a devaluation of the other. As I noted above, from this misguided orientation, not thinking becomes privileged and thinking requires eradication. Kim writes:

> If the cause for the arising of our predicament lies within discrimination, then the cause for the eradication of such a predicament lies within that discrimination itself, not outside. Discriminative thinking, delusory though it may be, possesses an intrinsic capacity within itself to overcome and transform its own limitations, for it is "ever already" within the process of realization itself, "not ever without." That is why discriminative thinking neither arrives or leaves.
>
> (2007, p. 84)

In *zazen*, we disengage our usual involvement in the ongoing operation of the mind. However, as we can easily observe, the mind continues to function as usual by itself. As Kim notes: "From this perspective, thinking is now free to be responsible, disciplined, fair, and compassionate in one's personal morality and social ethical thought and, furthermore, is even free to roam playfully throughout the universe in its mythopoeic imagination" (2007, p. 86).

Delusion, enlightenment, discursive thinking

Dogen argues cogently and clearly that delusion and enlightenment *alike* are rooted in discursive thinking.

Like it or not, you are bound to discriminate and differentiate things, events, and relations in a myriad of different ways. The activities of discrimination may be self-centered, discriminatory and restrictive. Yet, discriminative activities, once freed of substantialist, ego-centric obsessions, can function compassionately and creatively. Thus there are two kinds of discriminative thinking at an existential level, delusive and enlightened. To Dogen, whether or not we use discrimination in the Zen salvific project is not the issue; rather, how we use it is.

(Translated and quoted by Kim, 2007, p. 84)

Implications

How does the encounter dialogue between Hung-tao and the enquiring monk inform the psychoanalytic encounter? Psychic space opens to the relative experience of self and other; to the experience, which I describe in the example below, to "other as self," "self as other," which can be contained or articulated by the therapist.

Teaching, whether in the form of a Zen kōan or sutra or in the form of a psychoanalytic theory, is simply hearsay until the practitioner makes it personally real through experience, which derives from practice of *shikantaza* for the Zen practitioner, and from the felt impact of two unique individuals on each other in the consulting room. Bion cautions the psychoanalyst by prioritizing experience through the process of putting his mandates to relinquish memory, desire, and understanding into practice. He writes: "His interpretations should gain in force and conviction – both for himself and his patient – because they derive from the emotional experience with a unique individual and not from generalized theories imperfectly 'remembered'" (1967, p. 19).

Outside of the psychoanalytic encounter, from a globally all-inclusive perspective, Dogen notes that everything becomes practice. Washing dishes and taking out the garbage hold the same meaning and are equally important activities as sitting *zazen* and other formal religious practices. They require the same moment-to-moment awareness and the same attitude of reverence and are carried out with the same intention. All activities become expressions of and create opportunities to further bring out the realization of Buddha-nature; that is, "making real" presencing in each moment. *Zazen* creates a defined and structured space of this "real-making." It serves as a model that generalizes and influences our everyday lives. A movement occurs, over time, from self-centered desire to compassion. This movement applies to internal states as well, which we tend to think of as only self-oriented (desire based). When inner states are thought about from the shift in perspective to compassion, they clinically become also about the patient and reveal what might otherwise be inexpressible by the patient. Such internal states will then inform us with respect to how we might respond to the other. For instance, a feeling of helplessness that one might feel in the face of demands or attacks made by the other when thought about from a self-oriented perspective might result in doubt in our clinical acumen and knowledge, self-criticism, and a belief in a sense of inadequacy to respond to the other in ways that are helpful. From the perspective of compassion, however, one might ask: "where is the feeling of helplessness or inadequacy in the patient or other?" "Whose inappropriate demands and or aggression made the patient feel helpless at times in their life?" (e.g. when age-inappropriate expectations are forced on a child; the risk of punishment, ridicule, or withdrawal of love, attention, or affection looms large when impossible and inappropriate demands are not be met by the child). Of course, both aspects – desire and compassion – need to be considered regarding internal states, so such an investigation of internal states requires a process that includes getting clear on one's own personal response to internal states and, once clear, raising the questions: "Why is this issue coming up now with this particular individual?" "What does this particular internal state tell me about the other's inner life?" "Do I then contain this feeling and insight for the other until the appropriate time presents itself to share it back in the form of an interpretation?" "How do I know the timing is right?" It seems helpful to wait until what can be said can be framed within the context of the individual's conscious and expressed narrative.

This movement from desire to compassion depends on a major shift in attitude (feeling) and perception (insight). We need both to be well integrated. There is a conflict here that needs resolution that, from the psychoanalytic perspective, involves making peace with ungratified wishes and unmet needs coupled with a negative attitude about life in general. "I'm not achieving or getting what I need, require, demand, or deserve ..."

Taizan Maezumi, Roshi, summarizes this point regarding spiritual experience clearly in his elaboration of Dogen's writing. He notes that "Perhaps most cogently, as a body of religious work we see in these [Dogen's] writings that excellent state of well-accomplished enlightenment that transcends the duality of good and evil" (In: Cook, 2002, p. ix).

From Dogen's perspective, it is an ongoing activity of being; of moment-to-moment presence; an increasing magnification and sensitivity to experiencing; of being, not an "I got it made" or "this is it, I'm done!" Buddhists describe this attitude as the God Realm, which is characterized by intense arrogance and complacency. Notions of other-worldly transcendence are dualistic no matter how they are framed. They serve as yet another variation of the splitting of reality into these and those, a splitting that fosters a false perception of reality that caused problems in the first place.

The idea that splitting and reification are primary and fundamental factors is central and must be kept clearly in mind to fully understand the clinical ramifications of Zen in relation to psychoanalytic practice. As outlined above, Zen is fundamentally an experiential process supported by study, dialogue with a teacher, group involvement, and various ritual practices. This experiential emphasis serves to form the orientation toward technique in terms of how to work effectively and fully with splitting and reification clinically. Stated as simply as possible, the central question for the therapist becomes, "What is the emotional impact of the analyst on the patient and of the patient on the analyst?" The patient might not be aware of the impact on the analyst, but, as Wilfred Bion notes, the analyst is required to be aware of the patient's emotional impact. The analyst must in fact "suffer" the experience that the patient is not able to tolerate. From this perspective, everything else, including interpretation, is secondary. Additionally, as a function of ignorance (*avidya*), the active not knowing that unconsciously engenders the subject–object split and the associated reification of self and object in the first place, the analyst is equally subject to splitting and reification that, for the analyst, finds expression in notions of diagnosis, pathology, cure, and theory, all which serve to buffer and rationalize emotional experiences such as fundamental anxiety. I refer to what are traditionally referred to as "symptoms" as "expressions of self-experience" ("expressions" for short). For instance, expressions of self-experience become reified into, "He is a depressive," "She is a borderline," etc. This mode of explanation or description can interfere with the necessary deep contact where true emotional understanding takes place and that dissolves the perceived solidity of reified states; the deep contact that I speak about in Chapter 9, "Taste the strawberries," which Rhode describes as requiring letting go of an "adhesive clinging to surfaces" (1998, p. 18). I will unpack this aspect of the analyst's splitting and reification in terms of using specific techniques for understanding and responding to the depressive self-presentation in order to demonstrate how symptoms (expressions) contribute to a reified sense of self and to a reified perception and experience of self and other by both analyst and patient and how these states can be effectively worked with. The first step is to see how the reification of expressions contributes to the form and experience of the sense of self. This requires wholehearted acceptance of what is. Total exertion as acceptance does not imply complacency, passivity, resignation, action or inaction. Each discrete situation requires its own action.

Sitting with a patient requires listening both to the patient's narrative and non-verbal cues and simultaneously feeling one's way into the patient's internal impact. I typically ask supervisees and analytic candidates, "What is it like for you to sit with or be with this patient?" This is a question that I need to ask myself.

For instance, in listening to an anxious and angry patient who is ragefully venting during her session, I feel helpless. This basic feeling of helplessness can get lost in the shuffle of my preoccupation with the patient's rage. I'm thinking, "How can I get this to stop?" "What does it mean?" "If I knew that I would be able to fix it," etc. However, "What is it like …?" leads me to the feeling of helplessness, and this raises very different questions related to the patient's feelings of helplessness when faced with the rage of a parent or caretaker.

This total exertion with no part left out given to each moment ties in with the ongoing "in the moment" orientation that one encounters in much of the literature on Buddhism and psychotherapy (e.g. Christensen & Rudnick, 1999). Much of this literature references popular Zen books by contemporary teachers such as the perennial favorite, *Zen Mind, Beginner's Mind* by Suzuki (1970), *Everyday Zen* by Beck (1989), or *Most Intimate* by O'Hara (2014). These books are geared toward the Zen practitioner and the lay public. However, a close look at the scholarly literature can facilitate deeper connections to basic foundational principles and demystifies connections. This clarity of understanding can contribute to making clear connections to psychotherapy and uncover the assumptions that remain hidden in simple procedures and techniques that are otherwise taken for granted. The moment-to-moment attention, described in this literature, seems to engender its own curative impact. This is not mystical or mysterious, but is practical and rooted in basic Buddhist philosophical and religious principles. First, for the most part, Buddhism is considered to be primarily psychological and therefore views problems as originating in the mind. The idea, then, with regard to psychotherapy technique, is to engender self-reflection. Different individuals vary greatly in their capacity for self-reflection. Self-reflection might require slow, patient, and careful development over time. My question "What is it like …?" might be too open or too much for some individuals, especially if the tendency is to over-intellectualize, obsessively think, or perseverate on ideas. "What is it like …?" moves immediately to "What is internal?" If the patient can't handle this, I find out pretty quickly by responses such as "I don't know," "What do you mean?" or use of metaphor that removes one from the direct experience. "What is it like …?" might need to be titrated at first with the very type of questions that I caution the reader away from above. However, an ongoing process of presencing requires development that is appropriate for each individual. Over time, the capacity for increased direct experiencing occurs. This is the natural direction for a Zen orientation in psychotherapy; that is, in prioritizing ontological concerns, Zen emphasizes being and is less interested in causes or history. The problem with a purely psychological point of view of mind is that it results in a nihilistic response to the influence of events outside of the individual mind, a negation of the world beyond mental processes. This view received a radical expansion in the later development of Zen phenomenology, which includes all experiences, all objects as being Buddha-nature, along with a simultaneous rendering of Buddha-nature as emptiness. This moved Zen more squarely in an ontological and soteriological direction, which shifted the central concern to being and salvation. This has implications for integrated studies. The purely mind-only perspective developed by earlier schools of Buddhism is evident in technical descriptions and approaches to psychotherapy that place the emphasis exclusively and totally on the patient's internal experience without taking into consideration the contextual influences of the actual relationship between therapist and patient, as if the patient has no impact on the therapist and vice versa – as if the therapist has no impact on the patient beyond technical interventions such as interpretation. Psychoanalysis addresses this impact in terms of the more modern conceptualization of "totalistic" countertransference (for details on a totalistic perspective on countertransference in relation to Buddhist practice and thought, see Cooper, 1999a). I conclude this chapter with the following vignette that emphasizes the Zen emphasis on the presently experienced moment. During his welcome talk at a retreat I attended at Hokyo-ji in Ono, Japan, Docho-san, the abbot, welcomed our group by saying, "I don't care who you are or where you have been before!"

Chapter 7

Zen musings on Bion's "O" and "K"

> *The preaching of the Dharma has no set form*
> *The Real Function is beyond sounds and sights*
>   – Nagarjuna, quoted in Dogen, 1241
>   (Nishijima & Cross, 1996, p. 15)

> *The psycho-analyst and his analysand are alike dependent on the senses, but psychic qualities, with which psycho-analysis deals, are not perceived by the senses ...*
>   – Wilfred Bion (1970, p. 28)

Introduction

Literature review

Authors who discuss the relation between various strands of Buddhist thought and practice in relation to Bion's psychoanalytic thinking and technical recommendations represent a diverse range of viewpoints, opinions, interests, and orientations (Adams, 1995; Alfano, 2005; Bobrow, 2002, 2004, 2007; Christensen & Rudnick, 1999; Christensen, 1999; Cooper, 1998, 1999a, 1999b, 2000, 2001a, 2001b, 2002a, 2002b, 2004a, 2004b, 2014a, 2014b; Epstein, 1984, 1988, 1995; Harrison, 2006; Lopez-Corvo, 2005, 2006; Mendoza, 2010; Moncayo, 1998, 2012; Nichol, 2006; Pelled, 2007; Rubin, 1985, 1996, 2009; Suler, 1993, 1995; Symington & Symington, 1996).

A diverse variety of Buddhist perspectives from specific schools of Buddhism find representation and include Zen (Adams, 1995; Alfano, 2005; Bobrow, 2004, 2007; Cooper, 2010; Lopez-Corvo, 2005, 2006; Moncayo, 1998, 2012; Suler, 1993, 1995), Southeast Asian Theravada Buddhism (Epstein, 1984, 1988; Pelled, 2007; Rubin, 1985, 2009), and Tibetan Buddhism (Mendoza, 2010). Additionally, some authors draw from a variety of orientations that include both Western and Eastern wisdom traditions in their discussions (Harrison, 2006; Nichol, 2006).

These articles reflect a wide range of interest, orientation, complexity, and depth. Examples include broad-based discussions such as Adams' work on what he describes as "revelatory openness" (1995, p. 465). Other authors emphasize Bion's work as a focal point of intersection between Buddhist thought and practice with psychoanalysis. For instance, Harrison speaks of "nondual therapy and western psychotherapy, focusing on Bion's work as a central pivot" (2006, first unnumbered page). Alfano writes in the context of what she describes as "traversing the caesura" (2005, p. 225). Bobrow (2002) from a Zen perspective and Mendoza (2010) from a Tibetan viewpoint draw comparisons between Buddhist emptiness and Bion's "O" and "K". Epstein (1984, 1988), Pelled (2007), and Rubin (1985, 2009) draw technical comparisons between Southeast Asian Theravada Buddhist *vipassana* or mindfulness meditation and psychoanalytic listening. Nichol (2006), Symington and Symington (1996), and Lopez-Corvo (2005, 2006) discuss Bion's technique and ideas with direct reference to Buddhist thought. For example, Symington and Symington draw comparisons between Bion's mandate to relinquish memory, desire, and understanding with the Buddhist notion of "*Dukkha*" or non-attachment (1996, p. 169). Lopez-Corvo draws comparisons between Bion's "O" and what he describes as the Zen notion of "origin" (2005, p. 315) and Zen meditation or "intuition" (2006, p. 174). Moncayo (1998, 2012) writes from a Lacanian perspective with many references to Bion's seminal ideas such as "thoughts without a thinker," "non-understanding," and "intuition of 'O'." Bobrow (2004) draws attention to convergences and divergences between Buddhism and psychoanalysis. Bobrow (2004) and Cooper (2000, 2014a) address the overall neglect of the unconscious dynamics and related ramifications for a deeper understanding of the identities, similarities, and differences between Zen and psychoanalysis.

As I see it, this diversity of response, including total dismissal, criticism, idealization, and what lies in-between verifies the infinite possibilities evolving and blossoming through the unsaturated space that Bion advocates and points to repeatedly and consistently in his writings. Additionally, the diverse and creative threads that these authors pull on demonstrate the highly subjective nature of all experience. This diversity seems to validate Bion's point that "Memory is always misleading as a record of fact since it is distorted by the influence of unconscious forces" (1967, p. 17).

Cautionary preface to defining Bion's "O" and "K"

During this period of Bion's writing and thought, described by Bleandonu as his "epistemological period" (1999, p. 141), Bion was primarily interested in "openings." A clear-cut definition would run counter to Bion's agenda. On this point, Ogden notes:

> Bion uses such terms as "the thing in itself," "the Truth," "Reality" and "the experience" to convey a sense of what he has in mind by O. But since

Bion also insists that O is unknowable, unnamable, beyond human apprehension, these nouns are misleading and contrary to the nature of O.

(2004, p. 290)

Ogden continues by noting that while speaking about "O," he has not defined it. He argues that one cannot approach "O" by imposing limiting definitions that can saturate the reader's psychic space with predetermined meanings. Rather, "O" can only be realized in the moment, according to Ogden, "… by allowing its meanings to emerge (its effects to be experienced) as one goes. The effects are ephemeral and survive only as long as the present moment, for no experience can be stored and called up again" (2004, p. 291).

Bion is interested in an infinite expansion of meaning, which any specific definition would, from his point of view, foreclose. Eric Rhode expresses this point clearly and succinctly in relation to the notion of psychoanalytic "cure":

As the variable, "O" activates a state of becoming unrelated to any claim to therapeutic progress or cure. From the mystical perspective nothing progresses or is cured. There is either an evasion or a recognition of "O" by way of a becoming.

(1998, p. 118)

These points should be kept clearly in mind as we approach any specific definition of Bion's use of "O" and "K."

"O" and "K" defined

Drawing from Kant's notion of the ineffable "thing-in-itself," Bion uses the symbol "O" to point to the ineffable, unknowable, constantly evolving emotional Truth of the psychoanalytic encounter. "O" and "K" function for Bion as two distinct ways for experiencing and speaking about what he describes as the data of psychoanalysis. As I understand it, "O" and "K" function to represent and to speak about the core experiential aspects of Bion's mandate to relinquish memory, desire, and understanding, as described in his brief but highly condensed article, "Notes on Memory and Desire" (1967) and further elaborated in *Attention and Interpretation* (1970).

For Bion, the fundamental ground of psychoanalysis is "O." This is a "groundless ground" (Braver, 2012, p. 194) that is constantly in motion and at once both empty and full. "O" designates the ultimate, ineffable, infinite reality. Bion (1970) uses "O" to keep the psychic space open and unsaturated with preconceived meanings. He defines "O" as follows:

I shall use the sign O to denote that which is the ultimate reality represented by terms such as ultimate reality, absolute truth, the godhead, the infinite,

the thing-in-itself. O does not fall in the domain of knowledge or learning save incidentally; it can be "become," but it cannot be "known."
(1970, p. 26).

By asserting that "O can become," Bion is emphasizing the dynamic activity of "O" over the notion of "O" as a static object or distinct state of mind. This is important in terms of understanding the dynamic, inclusive relationship between "O" and "K."

In contrast, Bion uses "K" to point to what can be known though the senses and expressed through language. He describes "K" as interfering with the realization of "O," except when "O" evolves into "K" (O → K), which otherwise remains unknowable. "K" then refers to what Zen teachings describe as relative reality, the object of perception, and representative of "O," and what can be known through the senses and discursive reasoning.

In this regard, ineffable "O" can only be known and spoken about indirectly when the intuited lived experience of "O" evolves into "K" and is spoken about. He cautions that language itself derives from sense-based experience and is also limited to "K."

This core assumption and theoretical distinction between "O" and "K" and the related technique of relinquishing memory, desire, and understanding derive from a dualistic assumption rooted in Kant's notion of "thing-in-itself," and, as I will discuss below, it represents a major difference from Dogen's non-dualistic assumptions. That is, for Bion, noumena and phenomena are fundamentally separate. A posited unknowable essence cannot be known, as Bion notes, only intuited. Bion writes:

> Restating this in terms of psycho-analytic experience, the psycho-analyst can know what the patient says, does, and appears to be, but cannot know the O of which the patient is an evolution: he can only "be" it. He knows phenomena by virtue of his senses but, since his concern is with O, events must be regarded as possessing either the defects of irrelevancies obstructing, or the merits of pointers initiating, the process of "becoming" O. Yet interpretations depend on "becoming" (since he cannot know O).
> (1970, p. 27)

Commenting on the relation that Bion posits between "O" and "K," Harold Boris writes: "As an article of faith – later termed "O" – he took it that there was an experience and an experiencer. This was akin to the Kantian noumenon, and the question of its evolution into a phenomenon" (1986, pp. 163–164).

In this manner, Bion "operationalized" the Kantian "thing-in-itself" as a noumenon through his use of "O" and "K" and through his distinction between what can be experienced through "intuition" and what can be known through the senses. He thus transforms psychoanalytic realizations from static objects of knowledge to a fluid, ongoing, evolving realizational experiencing, both beginningless and endless. Bion's realizational orientation is tersely, if not poignantly expressed clinically in the following observations: "Out of the darkness and formlessness something evolves" (1967, p. 136). "It shares with dreams the quality of being wholly present or unaccountably and suddenly absent" (p. 137). "What is 'known' about the patient is of no further consequence: it is either false or irrelevant. If it is 'known' by patient and analyst, it is obsolete" (p. 136). "Otherwise the evolution of the session will not be observed at the only time when it can be observed – while it is taking place" (p. 137). "The psychoanalyst should aim at achieving a state of mind so that at every session he feels he has not seen the patient before. If he feels he has, he is treating the wrong patient" (p. 138).

Experiencing "O"

In my experience, "O" unfolds at times with clarity; other times ambiguously, hidden from awareness, or quite obvious. Sometimes I completely miss the intuition and forget about it; at other times I stumble over it, like stubbing my big toe on a chair leg in the dark; other times it's so blindingly obvious that it can be embarrassing. Whether obvious or oblivious to me, "O" circles endlessly like the Zen *enzo*, a symbol and expression of emptiness and becoming; full and complete, yet translucent, almost transparent, simultaneously opening and closing; opening to new and unforeseen openings; opening to closings that transmute into new openings – all the while turning and being turned between delusion and realization; between somethingness and nothingness; all-inclusive everythings, whole being Buddha-nature; self, no-self; Big Self, small self; a moment of encounter; the cosmic infinite everythingness; the no-thing. "O" points to a psychoanalysis free of fixed positions, formulas, and preconceived techniques, and, to use two common Zen phrases, "O" functions to hold the empty space by "taking the backward step" (Dogen, 1227, quoted in Waddell & Abe, 2002, p. 3); empty space, so prone to becoming saturated, suffocated, and closed down with meaning and old habit formations. All of this brings the attention to the activity of Buddha-nature realization manifesting in the practice of just sitting in the present moment, whether with a patient during the psychoanalytic encounter or during formal sitting practice on the cushion.

For both Bion and Dogen, this reality is not objectifiable, not conceptualizable, and not realized through thinking or through other sensory modalities, although "O" is always present, evolving and functioning in all experience, including "K," whether realized or not.

Dogen's radical non-dualism

Dogen, as noted in previous chapters, advocates a radical non-dualistic perspective, a perspective that is central to his thirteenth century reformulation of Zen Buddhism. That is, as Dogen emphasizes, the task of the Zen practitioner involves realizing the presently existing unitive nature of reality and then acting upon this unitive realization in the everyday world of duality and multiplicity. This orientation raises the question as to how Zen practice affects the practitioner's mode of being in the world in general, and specifically, with respect to this discussion, what impact Zen practice might have on the psychoanalytic encounter. I will provide an example of this impact through a concluding clinical vignette, which will help to unpack and explicate the abstract aspects of the ensuing discussion.

The identity of the one and the many

This dialogue between a Zen master and his disciple provides an entry point into a discussion of Dogen's non-dualism:

> Once Yangshan was gazing at the moon with Shandao.
> Yangshan asked: "When the moon is a crescent where does the round shape go?
> And, when it is full, where does the crescent go?"
>
> (Translated and quoted by Leighton, 2015, p. 64)

In the Zen Buddhist literature, the full moon represents enlightenment, realization, wholeness, or the one, or what Bion describes as "at-one-ment" (1970, p. 30). The crescent moon represents duality, the "ten thousand things," a Zen expression for relative reality, diversity, differentiation, discrimination, delusion, and the world of objects. We can paraphrase this dialogue to read: "When realized, what happens to delusion; when in delusion, what happens to realization?" Or, if we use Bion's language, we can say: "When 'at-one-ment' engenders intuition of O, what happens to K? When transformation O → K occurs, what happens to O?" Bokusan captures the paradox and irony of the identity of the one and the many in terms of enlightenment and delusion as follows: "What is it that you realize? You realize delusion. Look. When you are deluded, what are you deluded about? You are deluded about enlightenment" (2011 p. 47).

In contrast to the gap between noumena and phenomena described by Kant and embedded in Bion's use of "O" and "K," drawing from the Hua-yen totality school of Buddhism, Dogen's basic assumption finds noumena and phenomena uniquely distinct, yet inseparably intertwined. The Hua-yen philosopher, Chengguan, uses the metaphor of ocean and wave to capture this relationship between noumena and phenomena: "Just as water and wave cannot come into being without the other, so it is with phenomena and noumenon [and just] as water is simply of waves and waves are just water, so it is with noumenon and phenomena" (Cheen, 2014, p. 31).

Extrapolating to Bion's "O" and "K," from this non-dualistic perspective, while distinct, "O" is always present in "K" and "K" always present in "O."

This remains constant. It is our perceptual capacity that shifts. For Bion, this would mean shifts between intuition and sense perception and the movement between.

Foundational principles and techniques: similarities and differences

In a previous article (Cooper, 2014a), I demonstrated how technique serves as an expression of underlying assumptions and organizing principles. Bion writes:

> The analyst must focus his attention on O, the unknown and unknowable. The success of psycho-analysis depends on the maintenance of a psycho-analytic point of view; the point of view is the psycho-analytic vertex; the psycho-analytic vertex is O. With this the analyst cannot be identified: he must be it.
>
> (1970, p. 27)

Similarly, Dogen's frequent use of the expression "just this is it" (Leighton, 2015) or by Dogen (1242) in *Inmo* as "the matter which is it" (translated and quoted by Nishijima & Cross, 1996, Book 2, p. 119) points to an unknowable and ineffable suchness or thusness. Their approaches share identities, similarities, and differences. Neither can be stated directly or, as Bion writes, "indubitably or incorrigibly" (1970, p. 26).

Despite the differing core assumptions described above, both Bion and Dogen share quite similar practical starting points. Bion, drawing from the poet, John Keats, recommends sitting in "negative capability" until a "pattern emerges." Keats, in a letter to his brothers, describes negative capability as follows: "I mean Negative Capability, that is, when a man is capable of being in uncertainties, mysteries, doubts, without any irritable reaching after fact and reason" (1952). Bion recommends that the analyst patiently wait for the evolution from "O" to "K" to occur, and he is offering the technical tools to facilitate the necessary waiting "without any irritable reaching after facts and reason" (Keats, In: Bion, 1970, p. 125).

Similarly, as discussed in Chapter 3, Dogen promotes *shikantaza* (just sitting), a form of meditation that Kim describes as: "… objectless, subjectless, formless, goalless, and purposeless" (2004, p. 63). Further, this practice does not rely on any external or internal supports such as a mantra, visualization, or object of attention and is non-concentrative and non-directive. Not unlike negative capability, this practice keeps the Zen practitioner's psychic space open so that ultimate reality can be intuited, or known through *prajna*, the Sanskrit term for wisdom through intuition or "quick knowing" (Evans-Wentz, 1954). Quick knowing engenders a realization that is direct and has been described by Kasulis as "pre-reflective" (1981, pp. 56–60). So, from the analytic perspective, we are talking about a direct awareness of "non-sensuous reality" (Bion, 1970, p. 18) that is not mediated by the five senses, but rather by intuition, which from the Zen perspective functions as a sixth sense. *Prajna* dovetails with analytic intuition in terms of the process described by Stitzman: "The way intuition arises in the analytical space – defined as the encounter between Acts-of-Faith – suggests that we are speaking about a K knowledge that is direct and un-mediated" (2004, p. 1147).

However, differences between the two are also apparent. Bion struggles with the original catastrophe of psychic birth. Dogen points to an original fundamental anxiety that reifies experience that is then maintained by an active "not knowing" and that supports splitting. Bion, as noted above, advises waiting in negative capability until a pattern emerges through the evolution of "O" to "K," by which an interpretation can be made. In contrast, as discussed in Chapter 3, Dogen describes *shikantaza* as an expression or a "ritual enactment" (Leighton, 2008, p. 167) of our fundamental being or suchness. Dogen would say: "We already are it!" In the *Immo* fascicle of the *Shōbōgenzō*, he writes:

> If you want to attain the matter which is it, you must be a person who is it. Already being a person who is it, why worry about the matter which is it? [He adds:] Even worry is already the matter which is it!
> (Nishijima & Cross, 1996, Book 2, p. 119)

In summary, Bion advises waiting patiently and he offers the tools to facilitate such waiting. Dogen argues that there is nothing to wait for.

In this regard, Bion's technical mandate to relinquish memory, desire, and understanding serves as a tool to allow for the emergence of awareness of "O" through "O" to "K" evolution and is based on the underlying principle that "O" cannot be known. Dogen, in contrast, offers the technique of *shikantaza* to allow for the realization of ever-present, currently manifesting suchness. Of course, there is the obvious significant difference to keep in mind that the analyst's attention involves self and other, whereas the meditator's attention is on the wider present reality, including sense awareness.

From both Bion's and Dogen's shared perspectives, a definition would shut down the evolution Bion seeks. Similarly, for the Zen practitioner, choiceless awareness would also be interfered with by the imposition of an over-emphasis or saturation of didactic instructions, directives such as guided meditations, or definitions. It is with these points in mind, which apply equally to both Bion and Dogen, that Bion asserts:

> The foregoing is a brief account distilled from putting the precepts advocated into practice. The theoretical implications can be worked out by each psychoanalyst for himself. His interpretations should gain in

force and conviction – both for himself and his patient – because they derive from the emotional experience with a unique individual and not from generalized theories imperfectly "remembered."

(196, p. 19)

One reality

It must be clear that Dogen and Bion are not talking about two different realities. They are describing two ways that the one reality can be experienced: dualistically through the senses and thinking processes, non-dualistically, or, as noted above, "pre-reflectively" (Kasulis, 1981) through intuition.

Dogen often describes this experiential knowing as *"sho,"* or verification. He uses the term *"shūshō itto,"* or "the oneness of practice and verification," to speak about intuited knowing. This being the case, "O" is not a some-thing or a no-thing. At the same time, there is nothing that is not fundamentally "O." If "O" were a some-thing or a no-thing beyond our present existence, it could not truly be "O" as Bion defines it or as Dogen describes it in terms of his expression *"genjōkoan"* ("actualizing the fundamental point," Tanahashi, 1985; "Manifesting Suchness," Waddell & Abe, 2002; "Manifesting Absolute Reality," Cook, 1989).

Remember, Bion uses "O" to point to the ineffable infinite, so by definition nothing can be excluded. If we consider "O" as something or nothing beyond the present moment, it would become something limited to representation, and would not be as Bion (1970) describes it as ineffable and infinite.

Michael Eigen gives expression to the all-pervasive and infinite quality of "O" from a perspective that integrates psychoanalysis and mystical experience. He notes: "Yet unknowable O is our home. We may not know O, we can only be O. We are O [and even] if we try to get outside O, there is nowhere outside to get to" (1998, p. 17).

The Zen philosopher, Masao Abe, notes that Zen often expresses the ultimate, ineffable reality with questions such as "what," "where," or "whence." For example, consider this dialogue recorded in *Keitoku dentoroku* (Transmission of the Dharma Lamp) between the sixth patriarch, Eno (Hui-neng, 638–713) and Ejo (Nan-yüeh, 677–744) upon meeting for the first time:

"Whence do you come?"
"I come from Tung-shan."
"What is it that thus comes?"
Nan-yüeh did not know what to answer. For eight long years he pondered the question, then one day it dawned upon him, and he exclaimed, "Even to say it is something does not hit the mark."

(Translated and quoted by Abe, 1992, p. 45)

In a parallel to Bion's depiction of "O" as ineffable and unknowable, Abe comments:

> An interrogative "what" or "whence" is that which cannot be grasped by the hand, that which cannot be defined by the intellect; it is that which can never be objectified; it is that which one can never obtain, no matter what one does. Indeed, "what" or "whence" is unknowable, unnamable, unobjectifiable, unobtainable and therefore limitless and infinite.
> (1992, pp. 45–46)

The point regarding both Dogen's expression of suchness and Bion's expression of "O" is that they do not function as "nothingness" to be distinguished from sense-based perceptions of "somethingness," of "K." Yet, paradoxically, and at the same time, they are distinct and not distinct. In this regard, "O" and "K" are both somethingness and nothingness and beyond both somethingness and nothingness. This relationship is expressed in the practical instruction for *shikantaza* as exemplified in the following dialogue, which Dogen recorded numerous times in his writings and was discussed in Chapter 6. Here is the version from *Fukanzazengi*:

> A monk asked Yüeh-shan, "What does one think when sitting motionlessly in *zazen*?" Yüeh-shan replied, "You think of not-thinking." "How do you think of not-thinking?" asked the monk. "Nonthinking," answered Yüeh-shan.
> (Translated and quoted by Waddell & Abe, 2002, p.4)

The following comments will be focused on the dialogue and Dogen's radical non-dualism in relation to Bion's "O" and "K." Like thinking and not thinking, "O" and "K" are both at once completely distinct and one as lived, presently manifested reality (*genjōkoan*). Bion addresses this realization through his mandate to relinquish memory, desire, and understanding. In this way, he addresses the tendency to cling too tightly to sense-mediated experience at the expense of unitive experiencing or, as he notes, the experience of "at-one-ment" with evolving O (1970, p. 30).

Similarly, Dogen criticizes and warns against the tendency in Zen to overemphasize intellectual understanding at the expense of using our intuitive capacities, as he notes in *Fukanzazengi*: "No traps or snares can ever reach it" (Waddell & Abe, 2002, p. 4). The phrase "traps and snares" refers to the intellect and reasoning processes. On the other hand, Dogen also warns the Zen practitioner to maintain the middle ground, not be seduced by emptiness, and not to get lost in unitive experiencing, which he argues is at the expense of the dynamic tension and interplay of both cognitive and intuitive processes. Similarly, Bion reminds the psychoanalyst to apply binocular vision.

Stitzman (2004) views Bion's mandate, while stated in the negative, as the source for freeing up intuitive processes. Symington and Symington (1996) provide further elaboration in terms of the Buddhist notion of non-attachment. They discuss Bion's ideas from a clinical perspective and emphasize the notion of relationship that occurs between memory, desire, and understanding. Drawing from the Buddhist notion of non-attachment, they bring Bion's emphasis on relationships into direct alignment with Buddhist practice and thought. They write:

> Bion makes it clear that it is not the memory as such that blocks understanding but rather the attachment to it. What Bion recommends is that the analyst place on himself a discipline where he detaches himself from an addictive attachment to memory ... Bion says that it is the psychological state of attachment to the sensual that needs to be relinquished.
>
> (p. 169)

In a similar vein, Lopez-Corvo comments on what Bion describes as the "stubbornness present in many therapists during the act of listening to patients" (2006, p. 166). He describes this stubbornness as:

> [T]he analyst's inclination to cling to classical positions present in medicine, such as taking a clinical history in order to provide a classified diagnosis, thereby contaminating listening with previous memories and desires about the patient, such as the intent to cure or to understand.
>
> (p. 166)

On this point, Bobrow notes that both Bion and Dogen are after:

> ... bare awareness of mental, emotional and somatic states as the path to see into, unhitch and de-condition from desires and attachments, and liberate oneself from the delusive self-structures and suffering they engender.
>
> (2004, p. 19)

Bobrow describes presence as a central state of mind and an active process for both Bion and Dogen. He writes: "Presence of mind represents not only a way of being and communicating with others but reflects a way of regarding the processes and contents of one's own mind" (2004, p. 19).

From the Zen perspective, this sense of presence and active presencing is engendered by the intention to raise *Bodhicitta* (mind of awareness), the intention to simply sit with and to develop a reflective capacity to be with and to simply be aware of the rising and falling of all physical, sensory, and mental perceptions without attachment, aversion, or judgment.

Zen and realizational truth

Realizational truth can be experienced and expressed in a multiplicity of ways such as: "definite–infinite" (Cooper, 2010); "surface–depth" (Rhode, 1998); and "elusive–obvious" (Kim, 2007). Dogen uses the expression of "entwined vines" (Kim, 2004, p. 20) to express the interpenetration of intuitive/cognitive and rational/irrational functions. Bion speaks of "O"/"K" (1965, 1967, 1970) and the interpenetration of intuition and cognition through, as I noted above, what he describes as binocular vision. Bion does not offer answers. Rather, he advocates listening to our own truth evolutions through intuition of "O" until the analysand's "O" and the analyst's "O" evolve into what he describes, as I noted above, as "at-one-ment." In this regard, what he does offer is a new vantage point oriented toward "T" (Ultimate Truth); an orientation organized through the intuition of "O." Not unlike Dogen's "beyond thought," discussed in Chapter 6, Bion's "T" creates a third position that at once transcends and embraces "O" and "K." Similarly, Abe (1985) describes the dynamic tension between being and non-being and the third position that removes the dualism of an either–or dynamic.

At first glance, Bion seems to be describing a discontinuity between intuited reality and sense-based reality, between tangible and intangible. I believe that this reading of Bion has generated misguided critiques of his mandates. However, he describes an ongoing continuity in the experience of O → K evolutions where "O" and "K" constantly fluctuate between the perceptual and experiential foreground and background. The arrow suggests a linear progression and, perhaps ironically, whether intended or not, graphically demonstrates Bion's critique of the limits of sense-based language; in this case, words and symbols on a page that evoke preconceptions related to linearity.

From a non-linear perspective, "O" and "K" are two distinct vertices or focal points of one reality. Non-attachment to the senses through relinquishing memory, desire, and understanding facilitate the shift to intuited awareness. In *shikantaza*, the practitioner can become exquisitely aware of momentary shifts in the oscillating perceptual dynamics of "O" and "K." Radical non-dualism includes both the discontinuity and non-discontinuity. In contrast to classical psychoanalysis, which attempts to fill in all discontinuities by making the unconscious conscious, this approach strives to maintain openings. Bion criticizes an over-reliance on what he describes as the "medical vertex," his term for perspective or point of view and that parallels Kim's (2004, 2007) term, "foci." He cautions that the agenda to fill in gaps engenders a reification of continuity and forecloses the process of evolution. Taken out of context, Bion's advice appears to exaggerate discontinuity between intuition and sense-based K to the point of an either–or, antagonistically positioned polarization, which results in a failure to experience the realizational continuity that they engender and share.

"O" is viewed as realizing and expressing ultimate reality directly through "intuition," not as reality appears through the senses. This orientation does not negate the senses. Rather, this view places the senses in perspective. One view sets "O" and "K" apart, as if they were polar opposites (as if the full moon and the crescent moon were not the same moon). This reading of "O" and "K," taken out of the larger context of Bion's underlying assumptions, is problematic on a number of counts and has resulted in unwarranted critiques of Bion's intention. The problems include: the tendency to bifurcate and compartmentalize "O" and "K" as unrelated; the tendency to form a biased and limited view of Bion's position as exclusively negative and nihilistic; the tendency to over-value or idealize intuited "O"; and the tendency to devalue or discard "K." Additionally, unitive experience or, in Bion's terms, "at-one-ment" – what Zen considers being seduced by emptiness – tends to obliterate real and necessary distinctions that Dogen continuously and repeatedly articulates in his extensive writings.

With regard to at-one-ment, it is crucial to not lose sight of a sense of the dynamic relationship between "O" and "K." From the Zen perspective, an overvaluation of "O" would engender stasis due to the loss of subject and object distinctions. "O" and "K" are both "vertices" (Bion, 1970) and "foci" (Kim, 2007) in the realizational process that Dogen describes in *Bendowa* (1231) as "beginningless and endless" (Nishijima & Cross, 1996, Book 1, p. 12). Bion's critique of memory, desire, and understanding is directed toward an over-emphasis of "K" at the expense or loss of our intuitive capacities to experience "O" evolutions. He seeks a balance, not an overthrowing or discarding of "K."

Dogen and direct experience

Similarly, the Zen emphasis on direct experience and mind-to-mind transmission functioned historically as a critique of scholastic Buddhism, not as it is often misinterpreted as a wholesale disregard or annihilation of our capacity to think, reason, and make distinctions.

Dogen, not unlike Bion, endeavors to restore the balance and equilibrium so characteristic of the Middle Way Buddhist orientation by placing experiential and intuitive processes on an equal footing with study and cognitive processes. On this point, Kim notes:

> In its liberating process, nonduality embraces duality rather than abandons it. Consequently, nonduality is not extra-, trans-, pre-, post-, or antiduality. It is always necessarily rooted in duality ... Intellectual endeavor and critical rigor are intrinsic to enlightenment and, hence, part and parcel of practice.
>
> (2007, pp. 33, 38)

Dogen's position can be summarized as follows: realization through experientially intuited awareness demands that the practitioner apply the unitive experience in practice in terms of duality of revisioned relative reality.

Bion offers a parallel. He comments with regard to his description of the function of "O" for the psychoanalyst that: "No psycho-analytic discovery is possible without recognition of its existence, at-one-ment with it and evolution" (1970, p. 30). Again, to reiterate, "at-one-ment" or what I describe as "unitive experience" temporarily dissolves the perceptual awareness of subject and object distinctions. However, this alteration or shift in perception does not mean that subject and object distinctions do not exist. In terms of unitive experiencing, with respect to realization, Dogen describes it this way in *Genjōkoan*: "When Buddhas are truly Buddhas, there is no need for them to perceive they are Buddhas. Yet they are realized, fully confirmed Buddhas – and they go on realizing Buddhahood continuously" (translated and quoted by Waddell & Abe, 2002, p. 40).

In summary, the point here is that "O" and "K" function simultaneously: distinctly as two and unitively as one. The meanings and implications of this seemingly paradoxical statement can be unpacked as follows: they are both one and two. The unitive nature of "O" and "K" does not eliminate or dissolve the distinction between them. Separation always operates as realization oscillates between the two. From the Zen perspective, within the context of practice and realization, as the eighth century Ch'an master, Huai-jang, notes: "Practice and enlightenment are not obliterated but undefiled." By "undefiled," Huai-jang means without contrivances. Contrivances can include goal-oriented meditation techniques, such as breath counting or separating practice and realization, such as in a facilitative or instrumental orientation toward meditation. In contrast, as noted above, Dogen explicates an expressive or enactment orientation toward Zen meditation, which can be characterized as a ritual enactment of our fundamentally enlightened nature.

From Bion's perspective, "undefiled" would mean "free from memory, desire, and understanding," or, as noted above, free from over-attachment to sense-based experience, goals, or treatment plans. We live with the world of sense, language, and form. "K" remains fundamental to lived experience and expression. In this regard, "O" or unitive experiencing does not replace "K." Bion's concern points toward over-saturation or over-preoccupation with sense-mediated perception that can occlude the free awareness of intuited experiences. Kim describes this relationship between the "one" and the "many" that equally applies to the relationship between "O" and "K" as follows: "The dualistic world remains real, not dissolved. ... Confronted with thought and reality, the mind is ever-vigilant, deconceptualizing and deontologizing them as circumstances demand, and thereby attaining a state of freedom and purity" (2004, p. 64).

From this realizational perspective, to reiterate and review, "O" and "K" represent two oscillating focal points or "vertices" in Bion's realizational psychoanalytic process. The activities of "O" and "K" as realizational processes mutually inform and transform each other. The same holds true and extends into Bion's understanding of PS (the paranoid–schizoid position) and D (the depressive position), oscillations, introjection and projection, and container and contained (Hinshelwood, 1998; Klein, 1946). Stated experientially, the two people in the consultation room both impact each other, hopefully, but not always in beneficial ways. In this regard, "O" and "K" are activities formed as active relationships, not simply as psychological states or reified objects. Further, they are activities of one and the same reality.

The point here is that Bion's realization of "O" through intuited evolution is not limited to deconstruction through the temporary negation of the senses, distinctions, or intellect; a deconstruction that destroys every potentially sense-based, reified construct or representation. Rather, he also engages the reconstructive potential through his understanding of the realizational process embedded in his concept of "transformation" (1965). He operates intuitively, experientially, *and* conceptually and linguistically. This broad-based and comprehensive vision shared by both Bion and Dogen points toward Buddhist emptiness. On this point, Kim writes:

> Emptiness enables the practitioner to discern that the existential and spiritual predicament of hanging in empty space, however abysmal, frightening and uncertain, is none other than the liberating occasion of "right this moment" with an inclusive sense of efficacy.
>
> (2004, p. 45)

Bion similarly points to "right this moment" from the psychoanalytic perspective when he writes: "Psychoanalytic 'observation' is concerned neither with what has happened nor with what is going to happen but with what is happening" (1967, p. 17).

From the Zen perspective, the discriminative discernment regarding memory, desire, and understanding of our everyday lives does not operate outside of "O", is not extrinsic to what Bion describes as "at-one-ment." Dogen's radical non-dualism includes dualism. The idea is to get past reified polarizations through the realization that both operate synergistically and dynamically. Bion's psychoanalysis, particularly with respect to "O," "K," and "memory, desire, and understanding," as discussed here, serves as a specific and explicitly elaborated direct expression of Dogen's broader notion of *shūshō itto*, the oneness of practice and realization that destroys any goal-oriented view of *zazen*.

It is important to keep firmly in mind the dismissal of any hierarchical, cause and effect, primary/secondary, goal-oriented relationships that might be posited to exist between "O" and "K." As noted above, *zazen* and realization or "O" and "K" can best be viewed as two oscillating realizational focal points for experiencing and understanding reality. Thus, "K" does not wait on "O." "O" does not wait on "K." Rather, through the realizational process, they constantly inform and transform each other.

Speaking in parallel with the realizational perspective, Rhode notes that discontinuity "… can be indications of the becoming of 'O,' a mode of internalization that cannot be known and only inferred as a variable" (1998, p. 19). Thus, Rhode notes, "discontinuity may be a source of meaning" (p. 20).

Despite the significance that Rhode attributes to discontinuity from a realizational perspective, the tendency to polarize "O" and "K," as a result of dualistic linear thinking, and the need to create discrete categories to fit everything into can exaggerate discontinuity to the point that we can lose sight of the experiential realization that they are simply two vertices of one reality and that both are always operating regardless of our capacity for perception.

Exaggerated discontinuity limits "O" to its deconstructive function in terms of the obliteration of sense-based "K" reality and simultaneously limits "K" to a "screen" or a "cover" that veils "O" or ultimate reality. In this regard, "O" becomes isolated to the consultation room through the exclusion of memory, desire, or understanding and, along with it, a potentially associated disregard for everyday reality. This disregard, when it predominates psychoanalytic thinking, engenders a hesitancy to apply psychoanalytic thinking to the problems of everyday life on the individual, interpersonal, societal, and global levels. Dysfunctional institutional dynamics within psychoanalytic institutes that could be resolved through the application of psychoanalytic principles serves as a prime example of the failure of this disregard. From Bion's perspective of binocular vision, both "O" and "K" evolutions can and should be carefully examined in both their deconstructive and reconstructive modes through ongoing self-scrutiny. This orientation is elaborated and encouraged in Dogen's teachings in terms of dynamic, active relations in the everyday world and is rooted in the Mahayana Buddhist emphasis on the Bodhisattva vow: "Beings are numberless, I vow to free them."

Sitting with Ada: clinical vignette

The perspectives of both Zen and psychoanalysis influence my clinical work. In order to respond to an often-asked question – "How does Zen practice influence my approach to psychoanalysis?" – the following vignette emphasizes and highlights the Zen influence of "already present," discussed above. However, the reader is cautioned that the example exaggerates the Zen influence in order to bring it into the foreground. It is important to understand that I do not disregard interpretations. They serve an important, useful, and necessary function when the timing and context are appropriate. This is true within the long-term context of my work with Ada, from which this material is drawn. On the occasions when I would make interpretations, Ada would respond, for the most part, attentively and with wholehearted sincerity. However, despite the relevance or accuracy of the interpretations and the genuine nature of Ada's responses, they seemed to shift the shared feeling and energy of the moment away and to distract us from the simple act of shared presence. This vignette simply highlights one moment in a treatment that extended over many years. It is intended to exemplify my point and to demonstrate one way that Zen study and practice might influence my clinical work.

Ada expressed concerns regarding her feeling sensitive and vulnerable to what she feared as "violating boundaries." As she described it: "How can I make any impositions on you to ask for or expect any favors from you?" I responded, "In terms of what?" She then hesitatingly explained that she needed to reschedule our sessions to accommodate changes in a new work schedule. The required change was related to a promotion that she had successfully competed for and had just been awarded. Her increased responsibilities as a project manager demanded increased hours and a possibly unpredictable work schedule. We had covered various versions of this situation many times and both knew the transference origins of her sensitivity, vulnerability, and hesitation. We both knew why this felt to Ada like an imposition and evoked a fear of violating boundaries. This time, we simply continued to silently sit together with her concerns, with her feelings and with the situation; with her internal fears and her real needs. She soon began to describe a feeling of calmness and peace. The session ended and she left without further dialogue between us except for the usual, "See you tomorrow."

The following day, Ada arrived twenty minutes early (she usually arrives right on time, if not a few minutes late). She said that she had wanted to recapture the feeling of well-being that sitting with me had engendered the day before. She began the session by explaining her understanding of the transference dynamics. In her experience, any shift on my part – either toward or away – such as through making an interpretation, would have felt like an abandonment to her. There was a narrow tightrope of connection that my presence and silence seemed to maintain. Whether the interpretation was accurate or not, I would have been experienced by her as abandoning the experiential space of the lived moment; that I did not care to deal with her feelings or her presence. I would have disrupted the deep connection that she was feeling in the moment through the shared silence.

In this situation, I believe that an interpretation would have functioned as a counter-resistance on my part to the evolution of the Truth of the session and to the deepening intimacy of the unitive nature of the experiential moment. We pursued this shared understanding further in the following session. Ada's self-hatred, which she experienced as her greed and aggression, made her wish for making a request feel like a violation of our boundaries. She also felt that I would view her as greedy and aggressive for competing for the promotion and higher salary. She was afraid that I would view her negatively and that I would act out my negativity by withdrawal of attention and by harsh criticism. She experienced her promotion and her increase in salary as manifestations of her greed and aggression and imagined that I would be judgmental of her achievement. We both understood the early object relations that perpetuated her fears, as they had been spoken about many times during our work together. These self-perceptions and imagined expectations of my reactions, we discovered, despite their harshness, felt "safer" than the deeper, more vulnerable, shared feelings that were emerging through my undivided attention and silent presence no matter what. Ada imagined that she would be experienced as aggressive if she asserted these needs. As noted, she also considered her wish to express her needs as a violation of our boundaries. She was welling over with feelings and feared that she would "flood the room and wash me away." Not unlike her early objects, I simply could not and would not handle them. She wondered if I would be strong enough, compassionate enough, and present enough to willingly sit with and hold her feelings, which she felt as an acknowledgment of her needs, hunger, and longings. In short, would I love her unconditionally, no matter what? My capacity for acceptance and to love unconditionally meant sitting still, staying right where I was – in the present moment, attending to the moment, embracing the moment, in full acceptance. Together could we, as the old Zen teaching story asserts, "Taste the strawberries!" (Chapter 9). At this point, she said that she felt anxious but that it was a "good kind of anxiety, that there was something fundamentally anxious about feeling fully alive, mutually present, and loved."

From a Bionic perspective, we might say that Ada communicated the importance and significance of true and genuine presence in the not knowing and sitting with and patiently waiting for the evolution of the uniqueness of Ada's "O" or emotional Truth without "irritable grasping after facts" or making interpretations.

In contrast, Dogen views the truth as always present. Waiting for evolution is not necessary. In this regard, I could respond only to Ada, being-as-she-is, in the present moment as Ogden describes it as "… without trying to ferret out what the story was 'really about'; the story was not about anything; the story was the story; O is O" (2004, p. 297). In conclusion, we could say that Ada's experience I hope conveys the difference between talking about an experience, such as through interpretation, and simply being the experience in the evolving now of the emotional truth of presence, loving, and being loved.

Chapter 8

Two arrows meeting: Zen insight, psychoanalytic action

Since the mid-1980s, a number of articles have appeared in the psychoanalytic literature regarding the relationship between the Southeast Asian Theravada Buddhist technique of *vipassana* or "mindfulness meditation" and psychoanalytic listening (Epstein, 1984, 1988; Langan, 1997; Pelled, 2007; Rubin, 1985, 2009; Speeth, 1982). Although there are notable exceptions (Langan, 1997; Pelled, 2007), the basic thrust of these articles centers on the premise that psychoanalysis has no specifically described technical method to train and develop psychoanalytic listening. These authors then recommend that the psychotherapist who practices *vipassana* will develop this skill. This recent typical comment exemplifies this position:

> Freud (1912) delineated the ideal state of mind for therapists to listen, what he called "evenly hovering" or "evenly suspended attention." No one has ever offered positive recommendations for how to cultivate this elusive yet eminently trainable state of mind. This leaves an important gap in training and technique. What Buddhism terms meditation – non-judgmental attention to what is happening moment-to-moment – cultivates exactly the extraordinary, yet accessible, state of mind Freud was depicting.
>
> (Rubin, 2009, p. 93)

Recently, I reviewed these articles from a psychoanalytic perspective (Cooper, 1999a, 2010). This review focused on the context of the relationship between transference and countertransference in terms of fluctuating states of attention and inattention, with an emphasis on the various internal self and object dyads that these states reflect. That is, following Racker (1957), countertransference functions as an experience and expression of the analyst's identification with the analysand's internal self and object representations. In other words, as Racker notes: "Countertransference reactions have specific characteristics (specific contents, anxieties, and mechanisms) from which we may draw conclusions about the specific character of the psychological happenings in the patient" (pp. 304–305). I also provided extended case material to exemplify this point. For example, the experience of a loss of interest in the patient's narrative might signal the activation of an inattentive parental object.

These authors offer the reader clear, cogent, and convincing arguments that seem to support the cultivation of evenly hovering attention through the practice of *vipassana* by demonstrating remarkable descriptive similarities between these two techniques. However, the primary deficiency in this series of articles, as I see it, is a pervasive lack of consideration of the dynamic unconscious and the accompanying and related factor that it is the psychoanalyst's own personal analysis that contributes to a deeper understanding of one's own unconscious processes and that serves to clear up obstacles to psychoanalytic listening. In fact, there is no discussion in any of these articles of the dynamic unconscious, which Freud describes through his early notion of countertransference that "every unresolved repression in him constitutes ... a 'blind spot' in his analytic perception" (1912, p. 116) that the perspective analyst must resolve through the requisite personal analysis. In this regard, Freud articulates a clear and insistent mandate for facilitating and training evenly hovering attention.

Despite the diverse and contradictory theories that have evolved since Freud's original peregrinations into the influence of the dynamic unconscious in understanding the psyche, the role of unconscious processes continues to serve as a central organizing principle that defines psychoanalysis as a unique and independent field among the various psychologies. Despite differences in theory and technique, the experience of personal analysis continues to serve as the sine qua non of effective psychoanalytic training. Bion expresses the primacy of personal analysis cogently. He writes:

> The experience of psycho-analysis affords material impossible to equal from any other source. It follows that this material should be available in full to the psycho-analyst. The analysis that every psycho-analyst is obliged to undergo as part of his training is necessary because it removes obstacles to participation in the psycho-analytic experience; it has many facets, but for the psycho-analyst none can compare in importance with this ...
>
> (1970, p. 26)

It is a well-known fact that there exists a great variation in any analyst's capacity for effective psychoanalytic listening. This begs the obvious question of how do the many highly sensitive and attuned individuals who function effectively as psychoanalysts and who do not meditate develop such capacities? Most say through their own analysis. The other issue, which I have elaborated elsewhere, is the pragmatic over-valuation of attention and an accompanying unexamined devaluation of the analyst's experiences of inattention (Cooper, 2010). That is, if "attention" is depicted as the ideal state of mind for psychoanalytic listening and becomes overvalued at the expense of various states of "reverie" and simply written off as undesirable and dysfunctional states of "inattention," then we run a great risk of ignoring a valuable source of psychoanalytic data. On this point, Ferro notes: "Again, whereas on the one hand the analyst's mental 'dysfunction' is a painful fact for the patient, on the other it is a precious source of information on the mating of two minds ..." (2005, p. 10).

In this chapter, I intend to add texture to my previous discussions by further unpacking the issues at hand in terms of both Zen Buddhist and contemporary psychoanalytic conceptualizations of the various fluctuating mind states that occur during the psychoanalytic encounter with an eye toward weaving in recent psychoanalytic contributions that influence different conceptualizations of psychoanalytic listening. Additionally, I will discuss the significance and the influence of the notion of intention as a guiding principle in both psychoanalytic listening and intervention and in Zen study and practice.

The differences in the approach to understanding the influence of meditation on psychoanalytic listening – or should I say the influence between meditation and psychoanalytic listening – can be understood in terms of the basic question of how to employ the mind during the psychoanalytic encounter. I argue that the differences – either implied or explicitly stated by psychoanalysts and psychoanalytically oriented writers – cannot be reduced simply to matters of technique. While technical approaches to meditation, for instance, can partially account for differences, the deeper matter and more fundamental albeit no less complex question is interwoven into what Bielefeldt describes as "... disparate approaches to some fundamental issues in the interpretation of Buddhism – issues that have been debated in Zen since its inception" (1988, p. 79). For instance, the implicit underlying organizing principle behind the notion of random thoughts that appear in the mind as "useless chatter" reflects a model based on the belief in a pure enlightened state of mind that is purportedly covered over by discursive thinking. This, unfortunately, is a common misconception and belief system associated with many forms of meditation. This quietist image of meditation and its goal – to free the mind of thought – has been seriously questioned historically since the inception of Zen (Schlütter, 2010).

In contrast, the Soto Zen technique of *shikantaza* (just sitting), as I discussed in Chapter 3, derives from a radically non-dualistic, all-inclusive orientation, which emerged out of Eihei Dogen's radical non-dualistic foundational principles, which describes and advocates an all-inclusive approach to meditation practice and therefore does not distinguish between wholesome and unwholesome mental states and makes no effort to eliminate so-called afflictive states or to cultivate, as the American Zen teacher and psychoanalyst, Diane Martin, describes them, "preferred emotional states" (personal conversation). This position reflects a Middle Way perspective that advocates non-attachment and non-aversion to all mind moments, including attachment, aversion, non-attachment, or non-aversion, as well as the judgments that might accompany or follow them. All experiences simply rise and fall.

For example, an early Ch'an meditation manual, *Tso Ch'an I* by Tsung-Tse, warns the meditator of "demonic states" (see Bielefeldt, 1988). As Dogen's thought matured over time, he eliminated any discussion of such sates. In a later revision of *Fukanzazengi*, he also edits out any discussion of the health-promoting benefits of meditation. He describes *shikantaza* simply as "the dharma gate of ease and joy," which refers to "not idle sitting, but rather heightened awareness and aliveness" (Kim, 2004, p. 60).

Tsung-Tse continues, to quote Bielefeldt, that "… he [the meditator] can prepare himself by reading their description in the Buddhist literature and he can overcome them by maintaining right thought" (1988, p. 134).

Doctrinally speaking, this view, which supports cultivation of "right thought" and the active aversion and elimination of "demonic obstructions," is not consistent with a Middle Way view that promotes "neither attachment nor aversion," a doctrine that is reflected and finds expression in *shikantaza*, which functions as a practice of choiceless awareness.

Distinctions such as this are crucial for understanding the richness and diversity of Buddhist beliefs and associated practices and for understanding the differences between various recommendations as they are explicated in these articles and, for our purposes, for understanding the various relationships that exist between Zen and psychoanalytic theory and practice.

For the Soto Zen practitioner, this means that what shifts is the *relationship* to internal experiences such as thoughts, preoccupations, feelings, or wishes. The shift is from a judgmental stance that views these states as "interferences" or "afflictive" to a non-judgmental stance. This orientation finds expression in the following:

> The Zen standpoint is like an empty mirror which "maintains not only impartiality and discrimination simultaneously but also mindlessness and nonattachment; nothing at all is left on its surface though it actually has reflected the image."
> Soiku Shigematsu (1981, In: Heine, 1994, p. 95)

Similarly, from the psychoanalytic perspective, the following parallel line of thinking can be observed in Antonino Ferro's work: "For me, this listening to the listening is an exploration of the continuous, dreamy interplay at work in analysis, without a particular concern for "misunderstanding" or "appropriate understanding" (Ferro & Basile, 2006, p. 483).

Hence, no judgment is brought to bear on what might be described as "appropriate distraction-free attention" or "inappropriate distracted inattention." We need to be mindful that "inappropriate" (and "appropriate") is a judgment, which is nothing more or less than a mind-moment not unlike any other mind-moment. We need to be mindful that we are being inattentive. This ongoing awareness of fluctuations in the depth, intensity, and quality of attention reflects the operation of *hishiryo* (non-thinking, beyond thought). *Hishiryo* keeps us from getting caught in the dualism between attention and inattention. Both, in their rising and falling, are subjects of awareness. Despite this similarity between Zen and this particular version of psychoanalysis, it is important to keep in mind that, in contrast to the Zen practitioner, the psychoanalyst takes the additional step to understand what meaning such thoughts, feelings, fantasies, or preoccupations might have for the patient as they arise in the interdependently arising context of the therapeutic dyad.

What is psychoanalytic listening?

What do psychoanalysts mean by "listening?" Madeleine Baranger provides the following general explanation:

> We define the term "listening" in its widest sense, as the normally preferential attention we direct towards the patient's verbal discourse. But we also "listen" to his tone of voice – lively or depressed – the rhythm and pace of his delivery, his attitudes, movements and postures on the couch, and his facial expressions, in so far as we can see them from our vantage point.
>
> (1993, p. 18)

Another way to think about psychoanalytic listening is to note what feels the most immediate and the most real at any moment of contact regardless of the content. One way to become aware of these aspects is to tune in to what is happening internally as the patient speaks. For instance, are you feeling wide awake or drowsy? Do you feel physically light or heavy? I will question why I feel extremely tired and heavy in the body with one patient and alive and light as a feather with the next patient. Are you relaxed or tense, spontaneous or constrained? Are you feeling self-conscious or unselfconscious? What is your experience of time? Is the clock standing still – the second hand seemingly going backwards – or are you wondering where the time went? Is it moving fast or has it come to a dead standstill? During any psychotherapy session, one might fruitfully ask: "Why are these thoughts, feelings, and/or body sensations coming now at this particular time with this particular patient?"

Answering these questions can become a psychic struggle because often, in part, we don't want to know their answers. We can only allow ourselves to know what we feel we can tolerate. This is an ongoing psychic struggle and not a matter of technical deficit or mastery. We need to keep in mind that as part of the patient's struggle, the co-created situation also becomes our struggle. On this point, Bion notes, "the analyst can, and indeed must, suffer"

(1970, p. 19). No matter how much experience and technical proficiency we have as analysts, if the patient struggles, we will also struggle, or at least we will be made to feel the struggle deeply. This is a primary process function, not simply a matter of mastering a technique. There is no end point, just the ongoing "being-as-it-is-ness" of the psychoanalytic encounter influenced by the mutual impacts that both individuals exert on each other. Any of these internal experiences can point toward what might surface and become identifiable in the transference and countertransference dynamic.

What is being created as a result of the mutual impacts between analyst and analysand, both consciously and unconsciously? This approach to listening reflects more of an attitude on the part of the analyst; an attitude that might or might not be reflected in any particular technique. That is, as I have argued elsewhere (Cooper, 2010), our own meditation practice will influence our mode of being in the world and will, as a result, have an impact on how we listen or don't listen to a patient. As the Buddhist scholar, Sallie King, notes in her discussion of the *Buddha Nature Treatise*:

> Our world is the way it is because of the way we are; we are the way we are because of the way the world is. The two arise together and are mutually creative. However, it is stressed that this interplay may be broken by transforming oneself and the way one perceives the world, something over which one has total control and for which one's responsibility is also total.
>
> (1991, p. 45)

The distinguishing factor in psychoanalytic listening has been, despite a wide range of theoretical persuasions, to be able to access the patient's unconscious processes and to develop an understanding that will result in a beneficial response to the patient. Basically, for this to happen, the analyst's psychic space needs to remain open and as unsaturated as possible. Unsaturated here does not mean "empty," "dead," or "still." Rather, it means to be aware and to accept as freely as possible the rising and falling of all internal experiences without judgment or superimposed preconceptions. This rising and falling will include the emergence of the analyst's personal history, thoughts, feelings, memories, concerns, theoretical and technical leanings, and cultural, religious, political, and personal biases and allegiances, all flowing in and out of awareness in various permutations. All the material of reverie, and that from a judgmental/objective/scientific framework might be considered as "contaminants," "mental chatter," "distractions," "afflictions," and as obstructions to the listening process, but from a non-judgmental point of view, through the "objectification" of internal experience, are precisely the data of psychoanalysis.

Thomas Ogden characterizes this shift in our mode of being in the world and its resulting impact on the patient as a shift in perception. In describing his own work, he writes: "A good deal of my work as an analyst involves the effort to transform my experience of 'I-ness' (myself as unself-conscious subject) into an experience of 'me-ness' (myself as object of analytic scrutiny)" (1997b, p. 720). All mind activity, including the judgments that accompany the awareness of any mind-moment, are part and parcel of the analytic encounter and a valuable component of the analytic data.

The point here is that both Buddhist meditation techniques and psychoanalytic approaches to listening are numerous and diverse. Each meditation technique (and psychoanalytic technique) directly links to that particular system's foundational principles and reflects the religious goals of any given sect. As a result, the technique reflects specific biases regarding how any specific meditation practice is perceived, experienced, used, or depicted. In this case, the Theravada tradition that the above-mentioned authors draw from describes a dualistic approach to internal states by distinguishing internal experiences as either "wholesome" or "unwholesome" and advocates the dissolution of the unwholesome internal mental states through the development of wholesome states.

Similarly, from the psychoanalytic perspective, Thomas Ogden provides an excellent and moving description of his therapeutically efficacious use of seemingly distracting states, which, following Bion, he refers to as "reverie" (1997a, 1997b). Ogden describes a non-judgmental response to what from the Theravada perspective might be described as "afflictive and unwholesome." Regarding reverie, Ogden notes:

> For me, an indispensable avenue in my effort to get a sense of my unconscious experience in and of the analytic third is the use of "reverie."
>
> (1997b, p. 721)

> I include in the notion of reverie the most mundane, quotidian, unobtrusive thoughts, feelings, fantasies, ruminations, daydreams, bodily sensations and so on that usually feel utterly disconnected from what the patient is saying and doing at the moment.
>
> (p. 721)

> Reverie takes the most mundane, personal, and private of shapes, often involving the minutiae of everyday life.
>
> (p. 567)

The implication here is that reverie is not simply a didactically learned technique, but reflects a specific intention toward the psychoanalytic listening process based on a particular psychoanalytic theory that is explicitly non-dualistic, non-judgmental, and all-inclusive. As noted above, both Buddhism and psychoanalysis are highly subjective and experiential disciplines that prioritize experiential learning.

With regard to reverie in terms of "emotional truth" (Bion, 1970), Pelled (2007) points to the internal development of the psychoanalyst through developing a deep awareness of one's unconscious processes that interfere with taking in, containing, digesting, and feeding back the analysand's intolerable internal states that are communicated through ongoing cycles of projection and introjection and contribute to the development of reverie. She writes:

> It is impossible to develop without mentally "digesting" the experience, and impossible to digest the experience while an intensive drive to evacuate is activated. Undigested experience does not enable learning. Moreover, undigested experience is an experience in which the emotional aspect remains intolerable. For Bion, the absence of truth, or the lack of awareness to emotional truth, creates a real deficiency; the personality remains in a state of continual hunger and is deprived of the ability to grow mentally.
>
> (2007, p. 1513)

In other words, from this particular psychoanalytic perspective, the capacity for analytic reverie – a primary form of optimal analytic attention – depends on an analysis that will facilitate learning from experience in a manner that will engender awareness of what, until it is worked through, will remain intolerable and contribute to a limited capacity for effective and expanded psychoanalytic listening. This orientation finds expression in the contemporary Zen teacher, Shohaku Okumura's, commentary on Dogen's *Genjōkoan* that:

> When we give all of our attention and energy to the task or practice before us, we can truly penetrate it. We work on the practice, study it, experiment with it, and care for it. We do this over and over again with whatever we encounter, one thing at a time, each time.
>
> (2010, p. 176)

Similar distinctions appear in the psychoanalytic literature on attention and interferences to attention. For example, as I noted above, Freud considered countertransference as a "blind spot" requiring further analysis to facilitate deeper understanding of the analyst's issues. This in turn, he argued, would then free up the analyst to be more open to the unconscious aspects of the patient's narrative. This position views the experiences of the analyst and the analysand as completely unrelated. In this regard, we can consider the countertransference "blind spots," as Freud described them, and any accompanying reactions under the rubric of what Theravada Buddhism describes as "afflictive" or "unwholesome" mental states that need to be purged from the analyst's consciousness through personal analysis.

In contrast, from the "totalistic" (Kernberg, 1965; Racker, 1957) perspective, countertransference reactions serve as unconscious communications that, when understood, help to facilitate the psychoanalytic treatment. This latter orientation – that is, the totalistic view of countertransference – not unlike *shikantaza*, functions non-dualistically and reflects an all-inclusive approach to psychoanalytic experience. This position views both the analyst's experience and the analysand's experience as interrelated and co-created. Interestingly, none of the above articles address the issue of countertransference, despite its central position in contemporary psychoanalysis. This non-judgmental response is consistent with Dogen's more all-inclusive stance described above and points directly to the fundamental Buddhist notion of *pratītyasamutpāda* (dependent arising, interdependent co-arising), which, not unlike a totalistic understanding and use of countertransference, views all phenomena as contextual. This fundamental principle has, with few exceptions, been left out of the Buddhist and psychoanalytic conversation (Cooper, 1999a). In order to understand this connection, the notion of dependent arising requires unpacking.

Pratītyasamutpāda (dependent arising)

Pratītyasamutpāda, the complement to *sunyata* (emptiness, voidness), refers to the notion that all phenomena arise dependent on causes and conditions. Nothing arises independently. This fundamental Buddhist principle can contribute to our understanding and response to psychoanalytic listening. That is, reverie, for example, does not belong exclusively and solely to the analyst, but emerges in the dependently arising context of the treatment situation. Both the analyst and analysand contribute both consciously and unconsciously to the internal and external experience of the analytic situation. We are simultaneously separate and connected. In this regard, the analytic situation is a lived experiential expression of the unsolvable Buddhist paradoxical construct of the identity of the one and the many and the simultaneity of identity and difference. We are both one and two; both not one and not two. Ogden captures this basic Zen notion in his paraphrasing and extending of Winnicott's depiction that there is no mother without a baby and no baby without a mother. Ogden writes:

> ... we must live with the paradox (without attempting to resolve it) that there is no such thing as an analysand apart from the relationship with the analyst and no such thing as an analyst apart from the relationship with the analysand. At the same time, from another perspective, there is obviously an analyst and an analysand who constitute separate physical and psychological entities.
>
> (1997b, p. 720)

Similarly, from this radically non-dualistic perspective, we can extend this observation to internal experiences such as the analyst's reverie and note that consciousness and unconsciousness are also dependently arising. Thus, reverie is considered a link between conscious and unconscious. That is, we can make use of seemingly unrelated inner experiences such as what might be initially or superficially viewed as distractions to listening as dependently arising co-created by both analyst and analysand and an important aspect of psychoanalytic listening.

Who is the listener?

When a psychoanalyst listens, we cannot assume that it is simply or only the psychoanalyst who listens. In fact, from the Zen perspective, we can't assume that there is a psychoanalyst to do the listening as if listening were a separate activity from the activity of being a person. Any listening that occurs is filtered through a series of oscillating lenses, including the life experiences of the analyst, theoretical orientation, the analyst's internal object world coupled with the internal object world of the analysand, through mechanisms of evenly suspended attention, reverie, waking dream function, vicarious introspection, intuition, various cycles of projection and introjection, and infinite versions of complementary and concordant identification; all in various combinations that constitute the momentary and contextually arising experience of self. It would be naive to suggest that the analyst maintains a blank screen or that some version of meditation can facilitate a stable blank screen, as has been suggested by a number of authors representing a variety of points of view. This notion is simply a contemporary manifestation of what the sixth patriarch of Zen, Hui-neng (638–713), taught. That is, we don't keep the mirror (blank screen) free from dust; rather, there is no blank screen to dust with *vipassana* or any other meditative technique.

The movement that can be observed through the evolution of psychoanalysis is from a static, positivist-oriented, one-person psychoanalysis to a dynamic and alive, mutually interacting, two (or more)-person psychoanalysis. It might be more accurate to say that the experience of the blank screen reflects a lack of awareness of the background organizing principles that contribute to listening and various degrees of attention and inattention. Such a view reflects the illusion of reified self, which Buddhists describe as the primary source of suffering and, further, maintains the analyst as a separate non-conditioned entity, which supports the illusion of self or what has been described as the "illusion of the isolated mind" (Stolorow & Atwood, 1992). This assumption flies in the face of the basic Buddhist principle of no abiding self, which is ironic, considering that authors who promote this view are drawing from Buddhist thought and practice to make their claims.

Listening to listening

Haydee Faimberg (1996), for example, in an article on psychoanalytic listening with the apt title "Listening to Listening," argues cogently and thoroughly that the analysand listens through the filtration of whatever internal object representation is active at any given moment and notes that the analyst can determine this through the patient's responses to interpretations, observations, or interventions. Ferro (2009) details this expression by the analysand as "narrative derivatives" (Ferro, 2002a, 2002b), and he clearly describes the importance of how the analyst can use narrative derivatives to adjust how to listen to, understand and speak with any given patient at any given moment. Ferro adds a further complexity to the analyst's listening style, which includes a variety of permutations including external reality, the past, the patient's internal world, or the interpersonal situation created by the here-and-now of the analytic encounter. These diverse orientations to listening, according to Ferro, are all filtered through the child, adolescent, or adult state of the patient who is listening and speaking (Ferro & Basile, 2006). Racker (1957) reminds us that the analyst goes through similar processes as the patient. The same processes that influence the hows and whys of analytic listening that apply to the patient also apply to the analyst. He writes:

> We must begin by revision of our feelings about our own countertransference and try to overcome our own infantile ideals more thoroughly, accepting more fully the fact that we are still children and neurotics even when we are adults and analysts. Only in this way – by better overcoming our rejection of countertransference – can we achieve the same result in candidates.
>
> (p. 307)

Intention: Zen Buddhism

If we consider the intention behind Buddhist practice and psychoanalytic practice, we will see that communicating understanding through deciphering and interpreting the analysand's communications is specifically a psychoanalytic function. With regard to *zazen* and relevant to this discussion, Kasulis notes that "Since *zazen* does not reflectively conceptualize the content of experience, these categories do not even arise and cannot, therefore be either affirmed or denied" (1981, p. 79). Buddhist practice asserts a very different intention. One way this intention is stated from the Zen perspective is to "raise *Bodhicitta*," which refers to the activity of pre-reflectively maintaining a neutral and non-reactive awareness of the moment-to-moment rising and falling of all experience. This intention and the accompanying practice, according to Buddhist soteriology, together engender a realization of our true nature. Zen holds no intention to decipher or interpret another's internal experience.

In this regard, the absence of judgment and decoding processes is not to be thought of as a deficit. Within the soteriological intention of Buddhism as a religious system, which is expressed in the Soto Zen tradition as, for instance, Dogen's commonly used expression, *"shūshō itto"* (the oneness of practice and realization), the practice is complete in and of itself. When taken out of context of its religious function and exploited simply as a tool of psychoanalysis, we might consider that decoding and interpreting operate on multilevels and are not specifically or exclusively tied into listening.

Simply stated, the intention to raise *Bodhicitta* by maintaining moment-to-moment awareness of the rising and falling of experience engenders a magnified and deeper level of awareness of self and other. This deeper awareness, as an alteration in perception, serves to engender a shift in our mode of being in the world, which in turn meets the religious salvational goal of "saving all beings" through compassionate action. While there is no explicit need to decode experience and interpret as the psychoanalyst does to one degree or another, subtle shifts occur that will alter the way the committed Buddhist practitioner interacts with others. We could say that a natural "decoding" occurs as the Buddhist practitioner decenters from an exclusively self-orientation.

Anyone who has taken actual meditation practice seriously enough knows through self-reflection that over time it will influence how we listen to and respond to others. That is, we can act compassionately or selfishly at any given moment.

In terms of the analytic situation, Racker (1957), for instance, describes our responses to patients in terms of "concordant" and "complementary" identifications. In the former case, as Racker notes, we are in accord and empathically attuned to the analysand's sense of self. In other words, we are in a position to respond compassionately. In the latter case, we are, according to Racker, acting out an unconscious countertransference identification. In other words, we are reacting mindlessly and possibly selfishly. While it is true that Buddhist systems do not make these distinctions, which is one very significant way that psychoanalytic theories can contribute to Buddhist practice, deepened self-awareness of our inner lives and deeper sensitivity to the experience of others engendered through meditation practices will foster the enlightened activity reflected in how we respond to others both as therapists and as human beings in the world when we maintain a sense of intention.

Intention: psychoanalysis

In contrast to the Zen Buddhist religious goal to raise *Bodhicitta* and the accompanying meditation practices, psychoanalysis asserts a very different intention related to psychoanalytic listening. Psychoanalysis makes it clear that a significant object that complements the analysand's conscious narrative is the internal narrative that emerges in the mind of the analyst, which, from this particular theoretical standpoint, communicates unconscious aspects of the patient's internal world. This internal process of reverie leads to an interpretation that emerges as part of a dependently arising situation co-created by both analyst and analysand. This process points to a significant difference between psychoanalytic listening and Buddhist meditation. Madeleine Baranger describes it this way:

> Similarly, analytic listening is directed in advance towards an eventual interpretation, whose content is not yet known at the time of listening but which gradually takes shape up to the moment when the interpretation has to be formulated to the analysand.
>
> (1993, p. 15)

This intention is motivated through the expectation that the analyst will be able to assist the patient in some way to overcome and to come to terms with whatever is the trouble. In short, this goal and accompanying motivation articulate an intention that informs analytic listening. Interpretations serve to "editorialize" the ongoing process. They are both part and not part of the process. As "selected fact" (Bion, 1962, p. 73), they influence the future direction of the process. The ultimate goal for the interpretation is to facilitate a transformative process for the analysand.

Articles that discuss meditation and psychoanalytic listening that derive from a secular point of view do not address this fundamental and essential first step, except to view meditation as a facilitator of or as deficient in terms of its application to psychoanalytic listening. In this regard, attention based on intention reflects more of a total attitude or a mode of being with the patient; an attitude cultivated through practice and study. Similarly, psychoanalytic training also involves practice, study, and involvement in the form of personal analysis, supervision both individually and in groups, study, and class participation. While psychoanalysts can continuously work at sharpening technique, from the perspectives of both psychoanalysis and Zen, how we listen becomes more a matter of intention. From the psychoanalytic perspective, Ogden describes it this way:

> In order to do analytic work, the analyst must be able to experience and talk with himself (in as full a way as possible) about what it feels like being with the patient, and yet, for the most part, these experiences are unconscious.
>
> (1997b, p. 720)

This latter paradoxical observation raises important questions: does meditation address "blind spots" that might block psychoanalytic listening? Does meditation facilitate the analyst's awareness of unconscious experiences? These are complex questions with no definite answers. They require further discussion beyond the scope of this communication.

Conclusions

To reiterate, the point here is that each meditation technique (and psychoanalytic technique) reflects a background organizing structure of that particular system's foundational principles. In this case, this is from the tradition that the bulk of articles on Buddhist meditation and psychoanalytic listening primarily draws from – the Theravada tradition – which describes a dualistic approach to internal states by describing internal experiences as either "wholesome" or "unwholesome" and that advocates the dissolution of the unwholesome and development of the wholesome.

For example, during therapy, when inevitable states of inattention ensue, the therapist needs to clarify that state in terms of what meaning it might have for the patient. The opportunity for meaning evolution will be lost if the therapist imposes a negative judgment on the state of inattention and attempts to dismiss it as invalid or inappropriate to "proper psychoanalytic listening." Similarly, differentiation and discrimination are essential to responding to the ineffable, undifferentiated unitive experience that inattention might be a part of and can emerge with certain patients. What emerges demands the analyst's acceptance and respect, not dismissal.

The latter comprises an alteration in perception and an activation of *prajna* (quick knowing, intuition). This shift, in turn, will influence how the analyst understands and responds to analysand. Perhaps such shifts will not necessarily result in interpretation within the language constraints and conceptual limitations of a particular psychoanalytic theory; however, such limited and dogmatic (automatic) responses to a patient's narrative have been the subject of recent psychoanalytic criticism. In fact, the role of interpretation has seriously been questioned by an expanding group of psychoanalysts (Ferro, 2009; Roland, 1983).

Can we make effective clinical use of periods of inattention in the way that Ogden refers to in terms of his application of reverie? For instance, from the self psychological perspective, failures in empathic attunement – real or imagined – are necessary and essential to the process of cure. That is, through a process of "transmuting internalization" (Kohut, 1984), the analysand develops new psychic structures that contribute to a cohesive and flexible sense of self. In this regard, it is essential that the analyst accepts real and/or imagined periods of inattention and/or misunderstanding in a non-judgmental way.

Inattention can function as one of a wide variety of what Roland (1981) describes as "induced reactions." These reactions, according to Roland, can include various self states, emotional reactions, and thought trains. Rather than viewing these states as obstacles to evenly hovering attention, Roland views such reactions as part and parcel of the ongoing experience of psychoanalytic listening. He notes:

> For psychoanalysts frequently do experience a wide variety of both gross and subtle emotional reactions and attitudes toward many if not most

of their patients at one or another stage of the therapy. The important question is not whether these reactions exist, but rather how are we to understand them, and what uses are to be made of them.

(1981, p. 45)

Zen action, psychoanalytic action

For the Zen practitioner, *zazen*, or seated meditation, is *butsugyō*, or the activity of Buddha-nature itself. From this perspective – or at least from that promulgated by Dogen – we are less concerned with particular "states of mind" and more concerned with enlightened action; "less concerned with the Buddha as a symbol of pure consciousness than as example of liberated agent" (Bielefeldt, 1988, p. 170).

In this regard, evenly hovering attention functions as an activity that becomes sharpened and honed through the experiences available through each of these respective disciplines; an activity that manifests through the actual participation in the practices offered by each of these disciplines. For the Buddhist practitioner, as noted above, this process begins with intention; that is, the intention of raising *Bodhicitta* and through the active involvement with experiential practice, guided study, and direct interaction with a teacher both one on one and in groups. From this vantage point, attention reflects more of a total attitude or a mode of being with the patient; an attitude cultivated through personal analysis, practice, and study.

The relationship between attention and inattention as fluctuating aspects of psychoanalytic listening can become a psychic struggle. As Pelled (2007) observes, as noted above, we can only allow ourselves to know what we feel we can tolerate. This is an ongoing psychic struggle. This is a primary process function, not simply a matter of mastering a technique. There is no end point, just the ongoing "being-as-it-is-ness" of the psychoanalytic encounter influenced by the mutual impacts that both individuals exert on each other. No matter how much experience and technical proficiency we have as analysts, if the patient struggles, we will also struggle, or at least we will be made to feel the struggle deeply. How deeply can we allow ourselves to feel the struggle?

Chapter 9

Taste the strawberries

Introduction

The core myths that have informed psychoanalysis since its inception are the Oedipal and Narcissus myths. In this chapter, I discuss the clinical implications of two different types of myths, which I describe as "spontaneously arising, alternative, intuitive models." I describe them as "spontaneously arising" because they emerge freely, without thought, during the course of therapy. They have not been preconceived or imposed upon the treatment. Additionally, I describe them as "alternative" because they do not necessarily fall within the range of standard models such as the Oedipus myth or the myth of Narcissus. In fact, while highly useful from the psychoanalytic perspective, these latter models can often saturate an individual's psychic space and interfere with the spontaneous emergence of fresh, alternative ways of understanding how different people organize their unique inner psychic experiences. Finally, I describe them as "intuitive" because they typically emerge freely through the operation of what Zen practitioners refer to as *prajna*, which I described in Chapter 4, rather than through pre-learned cognitive processes or through discursive thinking.

One type of intuitive model includes the Zen kōan and related teaching stories. In this chapter, I discuss a particular Zen teaching story, "Taste the Strawberries," which emerged spontaneously as part of my reverie in my work with a young woman. The other type of myth emerges spontaneously as part of the analysand's narrative and can take various forms, such as a dream, a memory, a religious image, or the form of a culturally derived belief or story. For example, in the next chapter, I will describe the spontaneous emerging of the image of the water well as part of a graduate theology student's narrative during our work together. The water well as a spontaneously emerging, intuitive model then served as a central motif and driving force of the treatment. Teaching stories and myths are available in all cultures and most religious systems.

These various myths, images, and stories contain deep meanings and serve important psychic functions for patients. For instance, they might represent an unquestioned blueprint or guideline for approaching life. However, until they surface in the patient's narrative, they are simply taken for granted or remain unconscious. The common ground of these two types of myth – the Zen teaching story and the patient's dream – that constitutes the emphasis of this discussion centers on the notion of "the gap" (Cooper, 2001b), which I will describe along with implications for the psychoanalytic encounter. This discussion draws from the Zen story, "Taste the Strawberries." It emerged spontaneously in my reverie as I sat with the patient. The other story that I will draw from in this chapter derives from the patient's narrative in the form of a dream. I'll begin with the traditional Zen teaching story.

Taste the Strawberries

> A man, pursued by a tiger, found himself at the edge of a cliff. He leapt in order to escape the tiger, but suddenly, while in mid-air, he saw that a lion with jaws wide open was waiting threateningly at the bottom of the cliff. He grabbed at a vine growing out of the rocks at the edge of the precipice, where he found himself safely out of reach of the tiger. However, he became aware that two rats – one white, the other black – were gnawing away at the vine. Suddenly, he eyed wild strawberries growing out of the cliff side slightly out of reach. He would have to let go of his hold on the vine to grasp the strawberries. Boy, did they look juicy! Meanwhile, the vine was just about completely gnawed through. What did he do? The story ends here with the simple exclamation: *"Ah, taste the strawberries!"*

This traditional Zen teaching story reflects both the terror and the delight of a fully lived life and the gap between, or what prevents an individual from tasting life fully as one finds it. We live our lives whether engaged or not; whether we wholeheartedly reach for and taste the strawberries or not. As John Lennon noted in his last song, *"Beautiful Boy"* (1980), written just three weeks prior to his tragic death: "Life is what happens while we are busy making other plans." The ongoing cycle of passing days and nights, the white and black rats, eat away one's time no matter what.

Lennon's lyric serves as a poignant reminder that we are always, all of the time, living the reality that is our life happening in the present moment whether we are conscious or unconscious; whether we allow ourselves to believe it or not. Lennon points to our way of being in the world, which is the reality of our existence. From the Zen perspective, self is life and life is self. On this point, the Zen teacher, Kosho Uchiyama, notes in a parallel to John Lennon's lyric: "Self is what is there before you cook it up with thought" (2004, p. 30).

The gap

This simple Zen teaching story also exemplifies one version of the gap, which can be spoken about and revealed in many diverse, often seemingly contradictory ways, depending on one's perceptual and intuitive vantage point. For instance, drawing from psychoanalytic intersubjectivity theory and Zen practice, Magid (2002) characterizes the gap between surface and depth as an illusion. In contrast, Rhode speaks to the capacity of letting go of an adhesive clinging to surfaces and demonstrates the importance of "letting yourself go into deep space, the 'not knowing' of a session" (1998, p. 18). Lacan talks about the gap between conscious and unconscious, between preverbal and language, and between the "Real" and the "Imaginary." My work on the gap, as I mentioned above, centers on the relationship between intuition and cognition and between being and knowing (for elaboration, see Cooper, 2001b).

Whether illusory or real, as psychoanalysts, we are often faced with gaps and the need to unravel their relative reality and ultimate illusion. Even as illusion, the gap holds very real consequences that can keep an individual out of a fully lived life; out of tasting the strawberries.

For example, in the process of working through structural issues in an early draft of this chapter, I became aware of a gap that occurs between language that is emotionally evocative, performative, connected, simple, and light and language that can suddenly become highly informative, but flat, disconnected, convoluted, and dense. Such shifts can come unexpectedly, be subtle, or go unnoticed. They can be smooth or jarring. As psychoanalysts, we hope that our communications with our patients exert a beneficial impact. However, the knowledge/information/fact-hungry tiger of the scientific/medical model, when ruled by an over-reliance on discursive thought, can suddenly consume the life out of the performative potential of the Truth-based approach to human experience by oversaturating the psychic space from which intuition freely operates. Similarly, such gaps find expression in the quality of a patient's narrative with regard to the spaces between phrases, sentences, and words. With some individuals, the analyst becomes faced with a great, yawning abyss of silence that begins or appears during a session. Depending on one's point of view, silence might function to resist Truth or serve as an opening from which Truth evolves and becomes revealed. The Truth of the session might be the silence. What is the truth of the taste of the strawberry?

The gap finds expression in many traditions and, from the psychoanalytic perspective, may include subject and object and what connects (separates) them, pointing to the separation between different aspects of self and the oscillation between experiences of wholeness and fragmentation. From the Zen perspective, Charles Luk notes that "All of us are accustomed to the deep rooted habit of splitting our undivided whole into subject and object by clinging to the false ideas of the reality of an ego and phenomena ..." (1993, p. 11).

Fundamental anxiety

Zen teaches that this need for reification and separation derives from the fundamental anxiety of being, which is basic to the human condition. Anxiety looms large whether conscious or unconscious and can either be exacerbated or attenuated by how early relationships are internalized and played out in the present. For example, Bion (1959) notes that the quality of internalizations are contingent on the presence and quality of maternal reverie. The psychoanalytic literature provides examples of an unfortunate overabundance of gaps in both presence and quality. For instance, Rhode (1998) speaks evocatively of the traumatic nature of sudden gap-inducing shifts between the soft, nurturing breast and the cold, hard spoon in the absence of maternal reverie.

Fundamental anxiety engenders a need to cling to the precipice and becomes a clinging to the illusion of solidity of the false idea of who we imagine self and other to be. In this regard, embracing the gap has to do with seeing through the transparency of this sense of reified and alienated self and other and experiencing our connectedness with humanity and with nature.

Rhode poignantly describes anxiety-driven reification and separation. He writes:

> Some people seek to name and personify the gap, perhaps as a nameless dread. The continuum and any conceivable break in it begin to separate: the continuum transforms into the immanence of the natural world, while the break in the continuum gives utterance to a transcendental and supernatural order.
>
> (1998, p. 22)

From the Zen perspective, this reification and simultaneous polarization obscures the experience that transcendence is immanence and immanence is transcendence. As the Buddhist Heart Sutra asserts: "Form is exactly void; void exactly form." For Bion, the gap is the void, the formless infinite, the ineffable, that which he describes as "O."

Wholeness in this context requires acknowledging the simultaneous unity and duality that transcends linear polemic notions of concretized subject and object. Experiential resolution of the gap between subject and object becomes central to Zen practice and parallels Bion's (1970) notion of "at-one-ment," without which, he argues, the analysis remains incomplete.

No one is immune from the experience of reification and separation. I hope to demonstrate that this process can extend to diagnosis and occlude real contact in the analytic setting. Diagnosis is useful and important, but at an extreme it can foreclose openings through an over-saturation of the analyst's mental space and can create infinite distance between individuals.

Signs, symbols, functions

The gap charts an exploration that at once reveals and veils ultimate reality and addresses both real and imagined distinctions that apply equally to the various depictions of human experience. The gap evolves in infinite directions multiply layered with meaning and function. As symbol gap might point toward womb, abyss, death, breast, or the unknown. Precipice might function to represent common sense, umbilical cord, the extent of and limits of relationships, a closing off to the unknown, freedom, imprisonment, or clinging to life and death. Abyss might represent womb, depression, the object's narcissism, the path to creativity, freedom, and the unknown.

The gap functions as a metaphor for the relationship between being and knowing that can become polarized and reified at extremes, maintaining a state of fragmentation, alienation, and various forms that manifest as phobia, racism, torture, genocide, and holocaust; each fragment functioning as a still frame snapshot of a moment of the natural flow between being and knowing. However, thinking about the gap exclusively as symbol might represent a resistance to the actuality of the gap as a sign or expression of the futility of imprisonment, both psychically and as a human being caught in the space between life and death in the moment-to-moment drama of the multitude of ongoing lives and deaths of psychic states emerging, crystallizing, and dissolving. For instance, as both symbol and actuality, the psychoanalytic "weekend break" might represent intuited, perceived, actual, or fantasized gaps in the analyst's attention, reverie, intuition, empathy, or containment; the gap between structure and non-structure; continuity and discontinuity; what feels safe, predictable, known, but going nowhere; what feels unsafe, unpredictable, uncertain, but going somewhere toward the many unknown some-things and no-things that might evolve out of the gap; the search for the many deep "whatevers" that miss what is actually happening in the moment.

As Rhode notes in his striving to integrate both medical and mystical models, the gap can represent "the dis-continuity implicit in the concept of continuity. Or the gap represented the inconceivable, a truly metaphysical concept" (1998, p. 21).

The medical model and the mystical model both begin with radically different foundational assumptions. These diverging assumptions result in different priorities and responses to continuity and discontinuity. From the medical model, Rhode observes:

> Discontinuity tends to be related to meaningless, even to the destruction of meaning. In the religious vertex gaps have a different meaning. They can be indications of the becoming of "O," a mode of internalization that cannot be known and only inferred as a variable.
>
> (1998, p. 19)

Thus, from the religious/mystical perspective, Rhode writes "discontinuity may be a source of meaning" (p. 20). As a source of Truth, Bion quotes John Milton, who speaks of "The rising world of waters dark and deep. Won from the void and formless infinite" (1965, p. 151).

What evolves from the gap is experienced through "intuition." For instance, Rhode notes that the gap becomes accessible "… by forfeiting sensation, that is bodily knowledge" (1998, p. 22). For Rhode, "The religious vertex begins from the void" (p. 19). Zen practice, for instance, opens the practitioner to being one with the void, actually being the void, experiencing one's own voidness by cutting through logic, sense perception, and cause and effect thinking, which from this perspective are posited as interferences to "Truth."

Nadia's dream room

As I mentioned above, I refer to the gap as an alternative intuitive model because, as an image, it often rises spontaneously as an expression of the patient's inner experience. For Nadia, the gap emerged as a dream image of my consultation room. Before going further, it is important for the reader to understand that as an intuitive model, piece-by-piece deconstruction of the dream through interpretation of the specific elements can often be contraindicated. With this point in mind, from a clinical perspective, it can be extremely important to keep the dream intact and to allow its function as an intuitive model to facilitate a deepening of the patient's experience. In this respect, I am following Ferro's lead in terms of his arguments against what he describes as "a disease called compulsive interpretation" (2009, p. 171). That is, as he argues, the patient must first feel being clearly seen and deeply understood by the analyst on a concrete level. Deeper meanings will evolve naturally. In this respect, the dream functions as a vehicle for being seen and for creating the opportunity, as Ferro puts it, "… to see that the prevailing emotion is being brought into focus; and finally a level on which the emotion can be contextualized in the here and now" (p. 168). Premature interpretation can disrupt this process.

Nadia's very brief dream, one among a series, describes two areas in my consultation room. One area, for the most part, is consistent with the actual structure and appearance of the room. Another part of the dream room includes an "unfinished" area. In the dream, Nadia reports that she is sitting as she usually does during our sessions. This is all that she recalls. In terms of the gap, these two sections of the room might be viewed, albeit speculatively, as indicating the gap between complete and incomplete; between wish and perceptual actuality; between self-loathing and non-acceptance; in the liminal space between self and no-self; in-between the terror and delight of living and the lifetime disappointment of failed psychic birth. Experientially, Nadia struggles with the conflict between separation and fusion; in-between the need for separation and the intolerable loneliness that the thought of separation engenders.

We might think about the dream room in a linear way; that is, from unfinished to finished, or in the reverse as something complete and whole to something torn down and damaged, traumatized, or derailed, perhaps by a toxic object. The "evidence" is there for both of these perspectives, which in either direction of movement is consistent with the cause and effect linearity of the medical model dominated by secondary process. Both imply time, direction, and space. However, in the unconscious, the laws of time, direction, and space don't exist. They can be collapsed into condensations and/or magnified or dispersed into an infinite number of displacements.

Alternatively, we might think of the room as a concrete representation of the truth-revealing function of the gap with no relevance to past, future, time, or space. We might have fantasies about what it would take to finish or to unfinish the room, regardless of which perspective we take.

For Nadia, we can chart gaps between phrases, broken up by anxious laughter and sudden shifts in content; gaps between complete and incomplete rooms and by representation, aspects of self-experience between moments of feeling whole and moments of fragmentation; between moments of peace and moments of chaos; between projective identification as a form of primitive, preverbal communication and as an intrusion, an instance of destruction; as a resistance.

In terms of reversals in perspective, not unlike silence, Nadia's language often functions to resist the lived moment and the necessary silence from which Truth might evolve.

Nadia dreams into existence an empty, skeleton structure that is no different from another structure that might be full. She articulates a room and she designates it as mine, not hers. In another dream, the room becomes full of others bearing luggage, saturating the space and stealing time as she watches, speechless, her frozen immovability gnawing away her life and keeping the strawberries out of reach. Nadia has no recognition of these intruding strangers. Do they and their luggage represent the unformed thoughts that can't be linked to meaning? She floats in the void: no associations, meanings, thoughts, or feelings, just the lingering intrusive images: unrecognizable people with far too much luggage intruding into her space and time.

From the realizational perspective, however, this unfinished room might function as an opening where "O" might evolve from the formless void and infinite; as a threshold from which these strangers might be received and known. Reification that perpetuates gaps as resistance engenders the erroneous perception of mutual exclusivity. However, in terms of the identity of the relative and the absolute, trauma and damage co-exist with potentiality. They are not mutually exclusive. They are different aspects of one oscillation between definite and infinite. For Nadia, damage becomes a fertile ground, the broken and plowed up soil where Truth seeds might germinate, sprout, blossom into a psychic strawberry field, and spread new seeds.

Hallucination and intuition

As hallucination, Nadia's room can provide a mirror reflection that becomes and functions as a gap-filling projection, placing a some-thing where a no-thing might have been. No-things might also fill gaps where the dread of openness and what might follow operates unrelentingly. Room as hallucination, both complete and incomplete, fills the same psychic space where an object might have been but has disappeared. The room's function becomes one of proxy for what Nadia cannot put into or get from mother, lover, therapist, or life.

As intuition, the simultaneous emptiness and fullness of the room convey their own multiple meanings, frequently contradictory, depending on where one stands in shifting moments in which either the mystical or the medical model occupies the experiential foreground. Whatever meanings crystallize into awareness, they occur in-between the actualities and potentialities of life and death. However, what is at stake is their function in terms of destroying or engendering life or death potentials, connectedness, or alienation. Nadia is caught in this space, feeling outside the tightly knit ethnic, highly traditional community of her origin; feeling outside the perimeter of the larger culture. She identifies with both and neither. Room, whether accessible or not, remains an omnipresent given. However, crossing the threshold requires a certain amount of anxiety, as one must, in one way or another, confront and negotiate the gap. There is no getting around the tiger or the lion. One must let go of the vine to taste the strawberries. However, Nadia's vine, the entangled life she finds herself in, exerts a suffocating stranglehold.

Dream room and Nadia's perception suggest both aspects of the come-together/break-apart oscillation between finished, full room and fragmented, unfinished room. Bion developed a radical reorganization of Klein's linear evolution from the paranoid–schizoid (PS) position to the depressive (D) position into an ongoing oscillating dynamic that expresses synchronic non-linear operations. He uses double arrows (PS $\leftarrow \rightarrow$ D) to point toward oscillations between Klein's PS and D positions, between full and empty, finished and unfinished, and anything they might represent or signal.

My wish for Nadia's cure, my initial urge and associated push at finishing the unfinished room, derails the natural rhythm of oscillations and forecloses the potentials of what might evolve from the gap and ultimately negates the perspective provided by intuition of "O." Perhaps this loss of potential is what Nadia points to when she complains that I took her boyfriend's side. What does it mean to "take one's side – the boyfriend's side?" Nadia describes him as "rational, looks at the surface, seeks simple solutions, impatient, inattentive, leaving her feelings not taken seriously and not understood." Do I inadvertently over-privilege one side of the gap over the other? If so, what aspect is that? Nadia's protective, cynical, hopeless, immovable, "no-wish-to-change" self? She says, "I'm not going to change. You must acknowledge who I am." In this side-taking, does the vulnerable, not seen, not heard, not taken seriously, silent, hidden self who wishes but dreads contact remain unborn? Is this "taking the other's side" the actuality of the transference now transformed into a transference and countertransference dynamic? Is the failure to meet in mid-air between the groundlessness of the pursuing tiger and open-jawed lion collusion or coincidence? In this context, "coincidence" refers to an overlaying of the original relational dynamics.

Over time, shifts occur. Nadia moves into form reflected in her shifting self-perceptions from a nothing to a something; from a "something inexpressible" to "someone hateful." She moves from ungraspable, unsayable, unnamable, disgusting, to a self-described "bitch." The movement evolves from a disembodied feeling, a vague no-thing to a some-thing, evolving from the space from which life might spring forth; from the space where a self might have been; from the space foreclosed and filled in by resistance operating in the guise of a diagnosis as "depression." The issue of diagnosis in the present context requires further elaboration.

Diagnosis: steps and stumbles

Diagnosis functions to define the real experience of a patient and serves as an effort to create understanding, which might be influenced by various experiences, such as continued study, reading, supervision, peer group discussion, or attending conferences. This type of understanding can shift based on fluctuating "K" (knowledge of facts). The phenomenon that can be described as Nadia's depression lives as real experience whether it is understood and/or defined as depression or not. The definition or diagnosis "depression" is not depression itself. Let's not confuse the two.

Nadia's active destruction of hope, coupled with her despair and cynicism – symptoms typically associated with depression – become reified into a rigid and brittle sense of self that protects a vulnerable, sensitive, creative self from making real contact and becoming known and from being re-traumatized. She does not have to face the terror of unknown potentialities. In this regard, finished and unfinished rooms reflect hope/hopelessness oscillations as states of being used in the service of a precocious aspect of self that demonstrates Nadia's authentic insight and wisdom. However, this wisdom is skewed in the service of a cynical, antagonistic, depressive, hopeless self that prevents the needy, unfinished, isolated, frightened aspects of her being from being heard, understood, and taken seriously and from making real contact; a contact that permits the impact of the other in a way that would facilitate integration, wholeness, and self-fulfillment. Thus, natural oscillations remain disrupted and Nadia remains stuck, immobilized, unfulfilled, and generally terrified by life.

As a diagnosis, which ignores the Truth-based perspective, depression becomes reified and fills in the gap. In this respect, the notion of depression, despite its accuracy as a diagnostic category, lacks the richness of Nadia's lived experience and paradoxically deepens the distance away from real contact. In this regard, depression as diagnosis becomes useless. In contrast, Nadia's self-diagnosis of "bitch" is cogent, poignant, and accurate as it links self-loathing, disgust, and hopelessness as experiential states to a person living and creatively dreaming finished and unfinished rooms. "Depression" links to nothing. My preoccupation with diagnosis can serve as a counter-resistance to Nadia's lived, in-the-moment emotional truth. In this regard, the claims of Truth are not compatible with the notions of diagnosis and cure. As Rhode (1998) writes: "As the variable, ' "O" ' activates a state of *becoming* unrelated to any claim to therapeutic progress or cure" (1998, p. 118, emphasis in original). From the mystical perspective, nothing progresses or is cured. "There is either an evasion or a recognition of 'O' by way of a *becoming*" (p. 118, emphasis in original).

The diagnosis/cure sequence is linear and occludes awareness of non-linear, discontinuous evolution by over-saturating the psychic space where intuition occurs and that can utilize gaps as potent sources where "O" might evolve. Diagnosis reflects a need for what Bion, following John Keats, describes as an "irritable reaching after facts" and a failure to live with and "exercise negative capability" (1970, p. 125) that, in turn, occludes intuition. Could we imply that the medical model can function as hallucination by filling in the gap in knowledge with what we describe as diagnosis and treatment plan? From this vantage point, the empty space has no meaning or meaning-generation potential in itself until it becomes filled in, in which case the meaning is attached to the content, not the space itself. Thus, the fill becomes the carrier of meaning and consciousness of the gap. Even its existence is safely lost – covered over and saturated with meaning. Without this contact, Nadia remains lost, not taken seriously, not understood, alienated, lonely, sad, and hopeless.

I prefer to honor and work with Nadia's self-diagnosis of "bitch." I meet "bitch" head on as each session ensues. I get to know "bitch" through my direct experience of "bitch." "Bitch" exerts an impact on me and over time. I learn through the experience of sitting with Nadia what functions "bitch" serves in her psychic world. I learn through such experiences that "bitch" serves to block connections to the more vulnerable Nadia who, when she appears, is soft-spoken, sensitive, thoughtful, full of insight, and very well related. Nadia describes this aspect of her being as "much lighter." She says, "I don't have to watch myself and that feels very free." She has given herself more "emotional elbow room." In my experience, the feelings and sensations of heaviness and tension are completely gone from the room when this softer side of Nadia emerges.

Diagnosis serves an important function. My intention is not to "throw the baby out with the bathwater." Such exclusion would move the discussion in a dualistic and nihilistic direction. The critique here centers on the lifelessness that ensues from an over-emphasis, over-attachment, or over-reliance on diagnostic categories. This specific example parallels my point in Chapter 4 regarding an over-emphasis on cognitive understanding and a disregard for intuitive knowing. Functionally speaking, we can expect or observe or experience certain attitudes, behaviors, and self (other) perceptions when working with an individual who is diagnosed with, for instance, depression, such as in Nadia's case. Such individuals will fit, more or less, into preconceived categories, notions, or theories and meet certain expectations. In this regard, diagnostic categories facilitate communication with other professionals. However, something can so easily become lost; specifically, the raw uniqueness of the individual as well as our shifting, unique, moment-to-moment, day-to-day experience of the same individual; the intuited, emotional Truth ("O") of the person, which can become occluded, obfuscated, and layered over by over-conceptualization of diagnostic categories and by *a priori*, formulaic, prescriptive interventions. The situation can become further complicated by an over-reliance or unquestioned dogmatic adherence to a particular theory and related techniques that interfere with the lived immediacy of the moment. While useful, as Kasulis notes with respect to Zen experience, "the conceptual filter [of theory and diagnosis] like any filter useful for some special effect, *distorts* the original image" (1981, p. 56, emphasis in original). Kasulis' depiction of the Zen monk holds relevance for the psychoanalyst and supports the significance of the immediacy and presence of the psychoanalytic encounter. He writes:

> [T]he Zen monk is interested in preserving immediacy, but the myriad forms of life situations present a baffling assortment of possibilities to which one must respond ... Ideas, words and categories all have their place, but the Zen Buddhist, unlike other people, is trained to be explicitly aware of the limitations of concepts. The Zen monk recognizes that no new "___ism," not even Zen Buddhism, will be satisfactory.
>
> (p. 59)

Diagnosis from this perspective functions as a retrospective conceptualization of an experience that has already happened. Can we recognize this ongoing process, first note then relinquish the retrospective conceptualization, and return to the immediacy of the ongoing emerging moment?

Most experienced psychoanalysts, for example, agree that thinking theoretically during a session misses the point. Further, as theory and technique become internalized over time, the experienced analyst drops the mediation of such thinking and responds intuitively and spontaneously, albeit thoughtfully immersed in the evolving "O" of the session. In this case, dropping any notion of depression and responding directly to Nadia's expression of "bitch" engenders a deeper connection and furthers her growth in unexpected directions. She feels heard and seen and gradually softens, becoming less self-protective and increasingly more present and expressive of her vulnerabilities.

In my reverie, which do I hold: gnawed vine or strawberry? With regard to balance and counterbalance, Marilyn Charles writes, "My need to hold on to hope works in counterpart to the other's need to destroy it. The balance is only held to the extent that we hold firm to our respective sides" (2004, p. 15). For Nadia, this holding of a side creates a double bind, another form of side-taking, another gap. Holding hope risks her hopelessness not being taken seriously and not being attended to. The alternative is to collude with hopelessness and to remain at an impasse at the edge of the abyss, at the gap between a lived life and a dead life. Where, then, is the balance point that privileges neither side, that acknowledges both? It's so easy to be caught between lion and tiger!

Technical considerations

As I noted and described in previous chapters, Bion uses the term "O" as an expression of ineffable, unknowable reality. From his perspective, "O" is the reality of life prior to definition, prior to the intrusion of "K." That is why he asserts that "O" can be intuited, but not known. It can only be known through evolution into "K." However, Bion argues that "K" derived through memory, desire, or understanding occludes this evolution. Here is the caution. Psychoanalytic experience as it evolves into form produces diagnostic definitions. In this manner, all diagnostic categories are manifestations and reflections of psychoanalytic experience. Thus, for Bion, the emotional Truth of "O" only becomes intuited when the psychoanalyst relinquishes the "K" strivings mandated by the unquestioned assumptions of a rationalist episteme. Bion endeavors to accomplish this state of intuitive awareness by sitting fully in the reality of the life of the session through the practice of relinquishing memory, desire, and understanding (1965, 1970).

If, as analysts, we are thinking about diagnosis, theory, or possible interpretations, then we are not fully present and engaged with the patient and the experience of the patient. We are not, as Bion notes, *being* psychoanalysis. Rather, we are thinking *about* psychoanalysis. During the session, psychoanalysis is something we do, not something we think about. Eigen describes this process in terms of "the area of faith." He notes, in parallel to the Zen notion of total exertion, that, "By the *area of faith* I mean to point to a way of experiencing which is undertaken with one's whole being, all out, 'with all one's heart, with all one's soul, and with all one's might'" (1981, p. 413, emphasis in original). Uchiyama describes a similar stance toward *zazen* practice; that is, that we engage in *zazen* with our "flesh and bones" (2004, p. 49).

Does this emphasis mean that no fantasies, wishes, thoughts, or theoretically influenced formulations should ever occur? Does good enough psychoanalysis only occur when all of these possibilities are completely absent from mind? No, not at all! What this stance necessitates is the discipline to engage in ongoing self-scrutiny so that, as Uchiyama puts it with regard to *zazen* practice and that also has direct relevance to the psychoanalytic encounter, paralleling Bion's mandate to relinquish memory, desire, and understanding, "… we have to clearly distinguish 'chasing after thoughts and thinking' from 'ideas' or thoughts merely occurring" (2004, p. 49). As I noted in Chapter 4, spontaneously arising memories, for example, are clearly different from forced efforts to remember. Our response to spontaneously arising thoughts requires a further clarification. If a thought emerges spontaneously and we actively pursue it, we are not allowing for the evolution of "O" → "K" to occur through a natural process of reverie. Rather, we are simply pursuing thoughts.

Here is a concrete and lived example. We breathe whether we actively think about it or not. Thinking about breathing is not breathing itself. It is simply the mental process of thinking *about* breathing. "O," or the emotional truth of breathing, is the thought or un-thought actuality of breathing. Thinking about breathing brings "K" into the picture and obscures consciousness of the intuition of the "O" or the actuality of the lived experience of breathing. Breathing is only an explicit example. Bion uses the algebraic formulation "O" to represent any among infinitely possible evolving variable "O's." He describes this infinity of this ongoing, evolving possibility as a constantly moving evolution. Uchiyama puts it this way: "Life lives as real experience even if it is not understood or defined" (2004, p. 31).

The point to keep firmly in mind is that, despite their usefulness, psychoanalytic experience cannot be bottled up in diagnostic definitions. We need to be aware of the tendency to be led around by definitions rather than using them as secondary tools that facilitate working with the primary experience of "O" evolutions. I think it can be summed up in the Sufi riddle: "Does the man ride the donkey or does the donkey ride the man?"

Conclusions: openings and closings

We need to keep talking; we need to keep practicing. At the edge of the precipice, there are no reassurances and we don't know if the required leap of faith is a leap into death or a leap into life. Make no mistake: it's both! A shift occurs through practice, whether Zen, psychoanalysis, or both. This shift might be subtle or dramatic. However, even the most subtle shift, if one truly allows the practice to have an impact, feels like an infinite movement and we find life renewed, transformed and, in so doing, something is relinquished; it could be a wish, fantasy, claim, hallucination, but something is left behind, something dies. So the leap becomes an existential leap into a new way of being in the world in relation to our selves and others and it is simultaneously a death of old psychic and relational being that might manifest in attitude, behavior, thought, or feeling. In negotiating what needs to be left behind, we might need to face terror, disappointment, and fear related to the vulnerability that might initially occur in showing up for life, for therapy, for religious practice – for the open-jawed lion – and allowing this aspect of who one is to be known, heard, taken seriously, and made genuine contact with; to taste the strawberries. The admonishment that we keep talking, keep practicing might sound simplistic or glib, but it's not. Both practices exert their challenges, but they can render the existential leap more approachable. We might not notice the leap except in retrospect. So, talking and practicing *are* the leap. If we sit on our *zafus* (meditation cushions) imagining "enlightenment," we miss the enlightenment that we already are living. If we recline on the couch imagining that somehow we will be "better" in the future, we miss who we are as living beings now. Tasting the strawberries – simply being just who we are – requires self-acceptance, other acceptance, relinquishing agendas, and treatment plans. As psychoanalysts, this might mean facing our own feelings of grandiosity and inadequacy and relinquishing our attachment to knowing and certainty to make space for unknowing and uncertainty. Bearing witness to the Zen student's process, to the patient's process, both Zen master and analyst alike facilitate a sense of lived equanimity that provides the space for the individual to simply be as one is, simply for the sake of being. This creates a merging of continuity and discontinuity in terms of the ongoing process and attention of the analyst and the ongoing beginnings of the beginnings and endings of sessions.

Why believe that "O" evolves from a gap? Why should the infant believe in a capacity for maternal reverie from which a consistency of thinking of related self and other evolve?

We can consider Nadia's dream as a concrete representation of the fundamental paradox of being. Zen describes the conceptually non-solvable, yet experientially verifiable relationship between seemingly contradictory states, such as between "the identity of the one and the many" or being and non-being. Through meditation, Zen's primary experiential practice, one begins to realize that there is nothing to be solved, cured, interpreted, or resolved. Translated into the dynamics of the psychoanalytic encounter, Nadia's experience is actively attended to, witnessed, and lived. Over time, shifts in perspective occur. For Nadia, some shifts are sudden and jolting. Other shifts are gradual, gentle, and only known retrospectively. In conclusion, as Rhode notes, "Transition is between perspectives on the same state rather than between states" (1998, p. 91). Nadia's two rooms are experienced as one room. Over time she describes feeling a profound sense of wholeness.

Chapter 10

The abyss becoming well

Therefore, you will joyously draw water from the springs of salvation.
— Isaiah 12:3

It is like water turned to ice; all the ice is water, but it cannot be used to quench thirst.
This is mortal illness, before which ordinary physicians are helpless.
— Pai-chang (translated and quoted by Cleary, 1997, p. 9)

Introduction

The water well embodies a multifaceted and powerful mythology. This chapter touches on a few variations from world spiritual traditions as they interact with conceptualizations derived from psychoanalytic experience. Within the context of the psychoanalytic encounter, it serves to demonstrate the emergence of what I described in Chapter 9 as a "spontaneously arising, alternative, intuitive model" and how as an organizing principle of the patient's experience serves to structure the evolution of the treatment.

In ancient China, whole cities would be relocated, reoriented, rebuilt, or redesigned, but water wells remained immovable and unchanged in design, form, and location. They came to represent a symbol of constancy and life. The Taoist *I-ching*, or *Book of Changes*, asserts: "The well from which water is drawn conveys the further idea of an inexhaustible dispensing of nourishment" (Baynes, 1992, p. 185).

In Christian traditions, it is believed that the water from the baptismal font both cleanses away the stain of original sin and unlocks the gateway to spiritual life. The well forms the center of a concentric circle and functions as a place of meeting, a place where life happens and things change. Deals are made, marriages arranged, and gossip exchanged at the well. Taverns function as contemporary wells, "watering holes" that intoxicate.

The well represents a joining. The Old Testament chronicles Jacob and Rachel as well as Abraham and Rebecca meeting at the well. Therefore, as a symbol of life and wholeness, the well is associated with merging or intertwining of male and female, negative and positive, spiritual and physical. As a meeting place, the well provides a point of contact. Formulating and communicating this image functions as access to and expression of the ineffable.

Well images evoke a plethora of feelings: Rachel was guided by kindness, warmth, and compassion. Yet as Matthew Henry notes in his commentary on Genesis (Ge. 26:18–25), "Isaac met with much opposition in digging wells. Two were called Contention and Hatred." Further, he adds, "See the nature of worldly things; they make quarrels, and are occasions of strife" (1988, p. 14).

Psychoanalytic perspectives

From a realizational perspective that joins psychoanalytic and mystical notions, Bion (1965) speaks of emotional turbulence as essential for real growth. The well juxtaposes sense and non-sense (Cooper, 1999b). Both utilize the same imagic space differently, not necessarily compatibly. The well is bottomless and thus provides access to the infinite. Nothing ultimate, permanent, or essential remains. The contemporary American Zen teacher, Dennis Merzel, observes that: "Ultimately, there is no truth, only endless layers of self-deception" (1994, p. 120).

From a psychoanalytic perspective, the well functions and embodies both container and contained dynamics (Bion, 1965, 1970). As psychic location, it becomes a borderland where mystical and medical models merge and yet maintain their distinctiveness. Hence, they become useful as oscillating treatment forces (Cooper, 2001b, 2002a; Eigen, 1998; Rhode, 1994, 1998).

In Kleinian terms, the well might represent an idealized breast, always available, always full. However, a persecuting breast might also poison or drown. An unavailable or withholding breast becomes, in the subject's perception, a well run dry. In popular folk parlance, "You don't miss your water till your well runs dry" refers to separation, abandonment, the loss of love, and the souring of a relationship.

Zen perspectives

From the Zen perspective, Dogen frequently uses the image of the ocean to represent the infinite, the absolute, and at-one-ment. In contrast, the shoreline's infinite shapes and contours represent the definite, the relative and the many; in Zen parlance, "the ten thousand things." Ocean and shoreline together represent, in Zen parlance, "The identity of the One and the Ten Thousand Things."

The well represents a crystallized form of the infinite when transformed from infinite to definite; the myriad dharmas and the one. Water holds the conjunction of opposites: creation/life, destruction/death, hope/doom, wonder/cynicism, nourishment/poison. The well can function as an infinite void, a gateway to the abyss from which life forms. The well reveals the inner life force of the subject who projects a well image from fantasy life onto the real. The well constitutes an empty gap into which one can be born. Therefore, when looking through the lens of the mystical model, the well functions as a source of growth and life and as a gateway to unitive experience. From the perspective of the medical model, well images evoke very different associations. The well might transform into a source of regression, infantile merger, depression, or death.

Thresholds

The well, as a point of contact between medical and mystical models, embodies ultimate and relative, definite and infinite, form and formlessness in its wall and lining of stone and its moving, deep waters. Two contrasting images, when allowed to coexist, constitute a functional whole. Reversals in perspective occurring suddenly or gradually determine whether medical or mystical meanings predominate at a particular moment. The tension between the life and death functions of the well influences levels of contact and relatedness during the psychoanalytic encounter. Oscillating dynamics manifest as contact and withdrawal activities. While typically understood as representative of emerging transference/countertransference dynamics, they also reflect mystical/medical shifts in perspective that operate behind transference. Angels can easily become devils, life-giving liquids can be rendered toxic, and vice versa. In Zen parlance, "the bridge moves, the river remains still." "When Ching drinks, Li gets drunk." The therapist might contaminate or become contaminated. Water both drowns and quenches thirst. Linings contain and withhold and, at the extreme, suffocate. Relational dynamics that respect both coexisting possibilities and the momentary fluctuations between them seem to constitute a useful treatment stance with patients who get caught at the point of contact, where they might be immobilized in a life-and-death struggle.

Hallucination

As hallucination, the well can provide a mirror reflection that becomes and functions as a gap-filling projection, placing a some-thing where a no-thing might have been. Reified no-things might also fill gaps where the dread of openness and what might follow operates unrelentingly. Well as hallucination fills the same psychic space where an object might have been but has disappeared. The well's function becomes one of proxy for what one cannot put into or get from mother, therapist, or life. The emptiness of the abyss or the fullness of the well convey their own multiple meanings, frequently contradictory, depending on where one stands in shifting moments in which either the mystical or the medical model occupies the experiential foreground. Whatever meanings crystallize into awareness, they occur in between the actualities and potentialities of life and death. However, what is at stake is their function in terms of destroying or engendering life or death potentials, connectedness, or alienation. Water, whether accessible or not, remains an omnipresent given. However, visibility requires a certain amount of turbulence.

Symbol and sign

Eigen writes, "One can use symbols to represent or get rid of emotional reality ... Fertile symbols mix the known and unknown in productive ways. They hold the unknown open so that growth is possible" (1996, p. 54). It is not the intention here to ignore the symbolic communications of patients. Symbol formation is crucial to healthy psychic development and central to the psychoanalytic free-associative inquiry. However, overemphasis on the multifaceted layers of meaning and associations engendered by any symbol can overshadow a patient's actuality and occlude awareness of the patient's attempts to signal something that might be as basic as life and death. In this respect, preoccupations with symbolic meanings might function as a resistance to the agonies of lived truths by the analyst, analysand, or both.

Well images serve important treatment functions but eventually need to be relinquished. Ultimately, Zen teachers warn that the seeker must drink directly from the waters of life. For example, the traditional Buddhist saying, "Painted cakes do not satisfy the appetite," emphasizes the primacy of lived experience. From the Zen perspective, "painted cakes" refers to theories and concepts that can be used to understand and to explain reality. However, in terms of realization, the practitioner's own experience is necessary to be one in the flow of a totally exerted life.

Dan: beginnings

Dan struggles with psychic life and death. This struggle finds expression as represented in his use of the well as a symbol for the known and unknown, real or imagined, and as a graphic expression of experienced actuality. At thirty-one, Dan has spent the past ten years meeting for psychoanalytic therapy. He immigrated to the United States with his widowed mother and two siblings when he was in his teens. Dan's family roots include African, East Indian, Muslim, Hindu, and Christian influences. His father died due to alcohol-related complications when Dan was fifteen months old, just two months after the birth of his brother.

Their move to New York sounds more like a lunge for freedom soon after the death of a maternally related uncle, who, with his wife, dominated the extended family. Dan remembers his aunt as both suffocating and repressive. One wonders about the loss multiplying geometrically through the simultaneity of his father's death and his mother's grief. The attention required by his newborn brother complicated the situation. A significant theme for Dan revolves around his waiting around passively, hoping that he will be noticed and his needs, which he generally minimizes, seen and tended to. An assertive or active stance, Dan believes, would be burdensome and experienced by his mother as an inappropriate interruption. However, he also believes that activity ruins deeper, more intimate contact. He fondly recalls feeling deeply connected to her love, as she would sit silently reading while he would play on the living room floor.

Dan entered treatment complaining of depression and regret at an unfulfilled life, watching life slip by with no hope for the future, feeling frozen when rare opportunities would arise. Dan arrived at the consultation room door with the hope of reanimation. Not unlike any psychic process, Dan's deadness finds its roots in multiple sources. Speculations include his need to reassure his mother: "Don't worry, nothing is happening in my life. Nothing is changing. I don't rock the boat; I don't need anything. I am here for you." By remaining immovable, deadness might contain his mother's fears.

It is not clear whether Dan's deadness functions as a shutdown or whether he has constituted enough of a self to shut down. Perhaps some hidden fragments of self are subject to shutdown, while some have not been given birth to or have been killed off completely. Still others get him to the consultation room each week. At this juncture, mystical and medical models exert different forces with equal importance. Despite any speculations, Dan's deadness is not circumscribed, a passing cloud in an otherwise blue sky. It pervades his life space, choking his life force, and stops there. For Dan, the world is not a terrible place that will never change, a worldview typically associated with depression. He lacks the spark of life that can step him over the boundary into the light of life that he clearly perceives as there for the partaking, but not for him. Love and light exert themselves and shine in Dan's world. They are just beyond his grasp or can only be intuited, real or imagined, from a silent distance. He is left empty, thirsty for what he is unable to feel. His cakes are painted, one-dimensional and lacking in nourishment. For Dan, beginnings become aborted. This pattern repeated itself in a former therapy. Having dropped out of training, the therapist closed her practice and relocated out of state, in Dan's eyes, suddenly and without warning, thus creating another premature ending.

Eddie

About a year into our work together, Dan introduced Eddie, his hidden (unborn, aborted, murdered, miscarried) self. Past catastrophes and future unknowns can be traced simultaneously through both Dan and Eddie. In a sense, Dan's depression protects Eddie from being taken over or suffocated out of existence by others' demands, deficiencies, or deadness. Eddie remains a well-protected secret living safely in a wonderland inside walls of depression. I have learned to speak with Eddie directly with humor, childlike playfulness, or with a sense of wonder. At other times, communications are shunted through Dan, who acts as a mediator or guardian. It is doubtful, however, that Dan delivers all of my messages to Eddie or all of Eddie's messages to me. The mediating/guarding function strips life out of our interactions. Dan can just as easily destroy links to Eddie. The life and death contrast is shocking at times.

Conjunctions/disjunctions

Kleinian thought might place Dan, peering into the well, at the brink of the depressive position. The conjunction of container and contained, lining and water, might be perceived as too dangerous, so Dan remains immobilized. Water springs forth from sources much deeper than the well's lining. The ultimate is, after all, uncontainable. Dogen observes that, for the fish, the ocean is endless. On the threshold of the abyss or at the edge of the well, Dan embodies alienation and loneliness. For Dan, projection would be an overburdening intrusion into the therapist (or anyone else), so he has created the well as a substitute.

Dan finds the well's potency too intense for his brittle and fragile being. He takes in small doses when he can. The sacredness of well waters holds the potential for annihilation – not unlike the Holy Spirit striking Saul with such transforming energies that in a flash of sudden enlightenment he becomes Paul. Is this Saul transformer a potential Dan/Eddie destroyer? Dan, encumbered by pessimism, fear, and doubt, has little faith that Eddie could survive Dan without his suffocating containment. He turns away from the well and misses the gateway to depressive reorganization. He continues to view life as toxic. Oscillations become derailed. Pulverized into fragments, he remains a Saul, slaying himself each session.

Silence as chaos

Dan and Eddie arrive out of the chaos that is a void in the silence that accompanies the start of our sessions. The silence represents the one consistency from which he springs back to a moment of life. Dan always begins his sessions with silence, as if evolving out of formlessness into form. He drops in from a vast distance. At the close of our meetings, he evaporates back into the void. In the silence of a void, Dan safely avoids the frightening, nameless, uncertain vicissitudes of a lived life. However, life sparks drag his corpse back each week in the hope of reanimation. Dan's torment and anguish, however, parallel the emotional turbulence of the waters in the well that contains potentiality. Whether well images are understood or manipulated – as symbol or actuality – the transformation of hallucination/fantasy into an image embodies an individual's mythology. Myth images then allow for the articulation of an analysand's truth, particularly when derived spontaneously from one's own experience of lived truth as it crystallizes into spoken artifact. As manifest artifact, well thus embodies and carries the transference. As the artifact transference as experienced in the relationship in sessions is Dan/Eddie's internal state of mind. Dan, dead, fixed, rigid, reliable, unmovable, possible links destroyed; Eddie, alive, spontaneous, reachable through humor, in flux.

Will Dan make room for Eddie? Will Eddie dissolve Dan? Life and death images both serve their purposes. Both demand respect and need to be maintained. As a necessary pole, deadness serves a purpose. Attempting to eliminate deadness would constitute a disservice to Dan and Eddie. Efforts in that direction might represent non-acceptance of intolerable states by the analyst (Bion, 1959). Eigen observes:

> What emerges is not an end to deadness, but a new and better movement between aliveness and deadness, a rhythm or oscillation. The psyche cannot do away with its states, but it can grow to make more room for them.
>
> (1996, p. xvi)

If deadness, at times, functions as a defense against death, as Eigen describes, then Dan's deadness might be understood as a defense against his dead internal (introjected) father that covers him like a skin that can't be shed or that soaks him like alcohol, drenching every cell of his being. The phenomenon that appears as deadness (not to deny the actuality of dead states) may function as a membrane, a chrysalis cocoon that holds the potential that gives birth to Eddie. By honoring Eddie, we honor the infinite potentialities of being itself. In this respect, Eddie defines an area of the infinite that continues to spark in an otherwise dead emotional landscape. This spark keeps Dan alive and in treatment. In other words, Eddie might be understood as a reification or artifact drawn from the shapeless waters of a bottomless well into something definite and known. Through Truth transformations, the well as artifact crystallizes the unfolding of an analysis through the emerging form of emotional turbulence between the moment-to-moment sense and non-sense (no-sense) randomly occurring in any session (Cooper, 1999b, 2010).

Perceptual ambivalence

At the depressive threshold, Dan peeks out of the corner of his eye like a bashful child eyeing a last piece of homemade apple pie on the plate. His gaze then shifts. Fear and hunger emerge, hands clutched tightly, knuckles turning white, wondering, "Will there be any food left for me?" The breast is ambivalent at best, depending on the mother's emotional state and capacity for reverie. Oscillations occur between good and bad, nurturing and toxic, full and barren. The well, on the other hand, is a continuous, infinite, ever-flowing source of eternal life. Dan's well might function as a hallucination that defends against an imaginary fear, some nameless dread. For Dan, nameless dread might be life. Thus, as an actuality, the hallucinated well also functions as a resistance. Early Bion might say Dan is evacuating something. Later Bion would speak to the formless void out of which something will evolve. Dan resists living an unknown life while a known life pours out of him. Dan's passing life – an actuality – remains a source of anguish and regret. The well taps into worlds underground. What will Dan find there: a wellspring of eternal life – nourishment?

From a linear perspective, infinite life might be misperceived as a regressive return to infantile narcissism motivated by the urge for "oceanic merger." A circular perspective of constant oscillation demands other conceptualizations, like Alice's Wonderland, where anything can be anything else. Eternal life embraces the dead, undead, or yet to be born. As a tap into underworlds, the well becomes a phantasmagoric conduit between the dead and the living. Who is who? Picture image and negative – Dan and Eddie.

Intuition

As intuition, the well represents what new thing might evolve, what might be lived rather than imagined or hallucinated. When Dan peers into the well, he looks into himself; that is, into the depths of his own psychotic elements. What version of himself does he see? The stone wall that surrounds also contains and defines the well. Karma, the stone and mortar of his psychic and relational past, which he peers over, functions as a contact barrier. As contact barrier, the well becomes a point of contact with the ineffable, unspeakable. Here is the boundary between life and death, conscious and unconscious, linear and circular, Dan and Eddie. When linked to transformations of the infinite, the well takes on new significance. Has abyss, with its paranoid–schizoid implications, transformed, for the moment, into well: something empty, undefined, and persecuting transforming into something full, defined, and soothing, signaling movements between paranoid–schizoid and depressive positions? Has oscillation become engaged?

Dan is his own dead father to his child self. Eddie, who embodies all romantic notions about life and, therefore, the possibility for wonder, lives safely and securely hidden in an animal skin blanket of the dead Dan (father). Dead to the world like inert, impenetrable matter, Dan wards off the slings and arrows of what would destroy Eddie. Placenta burst, Eddie aborted – Eddie in a sarcophagus lost in a labyrinth unable to be given birth to. His tomb has been built from the stone and mortar of tragic reality and psychic givens.

How much of a father did Dan have before his death? Chaos and deprivation replace order and plenitude. Dan notes with regret: "I never got what sons are supposed to get from fathers – direction, guidance, advice." No structuring activity leaves only chaos and confusion. Dan finds himself withdrawing, hovering silently in the family background, hoping that a depressed and overburdened mother might notice and nourish him fortuitously. Her well, at least for Dan, dried up long ago. However, he continues to wait, experiencing psychic dehydration that contributes to deadening incrustation processes by destroying any emotional fluidity. Dan has no psychic lubrication, except for his visits to the well with me.

Dan finds himself waiting and silently starving to death. He starves me through his silences and brooding. Silences also give space for mutual reconstitution between sessions. When Dan finally speaks, he arrives from a void. I am relieved at my prodigal son's return. He has contained his live twin safely for his trip through life/underworld. The case that wraps (enraptures) him explains his stiff mummy-like body movements that appear as deadness. Inside the incrustations are signs of life. Deadness surrounds Eddie with protection and suffocation.

Death has claimed all of the significant men in his life – his father, uncle, disappearing cousin, and younger brother. They all have left except for Dan and Eddie. Dan has mother all to himself, at last. However, he has scored a Pyrrhic victory and finds himself alone with her deadness. Now deadness claims Dan and imprisons Eddie. Incrustations of deadness fill in the gap that a plunge into the well (wellness) implies. How has Dan internalized his dead father? Introjected deadness eats up his life and seeps back out again to the surface in the form of incrustation.

Multidimensional life flattens into cardboard. Eddie as spirit lives; despite its destruction, he has pushed deadness to the surface in an effort to maintain minimal life space in the depths. However, there is no object to accept, contain, or acknowledge his need to project deadness and its toxic hardening effect. It remains encrusted, spreading inwardly from the surface and out from the core. That is to say, the hardening processes move in both directions. He simultaneously holds and becomes his own projections. Thus follows an actual conflict of tensions between life and death. Life brings him to the consulting room and death gags him during long silences and then sends him off, lost in the void. Perhaps when announcing "time's up," we both die. In terms of repetition – that is, of transference – Dan fears overwhelming his "overburdened mother," not realizing how she has overburdened him. In terms of state of mind, transference reflects his own deadness. Evidence to the contrary has no effect. Dan finds such interpretations to be meaningless. He reciprocally replaced his dead father in effigy between self and mother (world) to ward off her toxic projections. He is already oversaturated with toxicity. In therapy, he does not want to overburden or to be overrun. The ensuing stalemate becomes lived transference in actuality and represents the unfortunate impasse that is his mind and his life. He thus communicates the vastness of empty space between Dan and Eddie, as well as between Dan/Eddie and the world in the excruciating eternal moments of impasse.

Amniotic infant

Is Dan the prenatal infant in his mother's womb, floating in amniotic space somewhere near the entrance to the birth canal? Is he some kind of introject inside his mother's psyche? Is the well a perceived entrance to/from the birth canal? It is hard to tell if he is on the outside looking in or on the inside looking out. He might be headed toward heaven or hell or to Wonderland, where inside and outside are reversible and differences do not exist. Dan views emotional attachments as dreaded hells. Womb functions both as regression and potentiality, a place or state of mind to emerge from or to return to. Womb might also be the emptiness of the infinite void in which creativity evolves, being formed in dark, unknown, amniotic waters like a fetus.

Pre-tragic mother

During a session, I experience myself as a pre-tragic mother, long hair flowing, jet black and beautiful, full hips and fertile breasts. I feel relaxed and poised to nurture and feed a hungry, reluctant infant. As we speak playfully, in my reverie, I imagine that, emotionally, he is bouncing on my knee, feeling safe and protected. His imagery has transformed an empty abyss to a water-filled well.

"Signs of life," I say when he first introduces the well. However, he fears falling into the well and drowning. He avoids drinking life and feels anguish as a result. How frustrating to know of the possibility and yet to be stuck so close, so thirsty. He avoids drinking life, but life is no longer an empty chasm – it is a full well, dangerously full. Sadness wells up as he speaks. He is conscious, yet he appears to not have the slightest clue. Will Eddie's sparks come through or will Dan's deadness destroy the potential for feelings to emerge, awareness to deepen, and insight to ripen? Is insight necessary for Dan? For now, the ripples of surfacing feelings seem to be almost more than Dan can bear.

Separations

It is the eve of my vacation, and Dan is for once able to speak. He misses his dead father, mostly as a source of inspiration and direction. Standing at the abyss of my impending vacation, he forms the words, "I will miss you." Water, for Dan, becomes a positive merger with the interconnectedness of life. It is simultaneously a death through oblivion-merger with the abyss of his mother's depression. She has infected him with death via her projections into his infant self (her ego). Alienation and salvation coexist in one boundless ocean. Dan can be cleansed or drowned, shattered or made whole "as a coincidence between opposites of creation and destruction" (Rhode, 1998, p. 171). He is liable to be overwhelmed by one or the other of them.

From the mandates and restrictions of the scientific model, Dan's well might represent an unconscious fantasy with origins in early bodily experiences related to the existence and/or non-existence of an object; that is, as transference, a prior object relation, and the associated affects and experiences of subject–object contact. Dan's experiences interpreted in terms of the genesis of subject–object transference relations fail to spark life, creative movements, or connectedness. Dan's deadness from this perspective might be understood as reactive and/or defensive.

An alternative view might consider deadness as a life not yet begun. Eddie, like a dormant seed, lies encased in a protective pod also known as Dan. The well in this view might be considered more fruitfully as an opening into life emanating from a void that is confused with deadness.

Deadness

Whether regressive or progressive, deadness remains an actuality. Time passes, leaving Dan unfulfilled and Eddie dormant. Deadness reaps deadness through the introjection of both father's and mother's depression. However, he also gives birth to mother. She finds the capacity to live through saturating Dan with all the toxicity that enables her to smile through life. As far as she is concerned, everything is just fine. Dan, now at thirty-two, feels hopelessly entrenched and unable to move. He finds himself stuck with her.

In the transference, the well takes in Dan's gaze and functions as a breast that absorbs his feelings – in this instance, sadness. His eyes both drink in and cry out. Through his eyes, he drinks life more as an observer than as a participant. Can the watered surface of the well, unlike the bottomless, imageless abyss, mirror Dan's image back to himself and reflect him into life? One might argue that Dan needs to grow into Eddie, or that Eddie might represent a derailed aspect of Dan's self-developmental process that has yet to be integrated and to grow into Dan. On the other hand, Dan and Eddie can be viewed as synchronic elements orbiting around each other like atomic electrons, forming a solidified wedge against existential anxiety that is actualized as treatment impasse. Impasse here becomes a place where awareness of the infinite potentially occurs, if we can tolerate remaining open to it. Dan can use my capacity for tolerance for the infinite silence to turn chaos into freedom.

Dan and Eddie, not unlike life and death from the Zen perspective of complementary opposites, both cause and affect each other non-sequentially in mutual co-creation. Dan and Eddie – birth and death – in this respect represent binary oscillations between being and non-being. Dan and Eddie as embodiment in reciprocal oscillation seal the gap and foreclose the possibility for intuitions to transform what evolves out of formlessness. Reification of the relative self (selves) occludes experiencing ultimate being. The location from which truth might evolve becomes reified, concretized, and experienced in the form of an Eddie, and represents Dan's efforts to keep from slipping off the edge of his world. Now the well forms in an area of experience denied in the scientific model, but that operates as part of Zen's articulation of everyday discourse and experience. Eddie as reification dissolves and leaves no reference points. Nothing remains for Dan to grasp in order to keep from slipping off the edge. Nothing remains to use in order to create more psychic ground to stand on even temporarily, as an illusion. The descent into the abyss is inevitable and holds the potential to transform the abyss into the well. However, it entails a loss of reference and requires unrelenting faith in the process, something perhaps I can provide by proxy for Dan. The realm of realizational experiencing holds no fixed reference points. It is discontinuous, timeless, flashing momentarily or for longer durations. Dan and Eddie aspects become integrated as one being, paradoxically, through separation through the function of the well as a contact barrier mediating intolerable Eddie/Dan aspects. The contact barrier creates a dislocation where a gap evolves and transforms, crystallizing the formless, bottomless abyss into the well image. The well respectively contains both Dan and Eddie functions of containment and definition at one extreme and of infinite effusiveness at the other. Dan/Eddie oscillates between these inevitable states of being.

Therapeutic stance

What becomes therapeutic for Dan is non-judgmental acceptance, my speaking freely to either Eddie or Dan. Additionally, humor, the free play of my own capacity to sit still with what is no matter what, and honestly believing in the well as actuality lend support to basic Dan/Eddie acceptance. Active interest in Dan/Eddie functions as a proxy for something he is unable to do consciously for himself. Feeling states have unspoken impacts. When they gather strength, they can clear blockages at the threshold between paranoid–schizoid and depressive positions and restore movements between them. Denial of either Eddie or Dan becomes a blockage or a no-place to move. Consciousness stagnates in Dan. This requires unrelenting faith. I am often a "doubting Thomas." Then we lose track of Eddie, and the infinite potentiality.

After my vacation, Dan is thirsty. He speaks mournfully of the waning summer. Winter is a stiff, cold, dry place. There is no in-between for him, only life or death – no threshold. "Things are freer, more fluid in the summer," "I am less restricted by clothing." The well is full, not empty or frozen over. But frozen over is frozen solid. He cannot imagine a crust or a thin ice layer that can be broken through. The frozen surface is the same as the frozen core. He cannot imagine or locate movements below. He cannot find the well, though he faces it. He can observe others drink, but he cannot.

New connections

We find a point of connection. He becomes interested in hiking. It is obvious to Dan that I resonate with hiking. He arrives at my office in a pair of new hiking shoes. The following week, he has a magazine devoted to hiking with a list of organizations that sponsor day hikes locally. Dan and I discuss a few possibilities. We explore his fantasies and fears. He has begun a journey. The notion of hiking, possibly following in my footsteps, speaks to his journey. Unlike his father's corpse, which lies motionless at the threshold to his home where he dropped dead one night, we can both put one foot in front of the other. Sometimes, this is all one can do. Sometimes, this is all it takes. He wants to climb to mountaintops and walk along edges. He imagines I have hiked more treacherous terrain and can guide him. We focus on the actuality of hiking. The transference operates silently in the background and need not be tampered with. He is thirsty for truth and has stopped at the well that, for the moment, is no longer an abyss. It is more contained than that. His real journey seems now to be just beginning.

Vastness

Dan can now do what Bion describes as "map the realization of mental space" (1970, p. 12). Not unlike the ancient Chinese landscape, the well in its immovability functions as his benchmark. Without a container function, Dan's emotions disperse into infinity. He has no awareness of feeling except for the frustration of no awareness where he believes something like a feeling should be. He has no words to express the vastness of his internal world. Vastness dissolves everything. All that remains is silence. He begins each session with a period of silence – not as long in duration now as when we began. However, the length of silence is no measure of its vastness, which becomes sensed in a moment of contact. Vastness dissolves both time and space. The well as container creates a place of definition, of emotional life. Emotions gather back together, form into awareness, and then crystallize into language structures. "I will miss you." "I am sad." "I guess this has to do with losing my father, no one to guide me." "Now I can talk to you, you can tell me things; I like that."

I respond, "I am touched by your expression of feelings." For Dan, this response might be too much. My silent attentiveness might already be too much. He imagines that his expressions of feeling might be too much for me.

"I will burden you," he answers. However, he is now able to tell me, "Oh no, not that, anything but that." "I don't want you to have those feelings about me, it's too much. I will be obligated to you."

I decide not to make a transference interpretation. For me, it would feel like a cold shutdown of emerging, heartfelt aliveness, and so I respond, "But I feel your sadness, knowing how thirsty you must be and I am glad that you feel, despite your anxiety and hesitation, OK enough to tell me."

Thirst for life raises issues of contamination and related confusion between the contaminated and the contaminator. A few sessions pass. Dan begins to speak of the burden he feels. Anger finds its way to the surface, forming into animated words: "Fuck the well, piss in the well." Dan's comments reveal his confusion between toxic wastes and life-giving fluids emanating from the same source. Fucking and pissing are the same to him. He finds himself in a room with a "whore" at a porno house. She says, "You can touch me." He could not touch his mother, only "intuit" her love from a distance, she being preoccupied with reading and he with his play toys. "With the whore," Dan continues, "I sucked her nipple and put my finger inside of her." Again, he simultaneously takes in nourishment and plugs up sources of toxicity (or a source of a birth that would interrupt his exclusive feeding). As he relates these events, I feel a deadly coldness in the room. It chills my bones. Dan has again obliterated Eddie. My capacity to make the connection is now spoken about here only in retrospect.

This dialogue follows the appearance of the well. Dan now begins to speak of the importance of such a place of meeting. Here, in his freed up speaking, is the biblical sense of the well spontaneously flowing forth. But the well is much more than a representation of the container/contained function. Container/contained speaks to the subject–object model and the relationship between the two. The creative aspects of the well emerging from the formless void speak to the unitive aspects of experience, or what Buddhists refer to as the identity of duality/unity, of ultimate/absolute, relative/empirical existence.

To view the well exclusively as resistance/defense transference, subject/object paradigm oversimplifies Dan's consciousness, unconscious dynamics, and uniquely forming psychic structuring activity. Such a simplification reflects Enlightenment positivism and disables the functioning of the realizational perspective. The fluid complexities of Dan's internal world reciprocally operate in relation to Eddie's pristine, naive simplicity. As family sacrifice victim, Dan fails to atone or to make right the loss of its members, except through the emerging materialization of early introjects.

Toxic introject

Following in his father's footsteps, Dan has recently taken to drink during lonely weekends. His father remains so much with him, a haunting, tormenting, shadowy ghost. As victim, Dan embodies both creation and destruction. Can Dan's well, through O evolutions, transform from something dangerous, toxic, and past into a source of reverie, intuition, life, something possible? Can the cynicism/wonder balance (Cooper, 2002a) be restored? In the evolutions toward balance, Dan locates a point of contact between his terror and his developing capacity for mourning. The associated shame functions as emotional fuel for igniting a threshold experience and regenerates wonder, represented as a thirst for life and an eagerness to enter his journey; for hiking along mountaintops. It is no accident that he begins hiking from the beach up to palisades along the cliffs, past waterfalls, and then up to a mountaintop. He now speaks of it being harder for others, not for him.

Being and non-being

Eddie and Dan live at the intersection of being and non-being. The electricity of life requires both charges. Eddie holds the positive, life-affirming aspects of this potential linkage. Dan holds the negative. They are embodiments of what Bion describes as "imaginary twins" (1956, p. 3). The well functions as an intermediary form of contact barrier, where Dan and Eddie might join under new circumstances. Dan's hallucination thus emerges on the edges between life and death. What might emerge in the spaces between the two? What tensions do they create for something new to evolve from? Neither life nor death can claim the well as exclusive territory. It remains a constant yet independent variable. Yet the well evokes a sense of the discontinuous in its turbulent waters. Here lies the potentiality for creativity that might point toward life. Reductive thinking limits the range of what the well might signify. Perhaps it serves to fill in a gap in history, a point of succession along a predictable continuum, a symbol for something else (transferences); when left to its own self-serving devices, the well ravages rampantly. The mystical quality of the gap becomes safely occluded. The fluidity of the well engenders infinite possibilities for speculation. So many theories, notions, ideas – not unlike the myriad fantasies that fill in the tapestry of a child's theories of the parents' sexuality or the mother's pregnancy or relationship with her newborn child. In a sense, the speculations are inconsequential. Reality remains, despite how it is defined, understood, or experienced. However, it does matter as a facilitator of imagination, fantasy, and the possibility to wonder together and, in Dan/Eddie's case, spark deadness into life. What, for example, does toddler Dan make out of the simultaneity of his brother's birth (appearance) and his father's death (disappearance)? Is that the price of life? If Dan's brother is so lethal to his father, does he then become a threat to his own being? Does infant become monster? Regarding the myth of Oedipus, Eric Rhode writes:

> The generalizing magnificence of the play is that it encourages us to be in sympathy with the older sibling, who would murder the foetus, and also with the foetus as well: the part of the foetus that wishes to come alive and not be death to the womb.
>
> (1990, p. 48)

Dan (through massive introjection) is his mother, who is pregnant with Eddie. Coming to life, Eddie is death to Dan and remains stillborn. In this sense, Dan might be a pregnant-mother killer. Birth potentials constitute the living moment as it presents itself. Moments dissolve into new moments along with potentialities. Potentialities, while ever present in the living moment, paradoxically become irretrievable as moments fade into lifetimes of lived moments; potentials actualized, failed, or aborted. In the totally exerted lived moment, life and death potentials continue.

Conclusion

Dan has created a center from which to work, a nexus, and a meeting place. He has created this center from fragments of emptiness and chaos, not so much by pulling them together through what we might otherwise describe as ego integration, but rather by allowing them to fall back into place in their eternal rhythmic orbits, like a solar system in a galaxy of distinct celestial bodies orbiting around a sun. Dan has made transitions that enable him to move from deadness to life. He spirals around, ascends, descends, transcends, and notes, "That's how life is." His journey of transformation, as it negotiates the ups and downs as participant rather than embryonic witness, traverses dry deserts, wastelands poisoned by toxicity, and past catastrophes – frozen, rigid, opaque to the extreme of excluding life. But Dan keeps on going, arriving at my door week after week; coming to life for a moment before leaving. Sometimes he reports moments of coming to life outside of our sessions. Dan drinks the little that he can from the well. He continuously re-establishes his orbit. As the well forms, he moves into fluidity, clarity, liquidity, and then back to a world of form, solidity, and substance of a lived life. There is nothing at the well to figure out, to enchant or entrance. Nothing remains to be interpreted – no past, no future, simply being as it is. "But first I want to say: After being, Doing and being done to. But first being" (Winnicott, 1971, p. 85). For Dan and Eddie, Winnicott's comment translates into "Just being together, meeting at the well. Eddie and Dan." In this respect, as Rhode notes:

> Hallucination focuses on radical juxtaposition. Its creativity is motivated by its need to create a center where no center exists ... In the religious vertex the way up and the way down are as dissimilar as the ascent to heaven or the descent to hell.
>
> (1998, p. 77)

Biblical figures meet at the well. Will Eddie meet Dan here also? Dan has created a center from which to work. As perimeter beings, Dan (Eddie) and I can move toward convergence points, like wheel spokes to a hub. As nodal beings in unity, we can move in diverging directions, expanding our edges. Perhaps we can find the spaces between spokes, hubs, and perimeters; the undefined, empty, in-between spaces where creative forces exert their pull. Movements are reflected in the ebb and flow of sessions. We come together, meet at the well, draw from its shared waters, make contact, and then part. Sometimes, our thirsts are mutually quenched. Moments of arriving from the void and departing light years away occur in the moment-to-moment ebb and flow of the session. Despite whatever changes occur in the psychic topographies of our separate lives, real or imagined, the movable cultures of two beings in the world find a fluid yet immovable meeting place at the well.

References

Abe, M. (1985). *Zen and Western Thought*. London: Macmillan.
Abe, M. (1990). Kenotic god and dynamic sunyata. In: J. Cobb, Jr. & C. Ives (Eds.), *The Emptying God: A Buddhist–Jewish–Christian Conversation* (pp. 3–65). Eugene: Wipf & Stock.
Abe, M. (1992). *A Study of Dogen: His Philosophy and Religion*. Albany: State University of New York Press.
Adams, W. (1995). Revelatory openness wedded with the clarity of unknowing: Psychoanalytic evenly suspended attention, the phenomenological attitude, and meditative awareness. *Psychoanalysis and Contemporary Thought*, 18: 463–494.
Aguayo, J. & Malin, B. (Eds.) (2013). *Wilfred Bion: Los Angeles Seminars and Supervision*. London: Karnac.
Aitken, R. (1991). *The Gateless Barrier*. New York: North Point.
Alexander, F. (1931). Buddhistic training as an artificial catatonia. *Psychoanalytic Review*, 18: 129–145.
Alfano, C. (2005). Traversing the caesura: transcendent attunement in Buddhist meditation and psychoanalysis. *Contemporary Psychoanalysis*, 41: 223–247.
Analayo (2004). *Satipatthana: The Direct Path to Realization*. Cambridge: Windhorse.
Baranger, M. (1993). The mind of the analyst: from listening to interpretation. *International Journal of Psychoanalysis*, 74: 15–24.
Baynes, C. F. (1992). *I-Ching*. R. Wilhelm (Trans.), Princeton: Princeton University Press.
Bays, J. (2004). Forward. In: M. Soeng (Ed.), *Trust in Mind* (pp. vii–xi). Boston: Wisdom.
Beck, C. (1989). *Everyday Zen*. New York: HarperCollins.
Benson, H. (1975). *The Relaxation Response*. New York: HarperCollins.
Bielefeldt, C. (1985). Recarving the dragon: history and dogma in the study of Dogen. In: W. LaFleur (Ed.), *Dogen Studies* (pp. 21–53). Honolulu: University of Hawaii Press.
Bielefeldt, C. (1988). *Dogen's Manuals of Zen Meditation*. Berkeley: University of California Press.
Bion, W. (1956). The imaginary twin. In: *Second Thoughts: Selected Papers on Psychoanalysis* (pp. 3–22). Northvale: Aronson.
Bion, W. (1958). On hallucination. *International Journal of Psycho-Analysis*, 39: 341–349.
Bion, W. (1959). Attacks on linking. *International Journal of Psycho-Analysis*, 40: 308–315.

Bion, W. (1962). *Learning from Experience*. London: Heinemann.
Bion, W. (1963). *Elements of Psycho-Analysis*. London: Heinemann.
Bion, W. (1965). *Transformations*. London: Karnac.
Bion, W. (1967). Notes on memory and desire. In: J. Aguayo & B. Malin (Eds.), *Wilfred Bion: Los Angeles Seminars and Supervision* (pp. 136–138). London: Karnac.
Bion, W. (1970). *Attention and Interpretation: A Scientific Approach to Insight in Psycho-Analysis and Groups*. London: Karnac.
Bion, W. (1980). *Bion in New York and Sao Paulo*. F. Bion (Ed.). Perthshire: Clunie.
Bion, W. (1992). *Cogitations*. London: Karnac.
Bleandonu, G. (1999). *Wilfred Bion: His Life and Works, 1897–1979*. London: Free Association Books.
Bobrow, J. (2002). Psychoanalysis, mysticism, and the incommunicado core. *Fort Da*, 8: 62–71.
Bobrow, J. (2004). Presence of mind. *International Journal of Applied Psychoanalytic Studies*, 1: 18–35.
Bobrow, J. (2007). The disavowal of the personal in psychoanalytic training. *Psychoanalytic Review*, 94: 263–276.
Bokusan, N. (2011). Commentary on the Genjo Koan. In: M. Weitzman, M. Wenger, & S. Okumura (Eds.), *Dōgen's Genjo Koan: Three Commentaries* (pp. 29–90). Berkeley: Counterpoint.
Boris, H. (1986). Bion re-visited. *Contemporary Psychoanalysis*, 22: 159–184.
Braver, L. (2012). *Groundless grounds: a study of Wittgenstein and Heidegger*. Cambridge, MA: MIT Press.
Buksbazen, J. (2002). *Zen Meditation in Plain English*. Boston: Wisdom.
Buswell, R. (1987). The "short-cut" approach of K'an-hua meditation: the evolution of a practical subitism in Chinese Ch'an Buddhism. In: P. Gregory (Ed.), *Sudden and Gradual: Approaches to Enlightenment in Chinese Thought* (pp. 321–377). Delhi: Motilal Banarsidass.
Carter, R. (2008). *The Japanese Arts and Self-Cultivation*. Albany: State University of New York Press.
Charles, M. (2004). *Constructing Realities: Transformations through Myth and Metaphor*. New York: Rodopi.
Cheen, G. (2014). *Translating Totality in Parts*. Lanham: University of America Press.
Christensen, A. & Rudnick, S. (1999). A glimpse of Zen practice within the realm of countertransference. *American Journal of Psychoanalysis*, 59: 59–69.
Christensen, L.W. (1999). Suffering and the dialectical self in Buddhism and relational psychoanalysis. *American Journal of Psychoanalysis*, 59: 37–57.
Clarke, R. (1973). *Hsin Hsin Ming: Verses on the Faith in Mind*. New York: White Pine.
Cleary, T. (1997). *The Five Houses of Zen*. Boulder: Shambhala.
Cohen, M. B. (1952). Countertransference and anxiety. *Psychiatry*, 15: 231–243.
Cook, F. (1977). *Hua-yen Buddhism: The Jewel Net of Indra*. University Park: Pennsylvania State University Press.
Cook, F. (1985). Dogen's view of authentic selfhood and its socio-ethical implications. In: W. LaFleur (Ed.), *Dogen Studies* (pp. 131–149). Honolulu: University of Hawaii Press.
Cook, F. (1989). *The Sound of Valley Streams: Enlightenment in Dogen's Zen*. Albany: State University of New York Press.

Cook, F. (2002). *How to Raise an Ox: Zen Practice as Taught in Master Dogen's Shōbōgenzō*. Boston: Wisdom.
Cooper, P. (1998). The disavowal of the spirit: wholeness and integration in Buddhism and psychoanalysis. In: A. Molino (Ed.), *The Couch and the Tree: Dialogues in Psychoanalysis and Buddhism* (pp. 231–246). New York: Farrar Straus/Northpoint.
Cooper, P. (1999a). Buddhist meditation and countertransference: a case study. *American Journal of Psychoanalysis*, 59: 71–85.
Cooper, P. (1999b). Sense and non-sense: phenomenology, Buddhist and psychoanalytic. *Journal of Religion Health*, 35: 351–370.
Cooper, P. (2000). Unconscious process: Zen and psychoanalytic versions. *Journal of Religion and Health*, 39: 57–69.
Cooper, P. (2001a). Clouds into rain. *Journal of Religion Health*, 40: 167–184.
Cooper, P. (2001b). The gap between: being and knowing in Zen Buddhism and psychoanalysis. *American Journal of Psychoanalysis*, 61: 341–362.
Cooper, P. (2002a). Between wonder and doubt: psychoanalysis in the goal-free zone. *American Journal of Psychoanalysis*, 62: 95–118.
Cooper, P. (2002b). The pervasion of the object: depression and unitive experience. *Psychoanalytic Review*, 89: 413–439.
Cooper, P. (2004a). The abyss becoming well: psychoanalysis and reversals in perspective. *Psychoanalytic Review*, 91: 157–177.
Cooper, P. (2004b). Oscillations: Zen and psychoanalytic versions. *Journal of Religion and Health*, 43: 233–243.
Cooper, P. (2010). *The Zen Impulse and the Psychoanalytic Encounter*. London: Routledge.
Cooper, P. (2014a). Taste the strawberries. *American Journal of Psychoanalysis*, 74: 147–161.
Cooper, P. (2014b). Zen meditation, reverie, and psychoanalytic listening. *Psychoanalytic Review*, 101: 795–813.
Cooper, P. (2014c). *Still Standing: Three Stones Haiku*. Honesdale: Three Stones Press.
Deshimaru, T. (2012). *Mushotoku Mind: The Heart of the Heart Sutra*. R. Collins (Ed.). Chino Valley: Hohm.
Dhargyey, G. (1974). *Tibetan Tradition of Mental Development*. Dharamasala: Library of Tibetan Works and Archives.
Dogen, E. (1227). *Fukanzazengi*. In: N. Waddell & M. Abe (Trans.), *The Heart of Dogen's Shōbōgenzō* (pp. 1–6). Albany: State University of New York Press, 2002.
Dogen, E. (1231). *Bendowa*. In: N. Waddell & M. Abe (Trans.), *The Heart of Dogen's Shōbōgenzō* (pp. 7–30). Albany: State University of New York Press, 2002.
Dogen, E. (1233). *Genjokoan*. In: N. Waddell & M. Abe (Trans.), *The Heart of Dogen's Shōbōgenzō* (pp. 39–45). Albany: State University of New York Press, 2002.
Dogen, E. (1240). *Uji*. In: N. Waddell & M. Abe (Trans.), *The Heart of Dogen's Shōbōgenzō* (pp. 47–58). Albany: State University of New York Press, 2002.
Dogen, E. (1241). *Kokyo*. In: G. Nishijima & C. Cross (Trans.). *Master Dogen's Shōbōgenzō: Book 1* (pp. 239–259). Woods Hole: Windbell, 1994.
Dogen, E. (1242a). *Zazenshin*. In: G. Nishijima & C. Cross (Trans.). *Master Dogen's Shōbōgenzō: Book 2* (pp. 91–106). Woods Hole: Windbell, 1996.
Dogen, E. (1242b). *Inmo*. In: G. Nishijima & C. Cross (Trans.). *Master Dogen's Shōbōgenzō: Book 2* (pp. 119–128). Woods Hole: Windbell, 1996.

Dogen, E. (1243a). *Zazengi*. In: G. Nishijima & C. Cross (Trans.). *Master Dogen's Shōbōgenzō: Book 3* (pp.167–169). Woods Hole: Windbell, 1996.
Dogen, E. (1243b). *Hossho*. In: G. Nishijima & C. Cross (Trans.). *Master Dogen's Shōbōgenzō: Book 3* (pp. 171–178). Woods Hole: Windbell, 1996.
Dogen, E. (1243c). *Butsudo*. In: G. Nishijima & C. Cross (Trans.). *Master Dogen's Shōbōgenzō: Book 3* (pp. 87–108). Woods Hole: Windbell, 1996.
Dogen, E. (1244). *Zanmai O Zanmai*. In: G. Nishijima & C. Cross (Trans.). *Master Dogen's Shōbōgenzō: Book 3* (pp. 371–375). Woods Hole: Windbell, 1996.
Eigen, M. (1981). The area of faith in Winnicott, Lacan and Bion. *International Journal of Psychoanalysis*, 62: 413–433.
Eigen, M. (1996). *Psychic Deadness*. Northvale: Aronson.
Eigen, M. (1998). *Psychoanalytic Mystic*. London: Free Association Books.
Epstein, M. (1984). On the neglect of evenly suspended attention. *Journal of Transpersonal Psychology*, 16: 193–205.
Epstein, M. (1988). Attention and psychoanalysis. *Psychoanalysis and Contemporary Thought*, 11: 171–189.
Epstein, M. (1995). *Thoughts Without a Thinker: Psychotherapy from a Buddhist Perspective*. New York: Basic Books.
Evans-Wentz, W. Y. (1954). *The Tibetan Book of the Great Liberation*. London: Oxford University Press.
Faimberg, H. (1996). Listening to listening. *International Journal of Psycho-Analysis*, 77: 667–677.
Faure, B. (1991). *The Rhetoric of Immediacy: A Cultural Critique of Chan/Zen Buddhism*. Princeton: Princeton University Press.
Faure, B. (1993). *Chan Insights and Oversights: An Epistemological Critique of the Chan Tradition*. Princeton: Princeton University Press.
Ferro, A. (2002a). Narrative derivatives of alpha elements: clinical implications. *International Forum of Psychoanalysis*, 11: 184–187.
Ferro, A. (2002b). Some implications of Bion's thought: the waking dream and narrative derivatives. *International Journal of Psychoanalysis*, 83: 597–607.
Ferro, A. (2005). *Seeds of Illness, Seeds of Recovery: The Genesis of Suffering and the Role of Psychoanalysis*. London: Routledge.
Ferro, A. (2006). Trauma, reverie and the field. *Psychoanalytic Quarterly*, 75: 1045–1056.
Ferro, A. (2009). *Mind Works: Technique and Creativity in Psychoanalysis*. New York: Routledge.
Ferro, A. & Basile, R. (2006). Unity of analysis: similarities and differences in the analysis of children and grown-ups. *Psychoanalytic Quarterly*, 75: 477–500.
Freud, S. (1912). Recommendations to physicians practising psycho-analysis. In: *The Standard Edition of the Complete Psychological Works of Sigmund Freud*, Vol. 12 (pp. 109–120). London: Hogarth.
Fromm, E. (1960). Psychoanalysis and Zen Buddhism. In: E. Fromm, D.T. Suzuki, & R. De Martino (Eds.), *Zen Buddhism and Psychoanalysis* (pp. 77–141). New York: Harper & Brothers.
Fromm-Reichmann, F. (1952). *Principles of Intensive Psychotherapy*. Chicago: University of Chicago Press.
Glass, N. (1995). *Working Emptiness*. Atlanta: Scholar's Press.

Gomez, L. (1987). Purifying gold: the metaphor of effort and intuition in Buddhist thought and practice. In: P. Gregory (Ed.), *Sudden and Gradual: Approaches to Enlightenment in Chinese Thought* (pp. 67–165). Delhi: Motilal Banarsidas.

Gregory, P. (1986). *Traditions of Meditation in Chinese Buddhism.* Honolulu: University of Hawaii Press.

Gregory, P. (1987). *Sudden and Gradual: Approaches to Enlightenment in Chinese Thought.* Delhi: Motilal Banarsidass.

Grotstein, J. (2007). *A Beam of Intense Darkness: Wilfred Bion's Legacy to Psychoanalysis.* London: Karnac.

Gunn, R. (2000). *Journeys into Emptiness: Dogen, Merton, Jung and the Quest for Transformation.* New York: Paulist.

Harris, M. & Bick, E. (1980). Bion's conception of a psychoanalytic attitude. In: M. Harris (Ed.), *The Tavistock Model: Papers on Child Development and Psychoanalytic Training* (pp. 45–50). London: Karnac.

Harrison, J. (2006). *Bion's O – An Open Gate between Eastern and Western Psychotherapy.* Tel Aviv: Tel Aviv University Press.

Heine, S. (1994). *Dogen and the Koan Tradition: A Tale of Two Shōbōgenzō Texts.* Albany: State University of New York Press.

Heine, S. (1997). *The Zen Poetry of Dogen: Verses from the Mountain of Eternal Peace.* Rutland: Tuttle.

Heine, S. (2002). *Opening a Mountain: Koans of the Zen Masters.* Oxford: Oxford University.

Heine, S. (2012). What is on the other side? Delusion and realization in Dogen's "Genjokoan." In: S. Heine (Ed.), *Dogen: Textual and Historical Studies* (pp. 42–74). Oxford: Oxford University Press.

Henry, M. (1988). *The Matthew Henry Concise Commentary.* Grand Rapids: Christian Classics Ethereal Library.

Hinshelwood, R. (1998). *A Dictionary of Kleinian Thought.* London: Free Association Press.

Hisamatsu, S. (1979). Ordinary mind. *Eastern Buddhist* 12: 1–29.

Horney, K. (1945). *Our Inner Conflicts.* New York: W.W. Norton.

Huxley, A. (1945). *The Perennial Philosophy.* New York: Harper & Row.

Joseph, B. (1989). *Psychic Equilibrium and Psychic Change: Selected Papers of Betty Joseph.* London: Routledge.

Issa, K. (no date). Haiku of Kobayashi Issa. D. Lanoue (Trans.), http://haikuguy.com/issa/search.php?keywords=the+sping+breeze+pushes&year=

Kasulis, T. (1981). *Zen Action; Zen Person.* Honolulu: University of Hawaii Press.

Katagiri, D. (2002). To live is just to live. In: J. Loori (Ed.), *The Art of Just Sitting: Essential Writings on the Zen Practice of Shikantaza* (pp. 101–104). Boston: Wisdom.

Kavanaugh, P. (2003). The dead poet's society: ventures into radioactive psychoanalytic space. *Psychoanalytic Review*, 90: 341–360.

Kavanaugh, P. (2004). Frankenstein's Genie-ology: the magical visionary experience and the associative method. *Psychoanalytic Review*, 91: 643–661.

Kavanaugh, P. (2005). Wang Fo and an ethic of free association: poetic imagination, mythical stories, and moral philosophy. *Psychoanalytic Review*, 92: 487–511.

Kavanaugh, P. (2009). The dramatic meaning of madness in psycho(analy)sis: the ear-rationality of treating illusion as reality. *Psychoanalytic Review*, 96: 983–1005.

Kavanaugh, P.B. (2010). Escaping the phantom's ghostly grasp: on psychoanalysis as a performance art in the spirit world. *Psychoanalytic Review*, 97: 733–756.

Keats, J. (1952). *Letters*, edited by M.B. Forman, 4th edition. London: Oxford University Press.

Kernberg, O. (1965). Notes on countertransference. *Journal of the American Psychoanalytic Association*, 13: 38–56.

Kim, H. (1985). The reason of words and letters: Dogen and koan language. In: W. LaFleur (Ed.), *Dogen Studies* (pp. 54–82). Honolulu: University of Hawaii Press.

Kim, H. (2004). *Eihei Dogen: Mystical Realist*. Boston: Wisdom.

Kim, H. (2007). *Dogen on Meditation and Thinking: A Reflection on his View of Zen*. Albany: State University of New York Press.

King, S. (1991). *Buddha Nature*. Albany: State University of New York Press.

Klein, M. (1946). Notes on some schizoid mechanisms. *International Journal of Psychoanalysis*, 27: 99–110.

Kohut, H. (1984). *How Does Analysis Cure?* Chicago: University of Chicago Press.

Komito, D. (1987). *Nagarjuna's Seventy Stanzas on Emptiness*. Binghamton: Snow Lion.

Kondo, A. (1952). Intuition in Zen Buddhism. *American Journal of Psychoanalysis*, 12: 10–14.

Lacan, J. (1981). *The Seminar of Jacques Lacan Book XI: The Four Fundamental Concepts of Psychoanalysis*. A. Sheridan (Trans.). New York: W.W. Norton.

Langan, R. (1997). On free-floating attention. *Psychoanalytic Dialogues*, 7: 819–839.

Lanoue, D. (no date). Haiku of Kobayashi Issa. http://haikuguy.com/issa/search.php

Leavy, S. (1964). *The Freud Journals of Lou Andreas-Salome*. New York: Basic Books.

Leighton, D. (2000). *Cultivating the Empty Field: The Silent Illumination of Zen Master Hongzhi*. Rutland: Tuttle.

Leighton, D. (2008). Zazen as an enactment ritual. In: S. Heine & D. Wright (Eds.), *Zen Ritual: Studies in Zen Buddhist Theory and Practice* (pp. 167–184). New York: Oxford University Press.

Leighton, D. (2011). *Zen Questions: Zazen, Dogen and the Spirit of Creative Inquiry*. Boston: Wisdom.

Leighton, D. (2015). *Just This Is It: Dongshan and the Practice of Suchness*. Boston: Shambhala.

Leighton, D. & Okumura, S. (1996). *Dogen's Pure Standards for the Zen Community: A Translation of Ehei Shingi*. Albany: State University of New York Press.

Leighton, D. & Okumura, S. (2004). *Dogen's Extensive Record: A Translation of the Eihei Koroku*. Boston: Wisdom.

Leighton, T. (2002). Introduction: Hongzhi, Dogen and the background of *shikantaza*. In: J. Loori (Ed.), *The Art of Just Sitting: Essential Writings on the Zen Practice of Shikantaza* (pp. 1–10). Boston: Wisdom.

Lennon, J. (1980). *Beautiful Boy: Double Fantasy (Record)*. New York: Geffen.

Little, M. (1960). Countertransference. *British Journal of Medical Psychology*, 33: 29–31.

Loori, J. (Ed.) (2002). *The Art of Just Sitting: Essential Writings on the Zen Practice of Shikantaza*. Boston: Wisdom.

Loori, J. (2011). *The True Dharma Eye: Zen Master Dogen's Three Hundred Koans*. Boston: Shambhala Publications.

Lopez-Corvo, R. (2005). *The Dictionary of the Work of W.R. Bion*. London: Karnac.

Lopez-Corvo, R. (2006). *Wild Thoughts Searching for a Thinker: A Clinical Application to W. R. Bion's Theories*. London: Karnac.
Low, A. (2006). *Hakuin on Kensho: Four Ways of Knowing*. Boston: Shambhala.
Luk, C. (1993). *Ch'an and Zen Teaching*. York Beach: Samuel Weiser.
Maezumi, T. (1978). *The Way of Everyday Life*. Los Angeles: Center Publications.
Maezumi, T. (2002). Forward. In: F. Cook (Ed.), *How to Raise an Ox: Zen Practice as Taught in Master Dogen's Shōbōgenzō* (pp. ix–x). Boston: Wisdom.
Magid, B. (2000). The couch and the cushion: integrating Zen and psychoanalysis. *Journal of American Academy of Psychoanalysis*, 28: 513–526.
Magid, B. (2002). *Ordinary Mind: Exploring the Common Ground of Zen and Psychotherapy*. Boston: Wisdom.
Matte-Blanco, I. (1975). *The Unconscious as Infinite Sets*. London: Duckworth.
Matte-Blanco, I., (1988). *Thinking, Feeling and Being: Clinical Reflections on the Fundamental Antinomy of Human Beings and the World*. London: Routledge.
Mendoza, S. (2010). The O of emptiness and the emptiness of O. *British Journal of Psychotherapy*, 26: 305–320.
Merzel, D. (1991). *The Eye Never Sleeps: Striking to the Heart of Zen*. Boston: Shambhala.
Merzel, D. (1994). *Beyond Sanity and Madness: The Way of Zen Master Dogen*. Rutland: Tuttle.
Miner, E. (1968). *An Introduction to Japanese Court Poetry*. Stanford: Stanford University Press.
Moncayo, R. (1998). True subject is no-subject: the real, imaginary, and symbolic in psychoanalysis and Zen Buddhism. *Psychoanalysis and Contemporary Thought*, 21: 383–422.
Moncayo, R. (2012). *The Signifier Pointing at the Moon: Psychoanalysis and Zen Buddhism*. London: Karnac.
Morvay, Z. (1999). Horney, Zen, and the real self: theoretical and historical connections. *The American Journal of Psychoanalysis*, 59: 25–35.
Nichol, D. (2006). Buddhism and psychoanalysis: a personal reflection. *American Journal of Psychoanalysis*, 66: 157–172.
Nishijima, G. & Cross, C. (1996). *Master Dogen's Shōbōgenzō*. London: Windbell.
Ogden, T. (1997a). Reverie and interpretation: Henry James (1884). *Psychoanalytic Quarterly*, 66: 567–595.
Ogden, T. (1997b). Reverie and metaphor: some thoughts on how I work as a psychoanalyst. *International Journal of Psycho-Analysis*, 78: 719–732.
Ogden, T. (2004). An introduction to the reading of Bion. *International Journal of Psycho-Analysis*, 85: 285–300.
O'Hara, P. (2011). *Ten Talks on the Heart Sutra*. New York: Village Zendo.
O'Hara, P. (2014). *Most Intimate: A Zen Approach to Life's Challenges*. Boston: Shamghala.
Okumura, S. (2002). The simple but profound practice of zazen. In: Soto Zen Buddhist International Center (Ed.), *Soto Zen: An Introduction to Zazen*. Tokyo: Sotoshu Shomacho.
Okumura, S. (2010). *Realizing Genjokoan: The Key to Dogen's Shōbōgenzō*. Boston: Wisdom.
Okumura, S. (2012). *Living by Vow: A Practical Introduction to Eight Essential Zen Chants and Texts*. Boston: Wisdom.

Pelled, E. (2007). Learning from experience: Bion's concept of reverie and Buddhist meditation: A comparative study. *International Journal of Psycho-Analysis*, 88: 1507–1526.
Pollak, S. & Pedulla, T. (2014). *Sitting Together: Essential Skills for Mindfulness-Based Psychotherapy*. New York: Guilford.
Racker, H. (1957). The meaning and uses of countertransference. *Psychoanalytic Quarterly*, 26: 303–357.
Rhode, E. (1990). *The Generations of Adam*. London: Free Association Books.
Rhode, E. (1994). *Psychotic Metaphysics*. London: Karnac.
Rhode, E. (1998). *On Hallucination, Intuition and the Becoming of "O."* Binghamton: ESF.
Roland, A. (1981). Induced emotional reactions and attitudes in the psychoanalyst as transference in actuality. *Psychoanalytic Review*, 68: 45–74.
Roland, A. (1983). Psychoanalysis without interpretation: psychoanalytic therapy in Japan. *Contemporary Psychoanalysis*, 19: 499–505.
Rubin, J. (1985). Meditation and psychoanalytic listening. *Psychoanalytic Review*, 72: 599–614.
Rubin, J. (1996). *Psychoanalysis and Buddhism: Toward an Integration*. New York: Plenum Press.
Rubin, J. (2009). Deepening psychoanalytic listening: the marriage of Buddha and Freud. *American Journal of Psychoanalysis*, 69: 93–105.
Schlütter, M. (2010). *How Zen Became Zen: The Dispute Over Enlightenment and the Formation of Chan Buddhism in the Song Dynasty*. Honolulu: University of Hawaii Press.
Shigematsu, S. (1981). *A Zen Forest: Sayings of the Masters*. NY: Weatherhill. In: Heine, S. (1994), Dogen and the Koan Tradition: A Tale of Two *Shōbōgenzō* Texts (p. 95), Albany: State University of New York Press.
Soeng, M. (2004). *Trust in Mind*. Boston: Wisdom Publications.
Speeth, K. (1982). On psychotherapeutic attention. *Journal of Transpersonal Psychology*, 14: 141–160.
Stambaugh, J. (1999). *The Formless Self*. Albany: State University of New York Press.
Stolorow, R. & Atwood, G. (1992). *Contexts of Being: The Intersubjective Foundations of Psychological Life*. Hillsdale: The Analytic Press.
Stitzman, L. (2004). At-one-ment, intuition and "suchness". *International Journal of Psychoanalysis*, 85: 1137–1155.
Suler, J. (1993). *Contemporary Psychoanalysis and Eastern Thought*. Albany: State University of New York Press.
Suler, J. (1995). In search of the self: Zen Buddhism and psychoanalysis. *Psychoanalytic Review*, 82: 407–426.
Suzuki, D.T. (1949). *Essays in Zen Buddhism: First Series*. London: Rider.
Suzuki, D.T. (1960). Lectures on Zen Buddhism. In: E. Fromm, D.T. Suzuki & R. De Martino, *Zen Buddhism and Psychoanalysis* (pp. 1–76). New York: Harper & Brothers.
Suzuki, D.T. (1972). *The Zen Doctrine of No-Mind*. York Beach: Samuel Weiser.
Suzuki, S. (1970). *Zen Mind, Beginner's Mind*. New York: Weatherhill.
Symington, J. & Symington, N. (1996). *The Clinical Thinking of Wilfred Bion*. London: Routledge.

Tanahashi, K. (1985). *Moon in a Dewdrop: Writings of Zen Master Dogen*. New York: North Point.
Townsend, G.F. (2012). *Three Hundred and Fifty Aesop's Fables*. Hamburg: Ulan Press.
Trungpa, C. (1976). *The Myth of Freedom and the Way of Meditation*. Boston: Shambhala.
Uchiyama, K. (2004). *Opening the Hand of Thought: Foundations of Zen Buddhist Practice* (Translated and Edited) T. Wright, J. Warner, & S. Okumura. Somerville: Wisdom.
Uchiyama, K. & Okumura, S. (2014). *The Zen Teachings of Homeless Kodo*. Boston: Wisdom.
Ueda, Y. (1967). Two main streams of thought in Yogācāra philosophy. *Philosophy East and West*, 17: 155–165.
Waddell, N. & Abe, M. (2002). *The Heart of Dogen's Shōbōgenzō*. Albany: State University of New York Press.
Winnicott, D.W. (1949). Hate in the countertransference. *International Journal of Psycho-Analysis*, 30: 69–75.
Winnicott, D.W. (1960). Countertransference. *British Journal of Medical Psychology*, 33: 17–21.
Winnicott, D.W. (1971). *Playing and Reality*. New York: Routledge.
Wolf, C. & Serpa, G. (2015). *A Clinician's Guide to Teaching Mindfulness*. Oakland: New Harbinger.
Woods, J. (1914). *The Yoga System of Patanjali*. Delhi: Motilal Banarsidass.
Yakai, K. (2010). *Soto Zen Texts for Daily Services: A Study Guide*. Santa Cruz: Warm Jewel Zen Temple.
Yamada, K. (1979). *Gateless Gate*. Los Angeles: Center Press.
Yampolsky, P. (2012). *The Platform Sutra of the Sixth Patriarch*. New York: Columbia University Press.
Yen, S. (1987). *Faith in Mind: A Commentary on Seng Ts'an's Classic*. Boston: Shambala.
Yen, S. (2001). *Hoofprint of the Ox: Principles of the Chan Buddhist Path as Taught by a Modern Chinese Master*. New York: Oxford University Press.
Yen, S. (2008). *The Method of No-Method: The Chan Practice of Silent Illumination*. Boston & London: Shambala.

Index

Abe, M.: on *avidya* (active not-knowing) 87, 88; on dharma 9; on interrogatives 104–105; on language 5, 7, 28; on *prajna* (primary understanding) 47; on realization 68, 73, 75–76; on realizational truth 107; with Waddell 12, 37, 39, 43, 46, 47–48, 63, 66, 100, 105, 109
Aguayo, J. 47
Alexander, F. 55, 85
Alfano, C. 50, 97
alpha function 58, 59
Amida (Pure Land) Buddhism 38, 39
Analayo 35
Andreas-Salomé, L. 62
antithesis 57
anxiety, fundamental 3, 69–71, 77, 103, 132
Association for Spirituality and Psychotherapy, New York City 3
authentic selfhood 2
avidya (active not-knowing) 3, 30, 77, 87–88, 93

Baranger, M. 118, 126
Basile, R. 117
Baso Dōitsu 65
Baynes, C. F. 143
behavioral psychology 30
Benson, H. 25
Bielefeldt, C. 5, 10, 31, 37, 41, 44–45, 80, 116–117, 128
Bick, E. 61
bi-logic 49, 55, 60
Bion, W.: *Attention and Interpretation* 98; on gaps between thoughts 81; "imaginary twins" 157; influence of Hinduism 28–29; on internalizations 132; on intuition 46–47, 90, 134; and Klein 136; on negative capability 86, 87, 89, 138; "Notes on Memory and Desire" 98; on psychoanalysis 10, 23, 35, 84–85, 91, 115, 118; on reverie 132; on Truth 134; *see also* "K" (knowledge); "O"
Bleandonu, G. 28–29, 87
Bobrow, J. 58, 97, 106
Bodhicitta (mind of awareness) 106, 124, 125, 128
Bodhisattva Vow 31, 41, 111
Bokusan, N. 57, 60, 65, 66, 74, 101
Boris, H. 99
Buddha Nature Treatise 66, 119
Bodhisattva of Wisdom 52
Buddha-nature: as innate 42; "O" and 100; total exertion and 20, 34, 76, 79, 94; *zazen* (seated meditation) and 64, 77, 128
Buksbazen, J. 50, 58
Buswell, R. 25, 26, 27
Butsugyō (Buddha act) 128

Cafh Foundation 3
Ch'an Buddhism 9, 24–27, 29, 39, 46, 117
Charles, M. 140
Cheen, G. 101
Chengguan 101
China 2, 25, 63, 143
Chogyam Trungpa 57
Clark, R. B. 70
Cleary, T. 143
Cook, F. 15, 16, 18–19, 20, 71–72, 77, 79, 92
Cooper, P. 97, 102
countertransference 62, 95, 114–115, 119, 121–122, 124, 125
Cross, C. 24, 32–33, 53, 54, 96, 102, 103

'D' (the depressive position) 110, 136
declaratives 82–85
dehumanization 71–73
delusion 61, 65–66, 68, 72, 74, 75–77, 90–91, 101
Deshimaru, T. 35
dharma gates 37, 67–68, 117
dhyāna (meditation) 9, 23, 24, 27, 28, 29, 41, 43
Diamond Sutra 7
discursive thinking 54, 55, 57, 60, 90–91, 116
Docho-san 95
Dogen, Eihei, *Shōbōgenzō*: Abe on 73; and action 10, 72; *Bendowa* 39, 40, 43, 63, 108; on Buddha nature 68, 100; *Butsudo* 41, 44; Cook on 16, 77; on *dhyāna* (meditation) 41; and direct experience 108–111; on discursive thinking 90–91; *Fukanzazengi* 37, 39, 43, 45, 46–48, 63, 80, 105, 117; *Genjō-kōan* 12, 66, 74, 81, 109, 121; and *gūjin* (total exertion) 2, 9; Heine on 75; on *hishiryo* (beyond thinking) 81, 88, 89; *Hossho* 84; *Immo* 102, 103; influences 8; and *ippō-gūjin* (total exertion of a single thing) 14–15; Kim on 32, 76, 81; *Kokyo* 32; language 7; Maezumi on 79, 92; ocean imagery 144; on ordinary life 20; on perception 19; and *pratītyasamutpāda* (dependent arising) 122; radical non-dualism 2, 28, 33, 45, 62, 64, 65–66, 68, 77, 80, 82–83, 100–102, 105, 110; on realizational truth 107; on sensing 53–54; on *shikantaza* (just sitting) 23–24, 26, 28, 32–33, 41–46, 80, 83, 102, 103; on *shushō-ittō* (unity of practice-enlightenment) 37, 38, 72, 104, 110, 125; *Tashin-tsu* 41; *Tenzo-kyokun* 12–13; on truth 113; *Uji* 12; *Zanmai O Zanmai* 24; on *zazen* 37, 41, 42, 83, 91; *Zazenshin* 26, 32–33, 37, 53–54, 80, 84
"Dongshan's Hot and Cold" (*Shoyo Roku*) (*The Book of Serenity*) 19
dreams and psychoanalysis 58–60, 100, 130, 134–140
dualism: direct experience 108–111; Dogen on 40, 54; and intuition 57; in Kant 99; in psychoanalysis 55; realization and delusion 65, 68, 73, 75, 77, 79; realizational truth 107; *shikantaza* (just sitting) and 46; Theravada Buddhism 120; thinking and not thinking 88–90, 92
dun (readiness) 28

Eigen, M. 104, 140, 146, 149
Ejo (Nan-yüeh) 104
"emptiness tradition" 73–74
enlightenment: and delusion 101; Dogen on 20, 39–41, 43–45, 65, 66, 68, 69, 79, 90–91, 108–109, 128; Lam Rim and 30; realization and 74–77, 83, 89, 108–109; *shikantaza* (just sitting) and 24, 30–33, 43–45; *shushō-ittō* (unity of practice-enlightenment) and 72; Silent Illumination 40; and total exertion 10, 12, 20; *zazen* 37
Eno (Huineng) 104
Epstein, M. 97
existentialism 62, 91, 110, 141, 142, 153

Faimberg, H., "Listening to Listening," 124
Faure, B. 8, 24, 28, 46, 47
Ferro, A. 6, 116, 117, 124, 134
Four Universal Vows 67
Freud, S. 51, 55, 114, 115, 121
Fromm, E. 5
fushiryo (not-thinking) 48, 80–82, 84, 88, 89, 105

the gap 130–135
God Realm 72, 92
Gomez, L. 66, 88–89
goshō o negau (hope) 38, 39
Gregory, P. 25
Grotstein, J. 55, 59
gūjin (total exertion) 1–2, 9–22; anxiety and 16–18; case study 18–19; concept/action 11–14; definition 14–15; Dogen on 39, 42; and intuition 49–64; knowledge and truth 51; living in moment 20–22; practice 10–11, 17–20; and *prajna* (primary understanding) 51–52; psychoanalysis and dreams 58–60; realization and 65, 68, 72, 76–77
Gunn, R. 8

hallucination 136–137, 138, 145–146, 148, 149–150, 157, 158
Harris, M. 61

Harrison, J. 97
Heart Sutra 73–74, 132
heijoshin ("ordinary mind") 40, 49
Heine, S. 5–7, 15, 33, 50, 61, 62, 75, 117
Henry, M. 144
Hisamatsu, S. 16, 18, 40, 49, 57, 60–63, 70–71, 74
hishiryo (beyond thinking) 80–82, 84, 86, 87, 88–89, 118
Hōnen 38
Horney, K. 49, 54, 56
Hua-yen Buddhism 101
Hui-neng 25, 26, 40, 123
Hung-tao 80, 83, 84, 86
Huxley, A. 1

I-ching (*Book of Changes*) 143
ignorance *see avidya* (active not-knowing)
immanence 65, 68, 79, 132
Indian Buddhism 24
Institute for Expressive Analysis 3
intention: in Buddhist practice 124–125; in psychoanalysis 125–126
International Forum for Psychoanalytic Education 3
interrogatives 82–85, 105
intuition: action and 77; analytic 87, 103, 136–138, 150–151, 153; Bion on 47; centrality of 54; Dogen on 46; and the gap 134; hallucination and 136–138; Kim on 90; Kondo on 52–53; non-sensuous 53–54; and *prajna* (primary understanding) 47, 102–103; religion and spirituality 60; total exertion and 16, 49–64; and Truth 131; *see also* "O"
ippō-gūjin (total exertion of a single thing) 14–15
Issa 13–14

Joseph, B. 16–17
Jōshū, "Wash Your Bowls" 26–27
"Jōshū's Dog," *Gateless Gate* collection 27

"K" (knowledge): definitions 98–100; and intuition 52, 57, 61, 62–63, 101–103; and psychoanalysis 137, 140–141; and realizational truth 107–111; *shikantaza* (just sitting) 105
Kamakura era Japan 2, 8, 43
Kant, I. 98, 101
Kasulis, T. 24, 68, 72, 78, 102, 124, 139
Katagiri, D. 42

Kavanaugh, P. 6
Keats, J. 86, 102, 138
Keitoku dentoroku (Transmission of the Dharma Lamp) 104
kensho (enlightenment) 28
Kim, H.: on Dogen 7, 8, 12, 32, 33, 39, 40, 64, 66, 76, 84, 91, 117; on duality 108, 109; on emptiness 110; on *gūjin* (total exertion) 9, 10, 11, 14–15; on meditation 25, 34, 38; on not-thinking 81, 90; on practice 75; on realizational truth 107; on *shikantaza* (just sitting) 102
King, S. 51, 66, 119
Klein, M. 136
Kleinian approach 144, 148
Kohut, H. 127
Komito, D. 28
Kondo, A. 49, 52–53, 54
Kyoto Buddhism 49

Lacan, J. 131
Lam Rim 30
language 5–8; Bion on 52, 99, 107; and containment 155; *dun* (readiness) 28; Kim on 90; Lacan on 131; as tool 86
Lanoue, D. 13–14
Leavy, S. 62
Leighton, D. 29, 37, 39, 45, 75, 101
Lennon, J., "*Beautiful Boy*" 130
literature review 94, 96–97
Lopez-Corvo, R. 97, 106
Low, A. 50–51
Luk, C. 131

Madhyamika Buddhism *see* Middle Way Buddhism
Maezumi, T. 79, 92
Magid, B. 56, 131
Mahayana Buddhism 9, 31, 32, 41, 66, 111
Malin, B. 47
Martin, D. 43, 116
Matte-Blanco, I. 11, 19, 49, 55–57, 89
meditation 30–31; contemporary therapeutic 30, 53, 54, 59, 73, 116, 126; East Asian 39; goal-oriented 109; Indian 24, 39; and psychoanalytic listening 118–124, 126; and wisdom 37–38; Western adoption of 83, 85, 119, 125; *see also shikantaza* (just sitting); Silent Illumination; *zazen* (seated meditation)
Mendoza, S. 97
Merzel, D. 144

Metropolitan Institute for Training in
  Psychoanalysis and Psychotherapy,
  New York City 3
Middle Way (*Madhyamika*) Buddhism 6,
  45, 79, 82, 108, 116–117
Milton, J. 134
mindfulness 16, 17, 30, 35, 97, 114–115
mindlessness 16, 17, 117
Miner, E. 13
Morvay, Z. 55, 56
Mumon *see* Wumen Huikai
mushotoku ("no gaining mind") 35

Nagarjuna 6, 63, 96
Nan-yüeh Huai-jang 40, 109
Narcissus myth 129
National Psychological Association for
  Psychoanalysis *see* NPAP
Nichol, D. 97
nihilism 6, 84, 94, 108, 138
nirvana (highest enlightenment)
  10, 72, 74
nirvikalpajnana (non-discriminating
  wisdom) 88
Nishijima, G. 24, 32–33, 53, 54, 96,
  102, 103
non-duality/absolute emptiness 9, 32
nonthinking 80, 81, 105; *see also zazen*
  (seated meditation)
North America 83, 85
not-thinking *see fushiryo*
noumena and phenomena 99, 101
NPAP (National Psychological
  Association for Psychoanalysis) 3

"O": "at-one-ment" 28–29, 47, 109, 132;
  Bobrow on 58; definition 97–100;
  evolution of 62, 102–103, 141;
  experiencing 100; Grotstein on 55;
  intuition of 52, 57–58, 59, 61, 86, 101,
  136, 139, 140; literature on 97; Ogden
  on 113; reality and 104–105; realization
  and 41, 88, 110–111, 135; realizational
  truth 107–108; Rhode on 10, 133, 138
Oedipal myth 129, 157
Ogden, T. 85, 86, 89, 97–98, 113,
  119–120, 122, 126
O'Hara, E. 50
Okumura, S.: on Dogen 10, 13, 39,
  121; on delusion 65, 66, 74; on not-
  thinking 81; on *shikantaza* (just
  sitting) 41–42, 86; on *zazen* (seated
  meditation) 23
Old Testament 143–144

Pai-chang 143
paranoid–schizoid position *see* PS
Patanjali 85
Pelled, E. 97, 121, 128
"Polishing a Tile to Make a
  Mirror" 32–33
positivism 51, 123, 156
prajna (primary understanding) 49–52;
  and action 10, 75; intuition and
  47, 54, 59, 102, 103, 129; and *zazen*
  (seated meditation) 26
pratītyasamutpāda (dependent arising)
  122–123
pre-reflective knowing 24, 47, 50–51, 52,
  102, 104, 124
present moment 130; meaning and 98; in
  psychoanalysis 13; realization and 39,
  65, 68, 100; *shikantaza* (just sitting)
  and 42; total exertion and 12, 15
projective identification 46, 58, 59,
  85, 135
PS (the paranoid–schizoid position)
  110, 136
psychoanalytic listening 118–124, 126
Pure Land Buddhism *see* Amida
  Buddhism

quietism 30–31, 37, 39, 41, 42,
  84–87, 116

Racker, H. 114, 124, 125
Ramakrishna 1
realization: Cook on 16, 20; and
  delusion 61, 65–79, 100; Dogen
  on 13, 32–33, 37–40, 83–84, 101,
  109–110; *hishiryo* (beyond thinking)
  and 81–2; Hung-tao on 86; intuition
  and 47, 52, 54, 63–64; meditation
  and 31; practice 74–78; and *prajna*
  (primary understanding) 102; and
  psychoanalysis 53, 99–100, 110–111,
  135, 144; quietism 30; *shikantaza*
  (just sitting) and 41–43, 45, 103;
  subitism 24; and thinking 88–90; and
  transcendence 67–69
realizational truth 107–108
reflective knowing 50
reification: and anxiety 132; and
  continuity 107, 135; of relative self
  153; and reverie 50, 58; thinking
  and not-thinking 90, 92–93; and
  transcendence 72, 73
reverie: intuition and 56; meditation and
  85; psychoanalysis 58–60, 63, 116,

119–121, 123, 126, 141, 149; reification of 50, 58; maternal 58, 132, 142
Rhode, E.: on deep contact 93; on the gap 131, 132, 133–134, 142; on "O" 10, 98, 111, 138; on Oedipal myth 157; on oppositions 152; on truth 51
Rinzai Zen tradition 5, 30, 83
Roland, A. 127–128
Rubin, J. 85, 97, 114

samsara 10, 72, 74
satori (enlightenment) 31
Sawaki, K. 23
Seng-ts'an, *Hsin Hsin Ming* 70
Senne, *Goshō* (*Shōbōgenzō* commentary) 50
shamatha (calm abiding meditation) 30
Shen-Hui 88–89
Sheng Yen 40
Shigematsu, S. 117
shikantaza (just sitting) 23–24, 41–44; definitions 27–28; Dogen on 103, 105, 117; duality/unity 75; historical shift 25–26; instrumental and expressive orientations 31–33; and intention 33–35; and not-thinking 80–82, 84, 86–87; practice 45–46, 83; quietist and insight orientations 30–31; reality 35–36; realizational truth and 107; three marks of existence 28–29
shiryo (thinking) 81–82, 84, 88, 89
shōjō no shu ("practice based on enlightenment") 31, 33
shōzen no shu ("practice prior to enlightenment") 31
shūshō itto (oneness of practice and realization) 37, 38, 65, 72, 104, 110, 125
shuzen ("step-by-step") meditation 30
Silent Illumination 29, 40
sinification of Buddhism 42
Soeng, M. 7
Stambaugh, J. 14, 15, 71, 89
Stitzman, L. 52–53, 103, 106
Stolorow, R. & Atwood, G. 123
subitism 24, 39, 66
sunyata (emptiness) 122; *see also* "emptiness tradition"
Suzuki, D.T. 1, 5, 33–34, 54, 56, 57, 83
Symington, J. 97, 106
Symington, N. 97, 106
symmetrization 11, 19, 49, 55–57, 62, 89
synthesis 57

"T" (Ultimate Truth) 107
Ta-hui 7
Tamekane 13, 15
"Taste the Strawberries" (Zen teaching story) 129–130
Te-shan 7
Theravada Buddhism 97, 114, 120, 121
thresholds 145
Tibetan Buddhism 30, 97
total exertion *see gūjin*
transcendence 66, 67–69, 70–73, 75, 77, 92, 132
transference 119, 145; case studies 112, 137, 149, 151, 153, 155, 157
Tsung-Tse, *Tso Ch'an I* 117
tun see dun

Uchiyama, K. 23, 38–39, 62, 68–69, 130, 140, 141
Ueda, Y. 50

vipassana (mindfulness) 30, 97, 114–115
vipasyana (insight meditation) 30

Waddell, N. 12, 37, 39, 43, 46, 47–48, 63, 66, 100, 105, 109
water well mythology 143–158; hallucination and 145–146; psychoanalytic perspectives 144; symbol and sign 146; thresholds 145; Zen perspectives 144–145
Winnicott, D. W. 122, 158
Woods, J. 85
Wumen Huikai (Mumon) 26, 27

Yakai, K. 31, 67
Yamada, K. 26, 27
Yampolsky, P. 25, 26
Yangshan 101
yoga meditation 85

zazen (seated meditation) 23–36; Bielefeldt on 44; and Buddha-nature 128; definition 28; Dogen on 37, 41, 42, 44, 80, 83; and intention 33–35; and intuition 57, 64; Kasulis on 124; Kim on 46; and not-thinking 90; practice instructions 26, 47–48, 57, 77, 91; reality 35–36; realization 75; and total exertion 11, 16, 17; Uchiyama on 62, 140
zenki 15